365 Amazing Bar Cookie Recipes

(365 Amazing Bar Cookie Recipes - Volume 1)

Susan Perrin

Copyright: Published in the United States by Susan Perrin/ © SUSAN PERRIN

Published on October, 12 2020

All rights reserved. No part of this publication may be reproduced, stored in retrieval system, copied in any form or by any means, electronic, mechanical, photocopying, recording or otherwise transmitted without written permission from the publisher. Please do not participate in or encourage piracy of this material in any way. You must not circulate this book in any format. SUSAN PERRIN does not control or direct users' actions and is not responsible for the information or content shared, harm and/or actions of the book readers.

In accordance with the U.S. Copyright Act of 1976, the scanning, uploading and electronic sharing of any part of this book without the permission of the publisher constitute unlawful piracy and theft of the author's intellectual property. If you would like to use material from the book (other than just simply for reviewing the book), prior permission must be obtained by contacting the author at author@bisquerecipes.com

Thank you for your support of the author's rights.

Content

365 AWESOME BAR COOKIE RECIPES ... 8

1. 10 Layer Monster Bars Recipe 8
2. A Twist On Nanaimo Squares Recipe 8
3. APPLE CHEESECAKE BARS Recipe 9
4. Adult Peanut Butter And Cookie Bars Recipe 9
5. Alabama Chocolate Praline Jumbo Christmas Mud Squares Recipe 10
6. Alligator Cookie (peanut Butter Chew) Recipe 10
7. Almond Apricot And White Chocolate Decadence Bars Recipe 11
8. Almond Bar Cookies Recipe 11
9. Almond ChoCoconut Bars Recipe 12
10. Almonds Orange And Carrot Bars Recipe 13
11. Almost Candy Bars Recipe 13
12. Apple Crumb Squares Recipe 14
13. Apple Golden Raisin Cheesecake Bars Recipe 14
14. Apple Pastry Squares Recipe 15
15. Apple Pie Bars Recipe 15
16. Applesauce Bars With Orange Glaze Recipe 16
17. Applesauce Squares Recipe 17
18. Apricot Bars Recipe 17
19. Apricot Butter Bars Recipe 17
20. Apricot Oat Bars Easy Recipe 18
21. Apricot Oat Squares Recipe 18
22. Apricot Oatmeal Bars Recipe 19
23. Apricot Squares Recipe 19
24. Apricot Walnut Bars Supreme Recipe 20
25. BEST Granola Bars Ever Recipe 20
26. BUTTER PECAN BANANA BARS Recipe 21
27. Baby Ruth Bars Recipe 21
28. Banana Honey Bars Recipe 22
29. Banana Bars Recipe 22
30. Banana Bars With Cream Cheese Frosting Recipe 22
31. Banana Cream Brownie Squares Recipe ... 23
32. Banana Crunch Bars Recipe 23
33. Banana Pudding Squares Recipe 24
34. Banana Split Cheesecake Squares Recipe .. 24
35. Bettah Buttah Banana Bars Recipe 25
36. Black Forest Cheesecake Squares Recipe .. 25
37. Blarney Stones Bars With Vanilla Icing And Chopped Peanuts Recipe 26
38. Blitzen Bars Recipe 26
39. Blueberry Almond Bars Recipe 26
40. Blueberry Cheesecake Bars Recipe 27
41. Blueberry Cookie Bars Recipe 27
42. Blueberry Hummingbird Bars Recipe 28
43. Blueberry Oat Popcorn Bars Recipe 28
44. Blueberry Ricotta Squares Recipe 28
45. Blueberry Walnut Bars Recipe 29
46. Blueberry White Chocolate Squares Recipe 29
47. Bob Sykes Bar B Qs Hersheys Perfectly Chocolate Chocolate Cake Recipe 30
48. Bodacious Chocolate Marshmallow Bars Recipe 30
49. Brazil Nut Ebony Bars Recipe 31
50. Brownie Goodie Bars Recipe 31
51. Brownie Goody Bars Recipe 32
52. Buckeye Cookie Bars Recipe 32
53. Buster Bar Ice Cream Dessert Recipe 32
54. Butter Nut Bars Supreme Recipe 33
55. Butterscotch Banana Bars Recipe 33
56. Butterscotch Bars Recipe 33
57. Butterscotch Cashew Bars Recipe 34
58. CEREAL PEANUT BUTTER BARS Recipe 34
59. CHERRY COBBLER BARS Recipe 34
60. CHOCOLATE CHIP COOKIE BARS Recipe 35
61. CHOCOLATE COCONUT BARS Recipe 35
62. CREAM CHEESE BLUEBERRY BARS Recipe 36
63. Cafe Ole Rice Crispy Bars Recipe 36
64. Cake Bars Recipe 37
65. Canadian Three Layer Bars Recipe 37
66. Candy Bar Brownies Recipe 37
67. Candy Bar Cake Recipe 38
68. Candy Bar Filled Cookies Recipe 38
69. Candy Bar Pie Recipe 39
70. Cant Leave Alone Bars Recipe 39
71. Cappuccino Nanaimo Bars Recipe 39
72. Cappuccino Bars Recipe 40
73. Caramel Apple Bars Recipe 40

74. Caramel Bars Recipe 41
75. Caramel Candy Bars Recipe 41
76. Caramel Cashew Bars Recipe 41
77. Caramel Cashew Crispy Bars Recipe 42
78. Caramel Cheesecake Bars Recipe 42
79. Caramel Crunch Bars Recipe 43
80. Caramel Krispy Bars Recipe 44
81. Caramel Peanut Butter Bars Recipe 44
82. Caramel Squares Recipe 44
83. Carmel Fudge Squares Recipe 45
84. Carrot Bars W Cream Cheese Frosting Recipe 45
85. Carrot Cake Bars Recipe 46
86. Carrot Cake WannaBe Bars Recipe 46
87. Cashew Caramel Crunch Squares Recipe .. 46
88. Channel Lemon Squares Recipe 47
89. Cheerio Bars Recipe 47
90. Cheescake Bars Recipe 48
91. Cheesecake Squared Recipe 48
92. Cherry Bars Recipe 49
93. Cherry Oatmeal Bars Recipe 49
94. Cherry Pie Crumb Bars Recipe 49
95. Cherry Squares Recipe 50
96. Chips Ahoy Peanut Butter Cheesecake Squares Recipe 50
97. Chock Full Blondie Squares Recipe 50
98. Chocolate And Peanut Butter Dream Bars Recipe 51
99. Chocolate Bar Nut Brownies Recipe 52
100. Chocolate Bottom Banana Squares Recipe 52
101. Chocolate Cake Squares With Eggnog Sauce Recipe 53
102. Chocolate Caramel Cashew Squares Recipe 53
103. Chocolate Caramel Layer Squares Recipe . 54
104. Chocolate Cheesecake Candy Cane Bars Recipe 54
105. Chocolate Cheesecake Squares Recipe 55
106. Chocolate Chip Cheese Bars 55
107. Chocolate Chip Cheese Bars Recipe 56
108. Chocolate Chip Cheesecake Bars Recipe .. 56
109. Chocolate Chip Cookie Bars Recipe 56
110. Chocolate Chip Cream Cheese Bars Recipe 57
111. Chocolate Coconut Bars Recipe 57
112. Chocolate Dulce De Leche Bars Recipe ... 57
113. Chocolate Macaroon Squares Recipe 58
114. Chocolate Mint Bars Recipe 58
115. Chocolate Nougat Squares Recipe 59
116. Chocolate Peanut Butter Bars Iv From Allrecipes Recipe 60
117. Chocolate Peanut Butter Bars Recipe 60
118. Chocolate Peanut Butter Dream Bars Recipe 60
119. Chocolate Peanut Butter Oat Bars Recipe 61
120. Chocolate Peanut Fudge Bars Recipe 62
121. Chocolate Pecan Pumpkin Bars Recipe 62
122. Chocolate Raspberry Cheesecake Bars Recipe 62
123. Chocolate Snicker Bar Brownies Recipe .. 63
124. Chocolate Streusel Bars Eagle Brand Recipe 63
125. Chocolate Toffee Caramel Bars Recipe 64
126. Chocolate Dipped Deluxe Overnight No Bake Power Bar Recipe 64
127. Chocolate Caramel Layer Bars Recipe 65
128. Chocolate Cherry Bars Recipe 65
129. Chocolate Covered Cherry Bars Recipe 66
130. Chocolate Glazed Almond Bars Recipe 66
131. Chocolate Peanut Butter Dream Bars Recipe 67
132. Chocolatey Peanut Buttery Bars Recipe 67
133. Chunky Love Bars Recipe 68
134. Citrus Bars Recipe 68
135. Cobblestone Bars Recipe 69
136. Coconut Angel Bars Recipe 69
137. Coconut Bars Recipe 69
138. Coconut Blueberry Cheesecake Bars Recipe 70
139. Coconut Brownies 70
140. Coconut Candy Bar Cake Recipe 71
141. Coconut Dream Squares Recipe 71
142. Coconut Blueberry Cheesecake Bars Recipe 72
143. Coffee Crisp Bars Recipe 72
144. Coffeebreak Chocolate Coconut Cookie Bars Recipe 73
145. Congo Bars Recipe 73
146. Cran Kin Bars Recipe 73
147. Cranberry Cake Squares Recipe 74
148. Cranberry Pear Bars Recipe 74
149. Cranberry Squares Recipe 75
150. Cream Cheese Pear Bars Recipe 75

151. Cream Cheese Squares Recipe 76
152. Creamy Baked Apple Squares Recipe 76
153. Creamy Dreamy Candy Bar Dessert Recipe 77
154. Creamy Lemon Oat Bars Recipe 78
155. Crumb Topped Date Bars 78
156. Crunchy Peanut Brickle Bars Recipe 78
157. DOUBLE DELICIOUS COOKIE BARS Recipe 79
158. Dads Fave Sour Cream Raisin Bars Recipe 79
159. Date Bars Recipe 80
160. Date Nut Bar Delight Recipe 80
161. Date Squares Recipe 80
162. Delicious Raspberry Walnut Shortbread Bars Recipe 81
163. Diabetic Chocolate Chip Pumpkin Bars Recipe 81
164. Disappearing Butterscotch Chocolate Bars Recipe 82
165. Dotty Golden Squares Recipe 82
166. Double Chocolate Bars 83
167. Double Chocolate Peanut Butter Bars Recipe 83
168. Double Chocolate Squares Recipe 84
169. Double Trouble Chocolate Nut Bars Recipe 84
170. Double Chocolate And Caramel Bars Recipe 84
171. Dreamy Coconut Squares Recipe 85
172. Dried Fruit Oat Bars Recipe 85
173. Dulce De Leche Apple Bars With Browned Butter Icing Recipe 86
174. Dulce De Leche Frosted Squares Recipe .. 86
175. EASY EASY LEMON CHEESE SQUARES Recipe 87
176. Easy Blueberry Lemon Bars Recipe........... 87
177. Easy Cherry Dream Bars Recipe 88
178. Espresso Chocolate Squares Recipe 88
179. Frozen Chocolate Bar Cookie Cake Recipe 89
180. Frozen Chocolate Mousse Squares Recipe 89
181. Fruit And Nut Bars Recipe 89
182. Fudge Fantasy Bars Recipe 90
183. Fudgy Almond Bars Recipe 91
184. GERMAN LEBKUCHEN HONEY BARS Recipe 91
185. GOOEY COCONUT BARS Recipe 91
186. German Chocolate Bars Recipe 92
187. Ginger Pumpkin Praline Squares Recipe ... 92
188. Gingerbread Squares Recipe 93
189. Glendas Best Zucchini Bars Recipe 93
190. Gooey Coconut Bars Recipe 94
191. Granola Bars Recipe 94
192. Granola Nut Protein Bar Recipe Recipe ... 94
193. Grasshopper Bars Recipe 95
194. Gutte Kuchen Recipe 95
195. HEATH BAR CAKE Recipe 96
196. Halloween Magic Bars Recipe 96
197. Heath Bar Apple Dip Recipe 96
198. Heath Bar Brownies Dated 1964 Recipe ... 97
199. Heath Bar Coffee Cake Recipe 97
200. Heath Bar Poundcake Recipe 97
201. Heavenly Brownie On Shortbread Bars Recipe 98
202. Heavenly Candy Bar Cake Recipe 99
203. Hershey Bar Cake Recipe 99
204. Hershys Cookie Layered Bars Recipe 100
205. Ho Ho Bars Recipe 100
206. Holiday Magic Bars Recipe 101
207. Homemade Snickers Bars Recipe 101
208. Homemade Twix Bars Recipe 102
209. Honey Almond Bars Recipe 102
210. I Want That Recipe Bars Recipe 102
211. Ice Cream Crunch Bars Recipe 103
212. Ice Cream Marshmallow Bars Recipe 103
213. Jane Parker A P Spanish Bar Cake Recipe 104
214. Kahlua Praline Bars Recipe....................... 104
215. Key Lime Bars Recipe 105
216. Killer Hazelnut Brownie Bars Recipe 105
217. Kit Kat Bars Recipe 106
218. Lamington Bar Cake Recipe 106
219. Layered Chocolate Bars Recipe................ 107
220. Layered Chocolate Cheesecake Bars Recipe 107
221. Layered Chunks Of Chocolate Squares Recipe.. 108
222. Lemon Bars Recipe 109
223. Lemon Cheesecake Bars Recipe 110
224. Lemon Cream Cheese Bars Special Recipe 110
225. Lemon Custard Bars Recipe 110
226. Lemon Raspberry Cheesecake Bars Recipe

227. Lemon Squares Recipe 111
228. Lemonberry Jazz Bars Recipe 112
229. Linzer Torte Bars Recipe 113
230. Luscious Layer Bars Recipe 113
231. Macadamia Fudge Squares Recipe 114
232. Macadamia Layer Bars Recipe 115
233. Magic Cookie Bar Mix For Gifts Recipe 115
234. Magic Cookie Bars Recipe 116
235. Mals Magic Bars Recipe 116
236. Maraschino Cherry Bars Recipe 117
237. Marbled Chocolate Nut Bars Recipe 118
238. Mars Bar Chocolate Muffins Recipe 118
239. Mars Bar Squares Recipe 118
240. Marshmallow Creme Banana Bars Recipe 119
241. Marshmallow Whipped Hershey Bar Pie Recipe 119
242. Marzipan Bars Recipe 120
243. Melting Moments Lemon Bars Recipe 121
244. Mexican Bars Recipe 121
245. Meyer Lemon Bars Recipe 122
246. Michelles Vegan Granola Bars Recipe 122
247. Milk Chocolate Bar Cake Recipe 123
248. Milk Chocolate Candy Bar Cake Recipe . 123
249. Millionaire Shortbread Bars Recipe 124
250. Millionaire Squares Recipe 124
251. Mint Nanaimo Bars Recipe 125
252. Moms Apple Pie Bars Recipe 125
253. No Bake Butterfinger Bars Recipe 126
254. No Bake Cashew Brittle Bars Recipe 126
255. No Bake Chocolate Peanut Butter Bars Recipe 127
256. No Bake Chocolate Peanut Butter Oatmeal Bars Recipe 127
257. No Bake Cereal Bars 128
258. No Bake Chocolate Cookie Squares Recipe 128
259. No Bake Butterscotch Coconut Squares Recipe 128
260. No Bake Chocolate Peanut Butter Bars Recipe 129
261. Norwegian Apple Squares Recipe 129
262. Nut Goodie Bars Recipe 129
263. Nutella Butterscotch Bars Recipe 130
264. Nutella Rocky Road Bars Recipe 130
265. O Henry Bars Recipe 131
266. OHenrie Bars Recipe 131
267. Oh Henry Bars Recipe 132
268. Oreo Cream Cheese Brownie Bars Recipe 132
269. PEANUT BUTTER MARSHMALLOW BARS Recipe 133
270. PEANUTTY BROWNIE BARS Recipe 133
271. PECAN BARS Recipe 134
272. PECAN PIE BARS Recipe 134
273. Pay Day Bars Recipe 135
274. Peanut Butter Bars With Chocolate Ganache Recipe 135
275. Peanut Butter Buckeye Bars Recipe 135
276. Peanut Butter Candy Caramel Bars Recipe 136
277. Peanut Butter Caramel Bars Recipe 137
278. Peanut Butter Chocolate Bars Recipe 137
279. Peanut Butter Cookie Candy Bars Recipe 137
280. Peanut Butter Crunch Candy Bars Recipe 138
281. Peanut Butter Cup Bars Recipe 139
282. Peanut Butter Granola Bars Recipe 139
283. Peanut Butter And Jelly Oat Bars Recipe 139
284. Peanut Cake Bars Recipe 140
285. Peanutty Buttery Squares Recipe 140
286. Pecan Squares Recipe 141
287. Pecan Squares Courtesy Of The Barefoot Contessa Recipe 141
288. Perfectly Peanutty Banana Bars Recipe .. 142
289. Pina Colada Bars Recipe 142
290. Pineapple Coconut Squares Recipe 142
291. Pineapple Oatmeal Bars Recipe 143
292. Praline Cheesecake Cookie Bars Recipe . 143
293. Pumpkin Bars Can Be Made Gluten Free Recipe 144
294. Pumpkin Bars Recipe 144
295. Pumpkin Bars With Cream Cheese Frosting Recipe 144
296. Pumpkin Cheese Praline Bars Recipe 145
297. Pumpkin Cheesecake Bars Recipe 146
298. Pumpkin Marshmallow Squares Recipe . 146
299. Pumpkin Pie Squares Recipe 147
300. Pumpkin Squares Recipe 147
301. Pumpkin Carrot Snack Bars Recipe 148
302. Pumpkin Spice Bars Recipe 148
303. Quick Chocolate Cherry Bars Recipe 149

304. Raspberry Linzer Bars Recipe 149
305. Red Velvet Cheesecake Bars From Henrys Deli Recipe 150
306. Redhead Bars Recipe 150
307. Rocky Road Bars Recipe 151
308. Rocky Road OREO Bars Recipe 151
309. Rustic Nut Bars Recipe 152
310. Salted Cashew Caramel Bars Recipe 152
311. Salted Peanut Marshmallow Bars Recipe 153
312. Sara Lees Carrot Square Cake Recipe 154
313. Scarlett OHara Pecan Bars Recipe 154
314. Scotcholate Bars Recipe 154
315. Scrumptious Chocolate Layer Bars Recipe 155
316. Simple Apple Squares Recipe 155
317. Sinfully Delicious Caramel Bars Recipe .. 156
318. Smore Bars Recipe 156
319. Smores Bars Recipe 156
320. Snicker Bar Cheesecake Recipe 157
321. Snicker Bars Recipe 157
322. Snickers Bar Cheesecake Recipe 158
323. Snickers Cheesecake Squares Recipe 158
324. Snickery Squares Recipe 159
325. So Easy Lemon Bars Recipe 160
326. Sour Cream Cranberry Bars Recipe 160
327. Sour Cream Banana Bars Recipe 160
328. Southern Pecan Bars Recipe 161
329. Special K Peanut Butter And Chocolate Bars Recipe 161
330. Speedy Brownies 162
331. Spicy Applesauce Bars Recipe 162
332. Spicy Chocolate Bars Recipe 163
333. Spicy Gingerbread Squares Recipe 163
334. Spumoni Bars Recipe 164
335. St Pattys Mint Cheesecake Bars Recipe ... 164
336. Sticky Carrot Squares Recipe 165
337. Strawberry Cheesecake Bars Recipe 165
338. Stuffed Chocolate Chip Cookie Bars Recipe 166
339. Sunshine Lemon Or Lime Bars Recipe ... 166
340. Super Lemony Lemon Bars Recipe 166
341. Sweet And Salty Chewy Pecan Bars Recipe 167
342. THEYLL NEVER BELIEVE IT CAKE SQUARES Recipe 168
343. Tarzan Ape Man Bars Recipe 168
344. Thick And Custardy Lemon Bars Recipe 169
345. Three Layer Lemon Bars Recipe 169
346. Tiramisu Cookie Bars Recipe 170
347. Tiramisu Squares Recipe 170
348. Toffee Almond Turtle Bars Recipe 171
349. Toffee Pumpkin Squares Recipe 171
350. Triple Chocolate Cherry Bars Recipe...... 172
351. Turtle Bars Recipe 172
352. Turtle Fudge Bars Recipe 173
353. ULTIMATE RICE KRISPY SQUARES Recipe 173
354. Walnut Easy Bars Recipe 173
355. White Christmas Fudge Bars Recipe....... 174
356. Whole Wheat Banana Bars Recipe 174
357. Whole Wheat Blueberry Bars Recipe 175
358. Yummie No Bake Cereal Bars Recipe 175
359. Zucchini Bars With Almond Cream Cheese Frosting Recipe 176
360. Zucchini Bars With Spice Frosting Recipe 176
361. Chocolate Bar Cake Recipe 177
362. Chocolate Mint Bars Recipe 177
363. Coconut Syrup Squares Recipe 178
364. Frosted Banana Cake Bars Recipe 178
365. Yummy Healthy Apple Oat Bars Recipe 179

INDEX 180

CONCLUSION 182

365 Awesome Bar Cookie Recipes

***

1. 10 Layer Monster Bars Recipe

Serving: 12 | Prep: | Cook: 25mins | Ready in:

Ingredients

- 1/2 c. unsalted butter, melted
- 1 c. graham cracker crumbs
- 1 can (14 ounces) sweetened condensed milk
- 1 c. pecan halves
- 16 caramels, cut up (3/4 cup)
- 1 c. semi-sweet chocolate chunks
- 1 c. white baking chips
- 1/2 c. milk chocolate chips
- 1/2 c. coarsely chopped walnuts
- 1/2 c. cashews

Direction

- Heat oven to 350 degrees F.
- Line 13 x 9-inch pan with heavy-duty foil, leaving extra foil extending over edges. Spray with non-stick cooking spray; line bottom with parchment paper.
- Pour melted butter into pan; tilt pan to spread evenly.
- Sprinkle graham cracker crumbs evenly over butter; pour condensed milk over crumbs.
- Layer pecan halves, caramels, chocolate chunks, white baking chips, milk chocolate chips, walnuts, and cashews in pan; press gently.
- Bake 25 minutes or until edges of bars bubble gently. Do not over bake. Cool completely on wire rack.
- Using foil edges, lift bars from pan. Slide bars off foil onto cutting board; cut into 24 pieces. (If knife sticks during cutting, spray with non-stick cooking spray.)

2. A Twist On Nanaimo Squares Recipe

Serving: 24 | Prep: | Cook: | Ready in:

Ingredients

- Bottom Layer:
- 113 grams unsalted butter, room temperature
- 1/4 cup (50 grams) granulated white sugar
- 1/3 cup (30 grams) unsweetened cocoa.+ extra for dusting.
- 1 large egg, beaten
- 1 teaspoon pure vanilla extract
- 2 cups (200 grams) graham cracker crumbs (I used digestive crumbs)
- 1 cup (65 grams) coconut (either sweetened or unsweetened)
- 1/2 cup (50 grams) walnuts or pecans, coarsely chopped
- FILLING:
- 1/4 cup (56 grams) unsalted butter, room temperature
- 2 - 3 tablespoons milk or cream (I used heavy cream)
- 2 tbsp vanilla pudding powder
- 1/2 tsp vanilla extract
- 2 cups (230 grams) powdered sugar.
- TOPPING:
- 4 ounces (115 grams) semisweet chocolate, chopped
- 1 tablespoon (14 grams) unsalted butter
- ¼ cup chocolate drink

Direction

- Butter a (23 x 23 cm) pan.
- Bottom layer:

- In a saucepan over low heat, melt the butter. Stir in the sugar and cocoa powder and then gradually whisk in the beaten egg. Cook, stirring constantly, until the mixture thickens (1 - 2 minutes). Remove from heat and stir in the vanilla extract, graham cracker crumbs, coconut, and chopped nuts. Press the mixture evenly into the prepared pan. Cover and refrigerate until firm (about an hour).
- Filling:
- In your electric mixer cream the butter. Beat in the remaining ingredients. If the mixture is too thick to spread, add a little more milk. Spread the filling over the bottom layer, cover, and refrigerate until firm (about 30 minutes).
- Top layer:
- In a heatproof bowl over a saucepan of simmering water, melt the chocolate and butter. Spread over the filling and refrigerate.
- To serve:
- Dust the entire surface with chocolate drink. To prevent the chocolate from cracking, using a sharp knife, bring the squares to room temperature before cutting. Makes about 25 squares

3. APPLE CHEESECAKE BARS Recipe

Serving: 24 | Prep: | Cook: 25mins | Ready in:

Ingredients

- Makes 24 bars
- 1-1/2 cups rolled oats
- 3/4 cup all-purpose flour
- 1/2 cup firmly packed light brown sugar
- 3/4 cup plus 2 tablespoons granulated sugar, divided
- 3/4 cup butter flavor shortening or 3/4 stick
- 2 (8-ounce) packages cream cheese, softened
- 2 large eggs
- 1 teaspoon vanilla
- 1 cup chopped granny smith apples
- 1/2 cup raisins
- 1 teaspoon almond extract
- 1/4 teaspoon ground nutmeg
- 1/4 teaspoon ground allspice

Direction

- Heat oven to 350°F.
- Combine oats, flour, brown sugar, and 1/4 cup granulated sugar in large bowl; mix well. Cut in shortening with fork until crumbs form. Reserve 1 cup mixture. Spray 13x9 inch baking pan with cooking spray. Press remaining mixture onto bottom of prepared pan. Bake at 350°F for 12 to 15 minutes or until mixture is set. Do not brown. Place on cooling rack.
- Combine cream cheese, eggs, 1/2 cup granulated sugar, and vanilla in large bowl. Beat at medium speed with electric mixer until well blended. Spread evenly over crust.
- Combine apples and raisins in medium bowl. Add almond extract; stir. Add 2 tablespoons sugar, cinnamon, nutmeg, and allspice; mix well. Top cream cheese mixture evenly with apple mixture; sprinkle reserved oat mixture evenly over top. Bake at 350°F for 20 to 25 minutes or until top is golden. Place on cooling rack; cool completely. Cut into bars

4. Adult Peanut Butter And Cookie Bars Recipe

Serving: 16 | Prep: | Cook: 20mins | Ready in:

Ingredients

- 9 ounces chocolate wafer cookies
- 1/2 cup butter melted
- 2/3 cup seedless red raspberry jam
- Filling:
- 3/4 pound cream cheese softened
- 2/3 cup creamy peanut butter
- 1/4 cup sugar
- 2 large eggs
- 1 teaspoon vanilla

- 2 tablespoons flour
- Glaze:
- 1-1/2 cups semisweet chocolate chips
- 1/2 cup heavy cream
- 1 tablespoon light corn syrup plus 1 teaspoon

Direction

- Preheat oven to 325.
- Line 2 square baking pans with foil extending foil by 2" on opposite ends.
- Coat well with cooking spray.
- Crush cookies into fine crumbs then add butter and pulse until evenly moistened and crumbly.
- Divide in half then press onto bottom of prepared pans and bake 10 minutes until set.
- Let cool completely on wire rack then spread 1/3 cup jam evenly over each crust.
- Increase oven temperature to 350.
- In bowl on high speed beat cream cheese, peanut butter and sugar until smooth.
- Beat in eggs 1 at a time then beat in vanilla and flour until smooth.
- Divide in half and spread over jam.
- Bake 18 minutes then cool just until warm.
- Heat all glaze ingredients in microwave on high for 1-1/2 minutes then whisk until smooth.
- Spread half over each peanut butter mixture layer then allow to cool to room temperature.
- Refrigerate at least 4 hours or overnight.
- To cut lift cookie squares out of pans and cut each into 4 strips.
- Cut each strip into 4 bars then have diagonally.

5. Alabama Chocolate Praline Jumbo Christmas Mud Squares Recipe

Serving: 16 | Prep: | Cook: 60mins | Ready in:

Ingredients

- 3/4 cup graham cracker crumbs
- 3/4 cup finely chopped pecans
- 1/4 cup firmly packed brown sugar
- 1/4 cup butter, melted
- 1 (12 oz.) jar caramel ice cream topping
- 3 Tbsp. flour
- 1 tbsp butter
- 4 (1 oz.) squares unsweetened chocolate
- 1 1/2 cups sugar
- 1 cup flour
- 4 eggs, beaten
- 1 tsp. vanilla
- 1 can chocolate frosting
- pecan halves
- maraschino cherries

Direction

- In a medium bowl, combine the first 4 ingredients, stirring well.
- Press mixture into the bottom of a 7x11" baking pan.
- Bake at 350* for 6-8 minutes.
- Cool slightly.
- Combine caramel topping and 3 Tbsp. flour, stirring well.
- Spread topping on crust, within 1/4" from the edge of pan. Set aside.
- Combine the 1 tbsp. butter and the unsweetened chocolate in a heavy saucepan; cook over low heat until melted.
- Stir in sugar, 1 cup flour, eggs, and vanilla; pour over caramel in pan.
- Bake at 350* for 50 minutes.
- Cool slightly and spread with chocolate frosting.
- Garnish with pecan halves and cherries.
- Set cool completely.
- Cut into 16 bars.

6. Alligator Cookie (peanut Butter Chew) Recipe

Serving: 8 | Prep: | Cook: 1mins | Ready in:

Ingredients

- 1 c kayro syrup
- 1 c sugar
- 1 c peanut butter
- 4 c corn flakes (can also use rice crispies!)

Direction

- Bring karo syrup, sugar, and peanut butter to a boil. Let boil for one minute. (Very important: the longer you boil the mixture, the harder it is to chew)
- When minute is up, remove from heat and stir in corn flakes.
- Let mixture harden and cut into squares.

7. Almond Apricot And White Chocolate Decadence Bars Recipe

Serving: 36 | Prep: | Cook: 40mins | Ready in:

Ingredients

- cookie Base:
- 1 pouch (1lb 1.5 oz) Betty Crocker sugar cookie mix
- 1/2 c butter, melted
- 1/2 tsp almond extract
- 1 egg, slightly beaten
- Filling:
- 1 pkg (7 or 8 oz) almond paste
- 1/2 c sugar
- 1 c finely chopped dried apricots (6 oz)
- 6 oz. cream cheese, softened
- 2 eggs
- 1 tsp lemon juice
- Topping:
- 1 bag (12 oz) white vanilla baking chips (2 c)
- 2/3 c whipping cream
- 1/2 c sliced almonds

Direction

- Heat oven to 375 degrees. In large bowl, stir cookie base ingredients until soft dough forms. Spread dough in bottom of ungreased 13x9" pan. Bake 10 to 15 mins or till set. Cool 10 mins.
- Meanwhile, in large bowl, beat almond paste and sugar with electric mixer on low speed until crumbly but blended. Add apricots; beat on low speed just until combined. Add cream cheese, 2 eggs and lemon juice; beat on medium speed until well blended. Pour over warm cookie base.
- Bake 20 to 25 mins or till set. Cool 30 mins.
- Place baking chips in small bowl. In 1 qt. saucepan, heat whipping cream just to boiling over low heat, stirring occasionally; pour over baking chips. Let stand 1 min. Stir until chips are melted and mixture is smooth. Pour and spread over filling. Sprinkle with almonds. Refrigerate about 2 hours or till set. For bars, cut in 9 rows by 4 rows. Store, covered in refrigerator.

8. Almond Bar Cookies Recipe

Serving: 36 | Prep: | Cook: 40mins | Ready in:

Ingredients

- ½ cup packed canned almond paste (about 5 oz; don't use marzipan), coarsely crumbled
- ½ teaspoon salt
- ¾ cup sugar
- 2 sticks (1 cup) unsalted butter, softened
- 1 large egg, separated
- 1 teaspoon almond extract
- 1¼ cups all-purpose flour
- ½ cup sliced almonds (about 1½ oz)

Direction

- Pulse the almond paste in a food processor until it's broken up into small pieces. (No need to overdo it)

- Add salt and ¼ cup sugar and continue to pulse until finely ground, about 1 minute.
- Put oven rack in middle position and preheat oven to 350°F.
- Butter a 9-inch square baking pan, then line with foil, leaving a 2-inch overhang on 2 opposite sides, and butter foil. (Note: I use a Kaiser Springform square pan, which eliminates the need to line the bottom with foil. You can simply remove the sides, let the cookies cool, and slice them on the pan bottom -- it's pretty much impervious to scratching.)
- Beat together butter and remaining ½ cup sugar in a stand mixer fitted with a paddle attachment for about 3 minutes, or with a hand held mixer for about 6 minutes.
- Add almond mixture, egg yolk, and almond extract and beat until combined well, about 2 minutes.
- Reduce speed to low, then add flour and mix until just combined. (Don't overmix once you've added the flour.)
- Spread batter evenly in pan with an offset spatula.
- Lightly beat egg white in a small bowl, then brush some of it over batter and sprinkle evenly with almonds.
- Bake until top is golden, 35 to 40 minutes.
- Cool completely in pan on a rack, about 1 hour.
- Transfer with foil to a cutting board, then discard foil.
- Cut into squares or rounds.
- Note: These cookies will keep in an airtight container at room temperature for about 4 days.

9. Almond ChoCoconut Bars Recipe

Serving: 24 | Prep: | Cook: 25mins | Ready in:

Ingredients

- 1 box of Devil's food cake cake mix
- 1 teaspoon almond extract
- ----
- bag of sweetened shredded coconut
- 1/2 can of condensed milk
- 20 big marshmallows
- ----
- 1/2 cup of milk chocolate chips
- 1/2 cup of chopped almonds

Direction

- Cake/Bottom
- Prepare as indicated on the box but add the almond extract at the same time you add the eggs. Pour into prepared jelly-roll pan.* Bake at 350F for about 12 minutes or until a toothpick comes out of the cake clean. Cool. Keep the oven on.
- Filling/Middle
- Put the condensed milk into a small medium sized saucepan and bring to a low boil over medium heat. Stir often so that the bottom of the pan doesn't burn and turn the milk into caramel. Add the marshmallows and continue mixing until the marshmallows are completely melted. Add the coconut and mix well. Spoon the coconut mixture over the cooked the cake and put it back in the oven for 8 minutes. Cool. (Turn off oven).
- Icing/Top
- In small bowl, melt chocolate chips in the microwave for a minute at a time and mix well. Continue until completely melted. Drizzle over bars. Store in the refrigerator until ready to serve.
- * If you want to make a taller, layered dessert, try making this in a 9x13 pan. Bake half the cake batter and cool. Then layer it with the coconut mixture, add a few chocolate chips and nuts, and then top it with more cake batter. Bake again for 10-15 minutes or until the cake is cooked thoroughly. Then top the cake with the nuts and drizzled chocolate.

10. Almonds Orange And Carrot Bars Recipe

Serving: 36 | Prep: | Cook: 25mins | Ready in:

Ingredients

- 75g/3oz/6tbsp butter, softened
- 50g/2oz/ ¼ cup caster sugar
- 150g/5oz/ 1 ¼ cups plain flour
- finely grated rind of 1 orange
- For the filling
- 90g/3 ½ oz/7 tbsp unsalted butter, diced
- 75g/3 oz/ ½ cup caster sugar
- 2 eggs
- ½ tsp almond extract
- 175g/6oz/1 ½ cups ground almonds
- 1 cooked carrot, coarsely grated
- For the topping
- 175g/6 oz/ ¾ cup cream cheese
- ¾ cup caster sugar
- 1 tsp milk
- 2-3 tbsp chopped pecans

Direction

- Preheat the oven to 375F. Lightly grease an 11x7in shallow baking tin. Put the butter, caster sugar, flour and orange rind into a bowl and rub together until the mixture resembles coarse breadcrumbs. Add water, a teaspoon at a time to mix to a firm but not sticky dough. Roll out on a lightly floured surface and use to line the base of the tin.
- To make the filling, cream the butter and sugar together. Beat in the eggs and almond extract. Stir in the ground almonds and the grated carrot. Spread the mixture over the dough base and bake for about 25 minutes until firm in the center and golden brown. Leave to cool in the tin.
- To make the topping, beat the cream cheese and sugar together until light and fluffy, add the milk and spread over the cooled filling. Sprinkle with the chopped pecans. Cut into bars with a sharp knife.

11. Almost Candy Bars Recipe

Serving: 20 | Prep: | Cook: 30mins | Ready in:

Ingredients

- Canola cooking spray
- 2 tablespoons butter
- 3 tablespoons sour cream
- 3 tablespoons chocolate syrup
- 1 package moist supreme devil's food cake mix
- 1/8 cup powdered sugar
- 3/4 cup butterscotch chips
- 3/4 cup semisweet chocolate chips
- 1 cup coconut sweetened
- 3/4 cup chopped pecans
- 14 ounce can sweetened condensed milk

Direction

- Preheat oven to 350 degrees then coat a rectangular metal baking pan with cooking spray.
- Heat butter in microwave in 1 cup glass measure on lowest setting just until melted.
- Stir sour cream and syrup into the glass measure with melted butter and mix until smooth.
- Put cake mix in mixing bowl then drizzle butter mixture over top and beat on low 30 seconds.
- Press evenly in bottom of prepared pan.
- Sprinkle the top of crust evenly with butterscotch chips, chocolate chips, coconut and nuts.
- Pour sweetened condensed milk evenly over all ingredients.
- Bake until light golden brown about 30 minutes then cool completely and cut into bars.

12. Apple Crumb Squares Recipe

Serving: 8 | Prep: | Cook: 35mins | Ready in:

Ingredients

- 1 cup old-fashioned rolled oats
- 3/4 cup whole-wheat flour
- 3/4 cup unbleached all-purpose flour
- 3/4 cup packed light brown sugar
- 1 teaspoon freshly grated lemon zest
- 3/4 teaspoon baking powder
- 1/2 teaspoon salt
- 1/2 teaspoon ground cinnamon
- 1/4 teaspoon ground nutmeg
- 3 tablespoons canola oil
- 1/4 cup apple-juice concentrate, thawed
- 3 medium tart apples, such as Granny Smith, peeled and thinly sliced
- 1/4 cup coarsely chopped walnuts, toasted
- apple cider Sauce
- 1/2 c. dark brown sugar (less for sweet cider)
- 3 c. apple cider
- 3/4 tsp. ground cloves
- 1/8 tsp. ground cinnamon
- 1/4 tsp. ground nutmeg
- 7 tsp. cornstarch
- 2 Tbsp. water
- 1 1/2 tsp. lemon juice
- Remove sauce from heat. Stir in lemon juice.
- Serve with
- 2 cups low-fat vanilla ice cream or nonfat frozen yogurt

Direction

- Preheat oven to 350°F. Coat a 9-inch square or 7-by-11-inch baking pan with cooking spray.
- Whisk oats, whole-wheat flour, all-purpose flour, brown sugar, lemon zest, baking powder, salt, cinnamon and nutmeg in a large bowl. Work in the oil and apple-juice concentrate with a fork or your fingers until the mixture resembles coarse crumbs.
- Press 2 cups of the oat mixture firmly into the bottom of the prepared pan. Arrange apple slices over the crust in three overlapping rows. Mix the walnuts into the remaining oat mixture. Sprinkle over the apples and pat into an even layer.
- Bake until the top is golden and the apples are tender when pierced, 30 to 35 minutes. Cool completely on a wire rack.
- Meanwhile, make Apple Cider Sauce.
- To serve, cut into 8 pieces and place on dessert plates. Top with ice cream (or frozen yogurt) and drizzle with cider sauce.
- Recipe: Apple Cider Sauce
- Combine cornstarch and water in separate bowl. Slowly add cornstarch mix to boiling apple cider, stirring constantly until the sauce thickens slightly.
- Remove sauce from heat. Stir in lemon juice.

13. Apple Golden Raisin Cheesecake Bars Recipe

Serving: 18 | Prep: | Cook: 13mins | Ready in:

Ingredients

- 1 1/2 cups rolled oats
- 3/4 cup flour
- 1/2 cup brown sugar
- 3/4 cup plus 2 tbsp. white sugar
- 3/4 cup butter flavored crisco
- 2 (8 ounce) packages softened cream cheese
- 2 large eggs
- 1tsp vanilla
- 1 cup chopped granny smith apples
- 1/2 cup golden raisins
- 1 tsp. almond extract
- 1/2 tsp. cinnamon
- 1/4 tsp. ground nutmeg
- 1/4 tsp. ground allspice

Direction

- Heat oven to 350*
- Combine oats, flour, brown sugar and 1/4 cup white sugar in a large bowl, mix well.

- Cut in Crisco with fork until crumbs form. Reserve 1 cup.
- Spray 13x9 inch baking pan.
- Press remaining mixture onto bottom of prepared pan.
- Bake at 350* for 12 to 15 minutes or until mixture sets. Place on cooling rack.
- Combine cream cheese, eggs, 1/2 cup white sugar and vanilla in large bowl.
- Beat at medium speed with mixer until well blended.
- Spread evenly over crust.
- Combine apples and raisins in medium bowl.
- Add almond extract; stir.
- Add 2 tbsp. sugar, cinnamon, nutmeg, and all spice; mix well.
- Top cream cheese mixture evenly with apple mixture; sprinkle reserved oat mixture evenly over top.
- Bake at 350* for 20 to 25 minutes or until top is golden.
- Place on cooling rack; cool completely.
- Cut into bars.

14. Apple Pastry Squares Recipe

Serving: 12 | Prep: | Cook: 40mins | Ready in:

Ingredients

- 1/4 cup packed brown sugar
- 2 tablespoons cornstarch
- 1 cup water
- 5 cups thinly sliced peeled apples
- 1/2 teaspoon ground cinnamon
- 1/4 teaspoon ground nutmeg
- 1 tablespoon lemon juice
- PASTRY:
- 2 cups all-purpose flour
- 1/2 teaspoon salt
- 2/3 cup cold shortening
- 2 egg yolks, beaten
- 1/4 cup cold water
- 1 tablespoon lemon juice
- GLAZE:
- 1/2 cup confectioners' sugar
- 1 tablespoon milk
- 1 tablespoon butter or margarine
- 1/2 teaspoon vanilla extract

Direction

- For filling, combine sugar, cornstarch and water in a saucepan.
- Mix until well blended.
- Add apples; heat to boiling, stirring constantly.
- Reduce heat and simmer 5 minutes, stirring occasionally.
- Remove from the heat.
- Stir in spices and lemon juices; set aside.
- For pastry, combine flour and salt.
- Cut in shortening until mixture is crumbly.
- Combine egg yolks, water and lemon juice; blend into flour.
- Mixture will form a ball.
- Divided in half. On a lightly floured surface, roll the dough between two pieces of waxed paper to fit the bottom and halfway up the sides of a 13-in. x 9-in. baking pan.
- Spread filling over pastry.
- Roll remaining pastry to fit pan exactly; place on top of filling.
- Fold bottom pastry over top and press to seal.
- Cut a few small slits in top crust.
- Bake at 400° for about 40 minutes or until lightly browned.
- For glaze, combine all ingredients and drizzle over the warm pastry.

15. Apple Pie Bars Recipe

Serving: 35 | Prep: | Cook: 45mins | Ready in:

Ingredients

- Ingredients
- CRUST:
- - 2 1/2 cups all-purpose flour

- - 1 tablespoon sugar
- - 1 teaspoon salt
- - 1 teaspoon baking soda
- - 1 cup vegetable shortening (not oil)
- - 2 eggs
- milk (up to 2/3 cup)
- FILLING:
- - 1 1/2 cups crushed corn flakes
- - 12 to 14 apples (peeled, cored, and sliced)
- - 1 1/2 cups sugar
- - 2 teaspoons cinnamon
- GLAZE:
- - 1 cup powdered sugar
- - 2 teaspoons lemon juice

Direction

- Directions
- Preheat oven to 350 degrees.
- CRUST: In a large bowl, combine flour, sugar, salt, and baking soda. Cut-in 1 cup vegetable shortening. Separate the eggs. Place egg yolks in a one cup measuring cup and add milk to the egg yolks until milk and egg yolks equal 2/3 cups.
- Blend the egg mixture into flour mixture until it reaches a dough consistency.
- Divide the dough in half. Roll out 1/2 of the dough to fit the bottom of the jelly roll pan. The crust will be very thin.
- FILLING: Cover crust with crushed corn flakes. Cover corn flakes with prepared apple slices. In separate bowl, combine sugar and cinnamon. Sprinkle evenly over apple slices. Roll out the remaining dough and cover the apple mixture with it. The dough will be very thin.
- Beat remaining egg whites until they appear semi-stiff. Brush them onto the crust.
- Bake for 35 to 40 minutes. Remove from oven.
- GLAZE: in a small bowl, combine powdered sugar and lemon juice for glaze. Blend until smooth. Adjust consistency (add lemon juice if too dry; add powdered sugar if too runny). Drizzle glaze over the top of the warm bars.
- Bars can be served warm or cold, and they freeze well, too.

16. Applesauce Bars With Orange Glaze Recipe

Serving: 48 | Prep: | Cook: 30mins | Ready in:

Ingredients

- 2 cups flour
- 1 1/2 cups sugar
- 2 tsp baking powder
- 1 tsp baking soda
- 2 tsp ground cinnamon
- 1/2 tsp salt
- 1/4 tsp ground cloves
- 1/2 tsp nutmeg
- 4 eggs, beaten
- 15 oz applesauce
- 1 cup oil
- For glaze:
- 1/4 cup orange juice
- 1 tsp orange zest
- 1/2 cup water
- 1/2 cup sugar
- 2 tbs water
- 2 tbs corn starch

Direction

- Sift dry ingredients in mixing bowl, set aside mix all liquid ingredients in a mixing bowl combine wet ingredients to dry and stir until smooth pour batter into ungreased 15 x 10 x1 inch baking pan lined with baking paper.
- Bake at 350 for about 25 to 30 minutes or until a wooden toothpick inserted in center comes out clean.
- For glaze:
- Heat orange juice, zest, 1/2 cup water until simmering. Add sugar and stir until dissolved. Mix corn starch and water and slowly add to simmering juice. Cook about 4 or 5 minutes until corn starch thickens glaze.
- Spread over cake.

- Refrigerate

17. Applesauce Squares Recipe

Serving: 12 | Prep: | Cook: 30mins | Ready in:

Ingredients

- 1-1/3 cup sifted cake flour
- 1 teaspoon baking soda
- 1/2 teaspoon salt
- 1 cup. sugar
- 1/2 teaspoon allspice
- 1/2 teaspoon cloves
- 1 teaspoon cinnamon
- 1/2 cup shortening
- 1 cup sweetened applesauce
- 1 egg
- 1/2 teaspoon chopped raisins
- 1/2 cup chopped nuts

Direction

- Sift flour, baking soda, salt, sugar and spices into a large bowl.
- Add shortening and applesauce then mix to dampen flour then beat 2 minutes.
- Add remaining ingredients and beat one minute with electric mixer.
- Pour into a greased square pan lined with wax paper.
- Bake at 350 for 30 minutes then allow to stand for 10 minutes.
- Remove from pan and cool.

18. Apricot Bars Recipe

Serving: 10 | Prep: | Cook: 30mins | Ready in:

Ingredients

- 1/3 cup dried apricots, chopped
- 1 1/2 sticks butter, unsalted
- 2 tbls. honey
- 2 cups Rice Krispies
- 1 cup almonds, chopped
- 1 egg
- 1 egg yolk
- 2/3 cup flour
- 3/4 cup apricot preserves
- 1 tbls. lemon juice

Direction

- Preheat oven to 350.
- Spray 11x7 baking pan with cooking spray.
- Put apricots in a saucepan with butter and honey over low heat until butter melts.
- Put Rice Krispies in food processor and process until fine crumbs.
- Mix cereal crumbs in a bowl with almonds, egg, egg yolk and flour.
- In large bowl, mix cereal mixture and honey mixture.
- Put half in baking pan and press down with a spoon until compact.
- In small bowl, mix preserves and lemon juice.
- Spread it on top of cereal mixture in pan.
- Press remaining cereal mixture on top of preserves.
- Bake for 30 minutes or until the top is golden brown.
- Cool and cut into 2 in. squares.

19. Apricot Butter Bars Recipe

Serving: 24 | Prep: | Cook: 60mins | Ready in:

Ingredients

- 1 cup of dried apricots
- 8 tbsp of unsalted butter
- 1 1/4 cups of firmly packed brown sugar
- 1 1/3 cups of all purpose flour
- 1/2 tsp of baking powder
- 1/4 tsp of salt
- 2 eggs
- 1/2 tsp of vanilla extract

- 1/2 cup of walnuts, coarsely chopped

Direction

- Preheat oven to 350 degrees.
- Butter a nine inch square cake pan.
- Rinse the apricots, place them in a saucepan and cover with cold water. Bring to a boil and simmer for 10 minutes. Drain, cool, chop into 1/4 inch pieces.
- Cut the butter into 1/4 cup of brown sugar and one cup of flour until a crumbly mixture is formed.
- Press the mixture into the bottom of the pan and bake 25 minutes until golden.
- Meanwhile, sift remaining flour with baking powder and salt.
- Beat the eggs until well blended.
- Beat in the remaining cup of brown sugar and then the flour mixture until well blended.
- Add the vanilla, chopped nuts and apricots.
- Evenly spread the apricot nut mixture over the baked layer and continue to bake 30 minutes.
- Cool in the pan and cut into squares or bars.
- Makes 2 dozen.

20. Apricot Oat Bars Easy Recipe

Serving: 1620 | Prep: | Cook: 35mins | Ready in:

Ingredients

- 10 ounces dried apricots (about 1 1/2 cups)
- 3/4 cup boiling water
- 3 cups uncooked rolled oats
- 1/3 cup whole wheat flour
- 1/3 cup all-purpose flour
- 1 tablespoon kosher salt
- 1/4 teaspoon ground cinnamon (optional)
- 8 tablespoons unsalted butter (1 stick)
- 7 tablespoons honey (6 n 1)
- 6 tablespoons packed light brown sugar (I use 3 tab. Brown sugar Splenda)
- 1/3 cup apricot jam
- 3/4 teaspoon vanilla extract

Direction

- Heat oven to 350°F and arrange the rack in middle. Butter an 8-by-8-inch glass baking dish and set aside. Place apricots in a large mixing bowl and cover with boiling water. Set aside until apricots are plumped up and have absorbed almost all the water, about 25 minutes.
- Meanwhile, in a large mixing bowl, combine oats, whole wheat flour, all-purpose flour, salt, and ground cinnamon (if using); mix until evenly combined, and set aside.
- In a small saucepan, combine butter, 6 tablespoons of the honey, and sugar. Bring to a boil over medium-high heat and cook, stirring occasionally, until bubbling and foamy, about 5 minutes.
- Pour honey mixture over oat mixture, stirring until oats are well coated. Press 1/2 of the oat mixture (about 1 1/2 cups) into the bottom of the prepared baking dish. Use the bottom of a measuring cup or glass to help ensure an even layer.
- Combine soaked apricots, remaining 1 tablespoon honey, jam, and vanilla extract in the bowl of a food processor. Process until mixture is puréed (it will resemble baby food), about 1 minute.
- Spread apricot filling evenly over oat base and sprinkle with remaining oat mixture, pressing it gently with your fingers. Bake until the bottom is golden brown and the top is well browned, about 35 to 40 minutes. Remove from the oven and let cool in the baking dish, allowing at least 12 hours for it to fully set up. Slice into squares and serve.

21. Apricot Oat Squares Recipe

Serving: 16 | Prep: | Cook: 30mins | Ready in:

Ingredients

- 1 cup quick-cooking oats

- 1 cup all-purpose flour
- 2/3 cup packed brown sugar
- 1/4 teaspoon baking soda
- 1/4 teaspoon salt
- 1/4 cup canola oil
- 3 tablespoons unsweetened apple juice
- 1 jar (10 ounces) apricot spreadable fruit

Direction

- In a large bowl, combine the oats, flour, brown sugar, baking soda and salt. Add oil and apple juice; stir until moistened. Set aside 1/2 cup for topping.
- Press remaining oat mixture into an 11-in. x 7-in. x 2-in. baking pan coated with non-stick cooking spray. Spread the apricot fruit spread to within 1/4 in. of edges. Sprinkle with reserved oat mixture.
- Bake at 325° for 30-35 minutes or until golden brown.

22. Apricot Oatmeal Bars Recipe

Serving: 28 | Prep: | Cook: 25mins | Ready in:

Ingredients

- 1 C all purpose flour
- 1 c quick cooking oats
- 1 tsp salt
- 1/2 tsp cinnamon
- 1/4 tsp ground cloves
- 1 tsp baking soda
- 6 TBLS butter
- 6 TBLS canola oil
- 3/4 c white sugar - I use half sugar & half splenda
- 1/2 c brown sugar
- 2 eggs
- 1 tsp vanilla
- 1/2 c dried apricots, diced - any dried fruit will work here

Direction

- Preheat oven to 375. Spray a 9x13 with non-stick spray - pam.
- Combine first 5 ingredients in one bowl, set aside.
- Combine butter through vanilla in another bowl and mix with electric mixer till smooth and fluffy.
- Add dry ingredients to the wet and mix just till incorporated. Add dried fruit.
- Spread mixture evenly into prepared pan, bake for 20-25 min. Cool completely before cutting into bars.

23. Apricot Squares Recipe

Serving: 24 | Prep: | Cook: 10mins | Ready in:

Ingredients

- 1/2 cup margarine
- 1 1/2 cup brown sugar
- 1 1/4 cup flour (plus 3 tbsp.)
- 2 eggs
- 1 cup chopped, dried apricots
- 3/4 cup flaked coconut
- 1/2 cup chopped pecans
- 1/2 tsp. vanilla
- 1/2 t. lemon juice
- 1/4 t. salt

Direction

- Mix margarine, 1/2 cup brown sugar and flour (1 1/4 cup). Press into ungreased 13 x 9 " pan. Bake in preheated 350 F oven for 10 minutes. Blend remaining 1 cup sugar, eggs, apricots, coconut, pecans, vanilla, lemon juice, salt and 3 tbsp. flour and pour over top of crust. Bake an additional 8 minutes until top is done. Cool and cut into squares.

24. Apricot Walnut Bars Supreme Recipe

Serving: 40 | Prep: | Cook: 30mins | Ready in:

Ingredients

- Ingredients
- * 1 cup butter, softened
- * 1/2 cup packed brown sugar
- * 2-1/2 cups all-purpose flour
- * 2/3 cup apricot preserves
- * 4 eggs
- * 1-1/2 cups packed brown sugar
- * 1/4 cup unsweetened Dutch-process cocoa powder
- * 2 teaspoons vanilla
- * 1 teaspoon salt
- * 3 cups walnuts, toasted and finely ground*
- * 8 ounces bittersweet chocolate, chopped
- * 3 tablespoons butter
- * 1 tablespoon light-color corn syrup
- * 1 tablespoon rum
- * About 40 walnut halves, toasted (optional)

Direction

- Directions
- 1. Preheat oven to 375 degrees F. Grease a 13x9x2-inch baking pan; set aside. In a large bowl, beat the 1 cup butter with an electric mixer on medium to high speed for 30 seconds. Add the 1/2 cup brown sugar. Beat until combined, scraping side of bowl occasionally. Gradually add flour, beating on low speed just until combined (mixture will look slightly dry). Press mixture into prepared pan. Bake in the preheated oven for 10 minutes. Carefully spread preserves over hot crust.
- 2. In another large bowl, beat eggs on medium-high speed for 3 minutes. Add the 1-1/2 cups brown sugar, the cocoa powder, vanilla, and salt. Beat on low speed for 3 minutes. Gradually add the finely ground walnuts, beating just until combined.
- 3. Carefully spread chocolate mixture evenly over preserves. Bake about 30 minutes or until set. Cool completely in pan on a wire rack.
- 4. For icing: In a medium heavy saucepan, combine bittersweet chocolate and the 3 tablespoons butter. Cook and stir over low heat until melted. Stir in corn syrup and rum. Spread icing over cooled uncut cookies. If desired, top with the walnut halves. Let stand for 1 to 2 hours or until chocolate is set. Using a sharp knife, loosen edges of cookies from sides of pan. Cut into bars. Makes about 40 bars.
- 5. *Test Kitchen Tip: To prevent overgrinding the nuts and turning them into a paste, grind about one-third at a time.
- 6. To Store: Place bars in a single layer in an airtight container; cover. Store at room temperature for up to 3 days or freeze for up to 3 months.
- Nutrition Facts

25. BEST Granola Bars Ever Recipe

Serving: 14 | Prep: | Cook: 5mins | Ready in:

Ingredients

- GRAINS:
- 1 cup rice puffs
- 1 cup rolled oats
- 1 cup rolled wheat
- 1/2 chopped almonds
- 1/2 sunflower seeds
- 1/2 cup flax seeds
- 1/2 cup dried cranberries
- GLAZE:
- 2/3 cup light brown sugar
- 1/3 cup + 1 TBS honey
- 1/4 cup butter (half a stick)
- 1 tsp vanilla

Direction

- Toast any raw grains in the oven for about 5 min. at 400 degrees, mixing half-way thru.
- Line 13x9 inch pan with foil to spread granola in.
- Mix all dry ingredients in very large bowl, or stock pot (I like to use my 8 qt. pot).
- Heat all glaze ingredients in heavy sauce pan on stove top at medium heat.
- Bring to boil, reduce heat stirring constantly, and simmer 2 minutes.
- Pour glaze over dry ingredients, mix well.
- Spread in foil lined pan, smooth flat with back of spoon.
- Smooth a LOT, as you want the grains to be packed together so the bars don't fall apart!
- Let sit for 2 hours.
- Remove granola in foil and place on counter, using a large knife, cut into bars.
- I like to individually wrap the bars in sandwich bags, because I found out the hard way, that they stick together!

26. BUTTER PECAN BANANA BARS Recipe

Serving: 24 | Prep: | Cook: 35mins | Ready in:

Ingredients

- butter pecan banana BARS
- 2 1/2 cups flour
- 1 2/3 cups sugar
- 1 1/4 teaspoons baking powder
- 1 1/4 teaspoons baking soda
- 1/2 teaspoon salt
- 3/4 cup butter, softened
- 2/3 cup buttermilk
- 3 medium-size ripe bananas, mashed
- 2 eggs
- 1/2 cup chopped pecans

Direction

- Combine flour, sugar, baking powder, baking soda, and salt in large mixing bowl. Add softened butter, cut in chunks, buttermilk, and bananas, and beat well using an electric mixer.
- Add eggs and mix well. Stir in nuts. Bake in an ungreased 15 inches x 10 inches x 1 inch pan for 30 to 35 minutes. Cool.
- Frost if desired with a mixture of 1/4 cup soft butter, 1 ½ cups confectioners' sugar, 1/2 teaspoon vanilla, and enough milk to reach spreading consistency.
- Beat frosting ingredients until smooth, and fold in 1/2 cup finely chopped pecans.

27. Baby Ruth Bars Recipe

Serving: 36 | Prep: | Cook: 20mins | Ready in:

Ingredients

- 2 1/4 cups all-purpose flour
- 1 teaspoon baking soda
- 1/2 teaspoon salt
- 3/4 cup packed brown sugar
- 3/4 cup granulated sugar
- 1/2 cup butter OR margarine, softened
- 1/2 cup creamy OR chunky peanut butter
- 2 large eggs
- 1 teaspoon vanilla extract
- 6 (2.1-ounce each) Baby Ruth Candy Bars, coarsely chopped

Direction

- Preheat oven to 375° F.
- Grease 15 x 10-inch jelly roll pan.
- Combine flour, baking soda and salt in small bowl.
- Beat brown sugar, granulated sugar, butter and peanut butter in large mixer bowl until creamy.
- Beat in eggs and vanilla extract.
- Gradually beat in flour mixture.
- Spread dough evenly into prepared pan.
- Sprinkle with Baby Ruth; press in lightly.
- Bake for 18 to 20 minutes or until golden brown.

- Cool completely in pan on wire rack.
- Cut into bars.

28. Banana Honey Bars Recipe

Serving: 24 | Prep: | Cook: 20mins | Ready in:

Ingredients

- 1 ½ cups flour
- 1 tsp baking powder
- 1 tsp cinnamon
- pinch salt
- ½ cup butter
- 1/3 cup brown sugar
- ¼ cup honey
- 1/3 cup skim milk
- 1/2 tbsp vanilla
- 3 large over-ripe bananas, mashed

Direction

- Preheat oven to 350F.
- Grease and flour a 9×13" pan.
- Whisk together the flour, baking powder, cinnamon and salt. Set aside
- Cream together the butter and brown sugar.
- Beat in honey, milk, vanilla and mashed bananas.
- Gently mix in the dry ingredients.
- Bake for 20 minutes.

29. Banana Bars Recipe

Serving: 24 | Prep: | Cook: 30mins | Ready in:

Ingredients

- 1 stick butter
- 1 1/2 c sugar
- 2 eggs
- 3 1/2 c or 3-4 large bananas, mashed
- 1 c raisins
- 8 oz. sour cream
- 1 tsp vanilla
- 2 c flour
- 1/2 tsp salt, optional
- 1 tsp baking powder
- 1 tsp baking soda
- Frosting:
- 8-oz. pkg. cream cheese
- 2/3 c butter, softened
- 1 Tb vanilla
- 4 1/2 c powdered sugar

Direction

- Cream together butter, sugar and eggs.
- Mix together bananas and raisins, sour cream and vanilla.
- Mix dry ingredients and add banana mixture; then add to creamed mixture.
- Pour into greased (not floured) jelly roll pan.
- Bake at 350 degrees for 20-30 minutes.
- Frosting:
- Beat cream cheese, butter and vanilla until creamy.
- Add powdered sugar.
- Beat until light and fluffy.
- Spread over cooled bars.

30. Banana Bars With Cream Cheese Frosting Recipe

Serving: 24 | Prep: | Cook: 24mins | Ready in:

Ingredients

- Bars:
- ½ cup butter
- 1 cup sugar
- ½ cup brown sugar
- 2 eggs
- 1 cup mashed bananas (2 large or 3 medium bananas)
- ½ cup full-fat sour cream
- 1 teaspoon baking soda

- 2 cups flour
- ½ teaspoon salt
- 1 teaspoon cinnamon, optional
- Cream Cheese Frosting:
- 6 ounces cream cheese
- 4 tablespoons butter, softened
- 2 tablespoons milk or cream
- 2 cups powdered sugar
- 1 teaspoon vanilla extract

Direction

- For the bars, cream together butter and both sugars.
- Add eggs, mixing in well; stir in bananas.
- Dissolve soda in sour cream.
- Add flour, salt and cinnamon to batter alternately with sour cream mixture, until batter is well blended.
- Pour batter into greased 10x15 baking sheet.
- Bake at 350 degrees for 20 to 25 minutes.
- Cool completely before frosting.
- For frosting, mix all ingredients together with electric mixer (using a mixer will tend to give you a fluffier frosting than mixing by hand).
- Spread over cooled bars.

31. Banana Cream Brownie Squares Recipe

Serving: 1 | Prep: | Cook: 25mins | Ready in:

Ingredients

- 3/4 cup dry roasted peanuts, chopped
- 1 pkg (15 oz) brownie mix
- 3 medium bananas
- 1 1/4 cup cold milk
- 1 pkg (5.1 oz) instant vanilla pudding and pie filling
- 1 container (8 oz) frozen whipped topping, thawed
- 9 strawberries
- 1 plain chocolate candy bar

Direction

- Preheat oven to 350.
- Chop peanuts.
- Prepare brownie mix according to package directions; stir in 1/2 cup of chopped peanuts. Pour into 9" square baking pan. Bake 24-27 minutes. Cool completely.
- Slice 2 bananas. Layer over brownies.
- In bowl, whisk pudding mix into milk; beat until mixture just begins to thicken. Fold in 2 1/2 cups whipped topping. Quickly spread pudding mixture over sliced bananas.
- Refrigerate 30 minutes. Sprinkle remaining 1/4 cup peanuts over top of pudding mixture. Garnish with remaining whipped topping.
- To serve, cut into squares and grate chocolate over dessert. Slice remaining banana and strawberries. Top each square with banana and strawberry slices.

32. Banana Crunch Bars Recipe

Serving: 16 | Prep: | Cook: 10mins | Ready in:

Ingredients

- 1-3/4 cups crushed chocolate wafers (about 36 wafers)
- 1/2 cup sugar
- 1/4 cup unsweetened cocoa powder
- 1 teaspoon vanilla
- 1/2 cup butter, melted
- 3 tablespoons light-colored corn syrup
- 2 tablespoons butter
- 2 medium bananas, sliced (1-1/2 cups)
- 1 teaspoon rum flavoring
- 1/2 cup semisweet chocolate pieces
- 1/2 cup peanut butter-flavored pieces
- 1 teaspoon shortening

Direction

- Preheat oven to 350 degree F. In a medium bowl combine the crushed wafers, sugar,

cocoa powder, and vanilla. Stir in 1/2 cup melted butter. Press into bottom of a greased 8x8x2-inch baking pan. Bake for 10 minutes. Cool slightly on a wire rack, about 10 minutes.
- In a small saucepan combine corn syrup and 2 tablespoons butter. Stir over medium heat until melted and bubbly. Remove from heat; stir in bananas and rum flavouring. Spoon banana mixture in an even layer over baked crust.
- In a small saucepan combine the chocolate pieces, peanut butter-flavored pieces, and shortening. Stir over low heat until melted. Drizzle over the banana mixture. Cover and chill until set. Let stand at room temperature 20 minutes before cutting into bars. Serve the same day.

33. Banana Pudding Squares Recipe

Serving: 24 | Prep: | Cook: | Ready in:

Ingredients

- 35 vanilla wafers, finely crushed
- 1/4 cup (1/2 stick) margarine, melted
- 1 pkg. (8 oz.) cream cheese, softened
- 1/2 cup powdered sugar
- 1 tub (8 oz.) frozen non dairy whipped topping, thawed, divided
- 3 bananas
- 3 cups cold milk
- 2 pkg. (3.4 oz. each) vanilla flavor Instant Pudding & pie filling
- 1/2 square BAKER'S Semi-sweet chocolate, grated

Direction

- COMBINE: crumbs and margarine; press onto bottom of 13x9-inch dish. Refrigerate while preparing filling.

- MIX cream cheese and sugar in medium bowl until blended. Stir in 1-1/2 cups whipped topping; spread carefully onto crust. Set aside.
- Cut bananas crosswise in half, then cut each piece lengthwise in half. Arrange over Neufchatel cheese mixture.
- BEAT milk and pudding mixes with whisk 2 min. Spoon over bananas. Spread with remaining whipped topping; sprinkle with chocolate.
- Refrigerate 3 hours before serving. Refrigerate leftovers.
- * This recipe can be made with low-fat vanilla wafers, low fat cream cheese and low fat milk if desired to reduce the calories. It doesn't take away from the taste.

34. Banana Split Cheesecake Squares Recipe

Serving: 1 | Prep: | Cook: 30mins | Ready in:

Ingredients

- Crust:
- 2 cups graham cracker crumbs
- 1/3 cup melted butter
- ¼ cup sugar
- Filling:
- 3 pkgs (8 oz. each) cream cheese
- ¾ cup sugar
- 1 tsp. vanilla
- 3 eggs
- ½ cup mashed banana
- Topping:
- 1 cup sliced strawberries
- 1 banana, sliced, tossed with 1 tsp. lemon juice
- 1 can (8 oz.) pineapple chunks, drained

Direction

- Crust:
- Mix crumbs, butter and sugar. Press onto bottom of 13x9x2 pan.
- Filling:

- Mix cream cheese, sugar and vanilla with electric mixer on medium speed until well blended. Add eggs; mix until blended. Stir in mashed banana. Pour into crust.
- Bake at 350 for 30 minutes or until center is almost set. Cool.
- Refrigerate 3 hours or overnight.
- Topping:
- Top with strawberries, sliced banana and pineapple. Drizzle with melted chocolate. Cut into squares.

35. Bettah Buttah Banana Bars Recipe

Serving: 12 | Prep: | Cook: 1hours | Ready in:

Ingredients

- 3 tbsp butter
- 2 tbsp peanut butter
- 1/3 cup sugar
- 1 tsp vanilla
- 3 large, over-ripe bananas, mashed
- 3/4 cup flour
- 1/2 tsp baking powder
- 1/2 tsp baking soda
- 1/4 tsp salt
- 1/4 cup baking cocoa
- 1/4 cup chopped peanuts
- 10 miniature peanut butter cups, chopped

Direction

- Preheat oven to 350F, grease a 9" square pan.
- In a bowl, beat butter, peanut butter and sugar until fluffy.
- Add vanilla and bananas, beating well.
- Mix together flour, baking powder, baking soda and salt. Add to the creamed mixture, blending gently but thoroughly.
- Divide batter in half.
- To one portion of dough, add cocoa and stir in thoroughly.
- To the other portion of dough, fold in chopped peanuts.
- Spread chocolate batter in the bottom of the prepared pan. Top with peanut butter and sprinkle with peanut butter cups.
- Bake for 25-30 minutes.
- Cool completely in the pan before cutting.

36. Black Forest Cheesecake Squares Recipe

Serving: 1 | Prep: | Cook: 35mins | Ready in:

Ingredients

- 1 pkg Fudge marble cake mix
- 1/4 c oil
- 3 Eggs; divided
- 3 pk (8 oz.) cream cheese; softened
- 1/2 c sugar
- 1/2 c sour cream
- 1/2 c whipping cream
- 1 can (21 oz.) cherry pie filling

Direction

- Preheat oven to 350 degrees. Grease 13x9 inch baking pan.
- Reserve 1 cup dry cake mix and swirl pouch; set aside. In large bowl, combine remaining cake mix, oil and 1 egg at low speed until dough forms. Press in bottom and 1 inch up sides of greased pan. Bake for 8 minutes.
- In large bowl, beat cream cheese until smooth and creamy. Add 2 eggs, 1 at a time, beating well after each addition. Blend in reserved 1 cup cake mix, sugar, sour cream and whipping cream at low speed. Beat 3 minutes at medium speed until creamy.
- Reserve 2 cups cheese mixture. Spoon remaining cheese mixture over crust. Add reserved swirl pouch to reserved cheese mixture; blend well. Spoon chocolate mixture evenly over cheese mixture.

- Bake for 30-40 minutes until edges are set and center is almost set.
- Do not overbake. Run knife around sides of pan. Cool to room temperature on wire rack.
- Spoon fruit filling evenly over top of cheesecake. Refrigerate several hours or overnight before serving. Store in refrigerator.
- Makes 48 bars.

37. Blarney Stones Bars With Vanilla Icing And Chopped Peanuts Recipe

Serving: 36 | Prep: | Cook: 20mins | Ready in:

Ingredients

- 4 eggs, separated
- 1 cup granulated sugar
- 1 cup flour
- 1 1/2 teaspoons baking powder
- 1/4 teaspoon salt
- 1/2 cup boiling water
- 1/2 teaspoon vanilla
- .
- Frosting:
- 1 cup butter
- 2 to 2 1/2 cups confectioner's sugar
- 1 teaspoon vanilla
- crushed salted peanuts

Direction

- Beat yolks with hand held electric mixer until thick and lemon colored. Add sugar gradually, beating continuously. Add dry ingredients, sifted together, alternately with boiling water.
- Add vanilla and beat well.
- Fold in stiffly beaten egg whites.
- Bake 20 minutes at 350 degrees in shallow sheet cake pan.
- When almost cool, ice with frosting.
- Cut in squares.
- Frosting:
- Cream butter; gradually blend in sugar.
- Cream until soft and smooth.
- After spreading frosting on Blarney Stones, roll each Blarney Stone in crushed peanuts or sprinkle crushed peanuts over frosting.
- Yield 3 dozen squares

38. Blitzen Bars Recipe

Serving: 24 | Prep: | Cook: 20mins | Ready in:

Ingredients

- 16 oz. pkg caramels
- 1 chocolate cake mix
- 1 cup nuts, chopped
- 2/3 cup evaporated milk
- 2/3 cup butter, melted
- 1 cup chocolate chips

Direction

- Preheat oven to 350 F.
- Combine caramels in 1/3 cup evaporated milk in saucepan, heat and stir until melted. Combine cake mix, butter and 1/3 cup evaporated milk and mix well. Press 1/2 of this dough into a 9" x 13" pan. Bake 5 minutes at 350 F. Sprinkle nuts and chocolate chips on baked dough. Cover with caramel mixture. Spread remaining half of dough over caramel. Spread with fingers (does not spread well). Bake 15 to 20 minutes at 350 F.

39. Blueberry Almond Bars Recipe

Serving: 16 | Prep: | Cook: 35mins | Ready in:

Ingredients

- 1/2 cup butter or margarine
- 1 12-ounce package (2 cups) white baking pieces

- 2 eggs, slightly beaten
- 1/2 cup sugar
- 1/2 to 1 teaspoon almond extract
- 1 cup all-purpose flour
- 1/2 teaspoon salt
- 1/2 cup blueberry jam
- 1/4 cup sliced almonds

Direction

- In a small saucepan, melt butter over low heat.
- Remove from heat.
- Add 1 cup of the baking pieces (do not stir).
- Set aside.
- Grease a 9x9x2-inch baking pan.
- Set aside.
- In a medium mixing bowl, combine eggs and sugar. Add butter mixture to egg mixture; stir just until combined.
- Stir in almond extract.
- In a small bowl, stir together the flour and salt.
- Add flour mixture to egg mixture; stir just until combined.
- Spread half of the batter into prepared pan.
- Bake in a 325 degree F oven for 15 to 20 minutes or until edges are lightly browned.
- Remove from oven.
- Meanwhile, in a small saucepan, melt jam over low heat, stirring occasionally.
- Spread melted jam evenly over warm crust.
- Stir the remaining 1 cup of baking pieces into the remaining batter.
- Drop the batter in small mounds onto the jam filling.
- Sprinkle with almonds.
- Bake about 35 minutes more or until a toothpick inserted near the center comes out clean and top is lightly browned.
- Cool on a wire rack.
- Cut into bars.
- Makes 16 bars.

40. Blueberry Cheesecake Bars Recipe

Serving: 15 | Prep: | Cook: 30mins | Ready in:

Ingredients

- Crust:
- 3/4 cup butter, melted
- 1/4 cup sugar
- 2 1/2 cups graham cracker crumbs
- Filling:
- 2-8 ounce pkgs. cream cheese
- 1 cup sugar
- 2 tsp. lemon juice
- 4 eggs
- 1 tsp. vanilla extract
- 1-21 oz. can blueberry pie filling

Direction

- Combine butter, sugar and crumbs. Press into ungreased 11 x 15" jelly roll pan. Set aside.
- Cream sugar and cream cheese together. Beat in lemon juice, eggs and vanilla. Spread carefully over crumb crust. Bake at 325 degrees for 30 minutes. Cool. Spread blueberry pie filling over top.

41. Blueberry Cookie Bars Recipe

Serving: 16 | Prep: | Cook: 40mins | Ready in:

Ingredients

- 2-1/4 c flour
- 1 c blanched sliced almonds
- 1/2 c sugar
- 1/2 tsp baking soda
- 1/2 tsp salt
- 1-1/2 sticks (6 oz) cold unsalted butter, cut in pieces
- 1 cold egg
- 1 tsp pure vanilla
- 3/4 c blueberry preserves

Direction

- Preheat oven to 350 degrees. Line a 9" square baking pan with a 12" long sheet of foil. Using food processor, mix flour, almonds, baking soda and salt till nuts are finely ground. Add the butter and pulse until coarse crumbs form. Beat together the egg and vanilla; drizzle over dough mixture. Transfer the mixture to a large bowl and knead with fingertips until clumpy.
- Transfer 2/3 of the dough to the pan and press into the bottom to form an even later. Spread the preserves on top. Dot the top with the remaining dough in clumps.
- Bake till edges are lightly golden, 35 to 40 mins. Let cool completely. Turn out of the pan, remove foil and cut in squares.

42. Blueberry Hummingbird Bars Recipe

Serving: 48 | Prep: | Cook: 30mins | Ready in:

Ingredients

- 3 cups flour
- 2 cups granulated sugar
- 1 teaspoon baking soda
- 1 teaspoon cinnamon
- 1 cup vegetable oil
- 1/2 teaspoon salt
- 2 teaspoons vanilla extract
- 2 cups diced bananas
- 1 cup chopped nuts
- 1 cup blueberries
- 3 eggs, slightly beaten
- 1 (8 ounce) can crushed pineapple, undrained

Direction

- Heat oven to 350 degrees F. Grease and flour 15 x 10-inch jellyroll pan.
- Lightly spoon flour into measuring cup, level off. In large bowl, combine all ingredients. Stir until blended, spread evenly in pan.
- Bake 30 to 40 minutes until toothpick inserted in center comes out clean.
- Glaze: In small bowl, combine 1/4 cup softened butter or margarine, 1 1/2 cup powdered sugar and 1 to 2 tablespoons warm milk. Spread over warm bars. Cool completely, cut into bars. Store in refrigerator.
- Makes 48 bars.

43. Blueberry Oat Popcorn Bars Recipe

Serving: 18 | Prep: | Cook: | Ready in:

Ingredients

- 8 cups popped white popcorn
- 1 cup coarsely chopped dry-roasted peanuts
- 1 (5 ounce) package dried blueberries
- 2 cups uncooked quick oats
- 4 cups mini marshmallows
- 2 tablespoons butter or margarine
- 1/2 cup honey
- cooking spray

Direction

- In a large bowl, combine popcorn, peanuts, berries and oats. In a large saucepan, melt marshmallows, butter and honey over medium-high heat. Pour marshmallow mixture over popcorn mixture and stir until completely coated. Spray a 9 x 130inch pan with cooking spray and press popcorn mixture into pan. Refrigerate until set, about 1 hour. Cut into bars. Store in an airtight container.

44. Blueberry Ricotta Squares Recipe

Serving: 16 | Prep: | Cook: 55mins | Ready in:

Ingredients

- 1 c flour
- 3/4 c white sugar
- 1-1/4 tsp baking powder
- 1/3 c milk
- 1/4 c shortening
- 1 egg
- 1/2 tsp lemon extract
- 1-1/2 c blueberries
- 2 eggs beaten
- 1-1/4 c ricotta cheese
- 1/3 c sugar
- 1/4 tsp vanilla

Direction

- Preheat oven to 350 degrees. Grease 9" square baking dish.
- In large bowl, stir together flour, 3/4c sugar and baking powder. Add the milk, shortening, 1 egg and lemon extract and use electric mixer to mix on low speed for 1 min. then medium speed for 1 min. Pour batter into prepared pan, and spread evenly. Sprinkle blueberries over batter.
- In medium bowl, stir together 2 beaten eggs, ricotta cheese, 1/3 c sugar and vanilla. Spoon mixture over the blueberries and spread evenly.
- Bake 55 to 60 mins until knife inserted near center comes out clean, cool completely before cutting into squares and serving.

45. Blueberry Walnut Bars Recipe

Serving: 12 | Prep: | Cook: 11mins | Ready in:

Ingredients

- 2/3c ground walnuts
- 1/2c graham cracker crumbs
- 2 Tbs. plus 1/3c sugar, divided
- 1/3c old fashioned oats
- 3 Tbs reduced-fat butter, melted
- 1 pkg(8oz) reduced-fat cream cheese
- 1 Tbs orange juice
- 1/2 tsp vanilla
- 1/2c reduced-fat whipped topping
- 2 Tbs blueberry preserves
- 11/2c fresh blueberries

Direction

- Combine walnuts, cracker crumbs, 2 Tbsp. sugar, oats and butter. Press onto bottom of 8' square baking dish coated with cooking spray. Bake at 350 for 9-11 mins or till set and edges lightly browned. Cool on wire rack.
- In large bowl, beat cream cheese and remaining sugar until smooth. Beat in orange juice and vanilla. Fold in whipped topping. Spread over crust.
- In a microwave-safe bowl, heat preserves on high for 15-20 seconds or till warmed; gently sit in blueberries. Spoon over filling. Refrigerate till serving.

46. Blueberry White Chocolate Squares Recipe

Serving: 1 | Prep: | Cook: 10mins | Ready in:

Ingredients

- 2 cups Amaretto cookie crumbs
- 1/4 cup butter, melted
- 1 ½ cups fresh blueberries
- 1/3 cup whipping cream
- 8 oz. white chocolate, finely chopped

Direction

- Line an 8" square metal cake pan with parchment paper, leaving a few inches of overhang; set aside. In bowl, toss cookie crumbs with butter until moistened; press firmly onto bottom of prepared pan. Sprinkle with blueberries; set aside.

- In a saucepan, bring cream to a boil; pour over chocolate in heatproof bowl and stir until melted. Let cool slightly; spoon evenly over berries. Refrigerate until firm, about 2 hours. Cut into squares.

47. Bob Sykes Bar B Qs Hersheys Perfectly Chocolate Chocolate Cake Recipe

Serving: 12 | Prep: | Cook: 45mins | Ready in:

Ingredients

- 2 cups sugar
- 1 3/4 cups all-purpose flour
- 3/4 cup Hershey's cocoa
- 1 1/2 teaspoons baking powder
- 1 1/2 teaspoons baking soda
- 1 teaspoon salt
- 2 eggs
- 1 cup milk
- 1/2 cup vegetable oil
- 2 teaspoons vanilla extract
- 1 cup boiling water
- --- -
- "PERFECTLY CHOCOLATE" chocolate frosting
- ------------------
- 1 stick (1/2 cup) butter or margarine
- 2/3 cup Hershey's cocoa
- 3 cups powdered sugar
- 1/3 cup milk
- 1 teaspoon vanilla extract

Direction

- CAKE

48. Bodacious Chocolate Marshmallow Bars Recipe

Serving: 36 | Prep: | Cook: 20mins | Ready in:

Ingredients

- 3/4 cup butter
- 1-1/2 cups sugar
- 3 eggs
- 1 teaspoons vanilla extract
- 1-1/3 cups all purpose flour
- 3 tablespoons baking cocoa
- 1/2 teaspoons baking powder
- 1/2 teaspoon salt
- 1/2 cup chopped nuts, optional
- 4 cups miniature marshmallows
- Topping:
- 1-1/3 cup chocolate chips
- 1 cup peanut butter
- 3 tablespoons butter
- 2 cups crisp rice cereal

Direction

- In a mixing bowl, cream butter and sugar.
- Add eggs and vanilla; beat until fluffy.
- Combine flour, cocoa, baking powder and salt; add to creamed mixture.
- Stir in nuts if desired.
- Spread in a greased 15 x 10 x 1" pan. (I used a 9×13-inch pan)
- Bake at 350F for 15-18 minutes.
- Sprinkle marshmallows evenly over cake; return to oven for 2-3 minutes.
- Using a knife dipped in water, spread the melted marshmallows evenly over cake.
- Cool.
- For topping, combine chocolate chips, peanut butter and butter in a small saucepan.
- Cook over low heat, stirring constantly, until melted and well blended.
- Remove from heat; stir in cereal. Immediately spread over bars. Chill.

49. Brazil Nut Ebony Bars Recipe

Serving: 16 | Prep: | Cook: 35mins | Ready in:

Ingredients

- 1/2 cup extra Dutch-processed (black) cocoa
- 1/4 cup regular, unsweetened cocoa
- 2/3 cup flour
- 1 packet instant oatmeal
- 1 tbsp instant espresso powder
- 1/4 tsp baking powder
- 3/4 tsp salt
- 200g silken tofu
- 1/4 cup coconut oil
- 1/4 cup canola oil
- 1/4 cup melted margarine
- 1 1/4 cup brown sugar
- 1 tbsp vanilla
- 2 oz chopped brazil nuts
- ~Frosting~
- 1/3 cup extra - Duch processed (black) cocoa
- 1 1/2 cups icing sugar
- 3 tbsp melted margarine
- 3-4 tbsp brewed coffee

Direction

- Preheat oven to 350F, grease a 9" baking pan.
- Sift together the cocoas, then whisk into the flour, oatmeal, espresso powder, baking powder and salt.
- In a food processor, combine the tofu, oils, margarine, sugar and vanilla until smooth. Pour into a bowl.
- Gently stir in the cocoa mixture until almost blended, then fold in the chopped nuts.
- Bake 30-35 minutes, until a tester yields moist crumbs. Cool completely.
- ~Frosting~
- Sift together the cocoa and icing sugar.
- To the melted margarine, alternately add the cocoa mixture with the coffee, starting and ending with the dry mix.
- Add a touch of extra coffee if needed for spreading consistency.
- Spread over cooled bars (you may not use all the frosting).
- Refrigerate until ready to serve.

50. Brownie Goodie Bars Recipe

Serving: 12 | Prep: | Cook: 30mins | Ready in:

Ingredients

- 1 box (1 lb 6.5 oz) Betty Crocker® Original Supreme brownie mix
- water, vegetable oil and eggs called for on brownie mix box
- 1 container (1 lb) Betty Crocker® Rich & Creamy vanilla frosting
- 3/4 cup salted peanuts, coarsely chopped
- 3 cups crisp rice cereal
- 1 cup creamy peanut butter
- 1 bag (12 oz) semisweet chocolate chips (2 cups)

Direction

- Heat oven to 350°F. Grease bottom only of 13x9-inch pan with cooking spray or shortening. (For easier cutting, line pan with foil, then grease foil on bottom only of pan.)
- Make and bake brownies as directed on box for 13x9-inch pan, using water, oil and eggs. Cool completely, about 1 hour.
- Frost brownies with frosting. Sprinkle with peanuts; refrigerate while making cereal mixture.
- Measure cereal into large bowl; set aside. In 1-quart saucepan, melt peanut butter and chocolate chips over low heat, stirring constantly. Pour over cereal in bowl, stirring until evenly coated. Spread over frosted brownies. Cool completely before cutting, about 1 hour. For bars, cut into 6 rows by 4 rows. Store tightly covered at room temperature.

- High Altitude (3500-6500 ft.): Follow High Altitude directions for 13x9-inch pan on brownie mix box.

51. Brownie Goody Bars Recipe

Serving: 18 | Prep: | Cook: 40mins | Ready in:

Ingredients

- 1 box of any brownie mix (13 x 9 size)
- 1 container of whipped vanilla frosting
- 3/4 cup salted peanuts, coarsley chopped
- 3 cups chrispy rice cereal
- 1 cup cream peanut butter
- 1 bag (12 oz size) semisweet chocolate chips

Direction

- Heat oven to 350 degrees and make brownies per directions on box
- Cool completely.
- Frost brownies with vanilla frosting mix.
- Sprinkle with chopped peanuts.
- Refrigerate for a few minutes.
- Meanwhile into a large bowl measure out cereal and set aside.
- In quart size saucepan melt peanut butter and chocolate chips over low heat. Stirring constantly.
- Pour this hot mixture over cereal in bowl and mix thoroughly.
- Spread over frosted brownies.
- Let set for about 30 minutes then cut into bars.

52. Buckeye Cookie Bars Recipe

Serving: 36 | Prep: | Cook: 25mins | Ready in:

Ingredients

- 1 Package chocolate cake mix (18 1/2 oz)
- 1/4 cup vegetable oil
- 1 egg
- 1 cup Chopped peanuts
- 1 Can sweetened condensed milk (14 oz)
- 1/2 cup peanut butter

Direction

- Preheat oven to 350F (325F for a glass dish).
- In large mixing bowl, combine cake mix, oil and egg; beat on medium speed until crumbly. Stir in peanuts.
- Reserving 1 1/2 cups crumb mixture, press remainder on bottom of greased 13x9-inch baking pan.
- In medium bowl, beat sweetened condensed milk with peanut butter until smooth; spread over prepared crust.
- Sprinkle with reserved crumb mixture.
- Bake 25 to 30 minutes or until set.
- Cool.
- Cut into bars. Store loosely covered at room temperature.

53. Buster Bar Ice Cream Dessert Recipe

Serving: 1 | Prep: | Cook: 8mins | Ready in:

Ingredients

- 1 pound chocolate sandwich cookies, crushed
- 1/2 cup margarine, melted
- 1 3/4 cups confectioners' sugar
- 1 (12 fluid ounce) can evaporated milk
- 1 cup semisweet chocolate chips
- 1/2 cup margarine
- 1 teaspoon vanilla extract
- 1/2 gallon vanilla ice cream
- 1 1/2 cups dry-roasted peanuts

Direction

- Combined crushed cookies and melted margarine and press into a 9x13 inch dish. Chill 1 hour in refrigerator.

- In a saucepan over medium heat, combine confectioners' sugar, evaporated milk, chocolate chips and 1/2 cup margarine. Bring to a boil, stirring constantly, and boil 8 minutes. Remove from heat and stir in vanilla. Set aside to cool.
- Slice vanilla ice cream into 3/4 inch slices, and place them in a single layer over the chilled crust. Smooth the seams. Sprinkle the peanuts over the ice cream. Top with the cooled chocolate sauce.
- Cover and freeze 8 hours or overnight.

54. Butter Nut Bars Supreme Recipe

Serving: 10 | Prep: | Cook: 25mins | Ready in:

Ingredients

- 2 eggs, beaten
- 1 cube (1/2 cup) real butter, softened
- 1 1/2 cups flour
- 1 1/2 cups brown sugar
- 2 tsp. vanilla
- 2/3 cup pecans or walnuts, chopped

Direction

- Combine all ingredients and mix well. Pour into a greased 13 x 9 inch baking pan and bake for 20 - 30 minutes at 350 degrees. Allow to cool and cut into bars.
- The Skinny: Use your favorite egg and sugar substitutes.

55. Butterscotch Banana Bars Recipe

Serving: 16 | Prep: | Cook: 40mins | Ready in:

Ingredients

- 6Tbs. butter, softened
- 1c firm packed brown sugar
- 1 egg
- 1/2tsp. vanilla extract
- 1 large banana, mashed
- 1 1/2tsp. baking powder
- 1 3/4c flour
- 1/2tsp salt
- 1/2c chopped nuts(I use pecans)
- 1 6oz. pkg. butterscotch chips

Direction

- Preheat oven to 350.
- Beat butter and sugar in a large bowl with electric mixer till creamy. Beat in the egg, vanilla and banana. In another bowl, stir together all the dry ingredients. Gradually add dry ingredients to the butter mixture, blending thoroughly. Stir in nuts and chips. Spread in a greased 9" square pan.
- Bake at 350 for 35-40 mins. Cool before cutting. Store in an airtight container or cover with foil.

56. Butterscotch Bars Recipe

Serving: 36 | Prep: | Cook: 40mins | Ready in:

Ingredients

- Crust:
- 1 cup butter, softened
- 1 cup brown sugar
- 2 cups flour
- ½ teaspoon salt
- Filling:
- 4 eggs, beaten
- 2 teaspoons baking powder
- 2 cups brown sugar
- 2 cups coconut
- 1 teaspoon salt
- 4 tablespoons flour
- 1 teaspoon vanilla extract

Direction

- For the crust, cream together butter and sugar; add flour and salt, mix together well.
- Pat into an ungreased 10x15 baking sheet.
- Bake at 350 degrees for 15 minutes. While crust is baking, prepare filling.
- For filling, beat eggs well; add remaining ingredients and mix together until well blended.
- Pour over hot crust and return pan to oven for an additional 20 to 25 minutes, until bars are nicely browned.

57. Butterscotch Cashew Bars Recipe

Serving: 30 | Prep: | Cook: 15mins | Ready in:

Ingredients

- Bottom:
- 1 C plus 2 Tb butter, softened
- 3/4 C plus 2 Tb packed brown sugar
- 2 1/2 C flour
- 1 3/4 tsp salt
- Topping:
- 1 pkg butterscotch chips
- 1/2 C plus 2 Tb light corn syrup
- 3 Tb butter
- 2 Tsp water
- 2 1/2 C salted cashew halves

Direction

- In large bowl, cream butter and brown sugar for bottom.
- Combine flour and salt and add to creamed mixture.
- Press into a greased 15x10x1 pan and bake at 350 for 10-12 minutes. - Should be lightly browned.
- Combine chips, corn syrup, butter and water in a sauce pan.
- Stir over medium heat until melted.
- Spread over crust.
- Sprinkle on cashews and press down lightly.

- Bake for approx. 12 minutes or until bubbly and lightly browned.
- Cool and cut.

58. CEREAL PEANUT BUTTER BARS Recipe

Serving: 24 | Prep: | Cook: 120mins | Ready in:

Ingredients

- 1 c. sugar
- 1 c. light corn syrup
- 1 1/2 c. chunky peanut butter
- 8 c. corn flakes (or any cereal)

Direction

- Combine sugar and corn syrup in saucepan and bring to a boil. Remove from heat; stir in peanut butter. Pour over cereal in a bowl and mix well. Spread in greased pan. Cut into 24 (2x2 inch) bars.

59. CHERRY COBBLER BARS Recipe

Serving: 24 | Prep: | Cook: 35mins | Ready in:

Ingredients

- 1 CUP margarine
- 2 CUPS flour
- 1 TEASPOON vanilla
- 3 eggs
- 1-1/2 CUP sugar
- 1 CAN cherry pie filling (ABOUT 13+ OUNCE CAN)
- ***
- ************ glaze topping ******************
- 1/2 cup powdered sugar
- warm water

- mix together to make a thin glaze use small amts of warm water and stir until thin not watery.. icing ..drizzle over tops of bars

Direction

- Cream together all ingredients and put only 1/2 of mixture into the bottom of a greased 9 x 13 pan.
- Spread 1 can cherry pie filling on top .spread the other 1/2 of mixture on top of cherries.
- Bake at 350 degrees F. for 35 minutes.
- Drizzle icing glaze on top when removed from oven.
- Cut into bars when cooled.

60. CHOCOLATE CHIP COOKIE BARS Recipe

Serving: 16 | Prep: | Cook: 20mins | Ready in:

Ingredients

- chocolate chip cookiE BARS
- ½ cup (1 stick) butter, softened
- ½ cup vegetable shortening
- ¾ cup granulated sugar
- ¾ cup packed brown sugar
- 2 eggs
- 1 teaspoon vanilla
- 2 ½ cups all-purpose flour
- 1 teaspoon baking soda
- 1 teaspoon salt
- 2 cups (12 ounces) semisweet chocolate chips
- 1 cup chopped pecans or walnuts
- Preheat oven to 375. Grease a 9X13-inch baking dish. Set aside.

Direction

- Preheat oven to 375. Grease a 9X13-inch baking dish. Set aside.
- In large bowl, or in large bowl of electric mixer at medium seed, beat butter, shortening, granulated sugar and brown sugar for 3 minutes. Add eggs and vanilla. Beat 2 minutes. Reduce speed to low. Beat in flour, baking soda and salt. Fold in chips and nuts.
- Spread dough evenly in prepared baking dish. Bake 20 minutes or until golden brown and firm to the touch. Cool completely.
- Makes 16 (2X3-inch) bars
- Variations: Substitute peanut butter chips, milk chocolate chips or raspberry-flavored chips for all or half of the semisweet chocolate chips.

61. CHOCOLATE COCONUT BARS Recipe

Serving: 1 | Prep: | Cook: 25mins | Ready in:

Ingredients

- 2 C.graham cracker crumbs
- 1/2 C margarine, melted
- 1/4 C.sugar
- 2 C flaked coconut
- 1 can (14 oz.)swt. condensed milk
- 1/2 C pecans, chopped
- 1 (7 oz.) plain chocolate candy bar
- 2 T. creamy peanut butter

Direction

- Combine the crumbs, margarine and sugar. Press into a greased 13" x 9" x 2" baking pan.
- Bake at 350 degrees for 10 minutes, meanwhile, in a bowl, combine coconut, milk and pecans; spread over the crust. Bake at 350 degrees for 15 minutes; cool completely. In a small saucepan, melt candy bar and peanut butter over low heat; spread over bars. Cool until set. Yields about 3 dozen.

62. CREAM CHEESE BLUEBERRY BARS Recipe

Serving: 12 | Prep: | Cook: 30mins | Ready in:

Ingredients

- Ingredients:
- 1 ½ cups all-purpose flour
- 3-oz quick oats
- ¼ cup firmly packed light brown sugar
- ½ tsp. cinnamon
- ½ cup reduced-calorie tub margarine, well chilled
- 8-oz non-fat cream cheese
- 2 Tbs. sugar
- ½ egg substitute
- 2 Tbs. grated lemon zest
- 1 tsp. vanilla extract
- 1 ½ cups fresh blueberries

Direction

- 1) Preheat oven to 350. Spray an 11" x 7"-inch baking pan with non-stick cooking spray.
- 2) In a medium bowl, whisk together flour, oats, brown sugar and cinnamon. With pastry blender or 2 knives, cut in margarine and 2 tablespoons of water until mixture forms a crumbly dough. Press dough into the bottom of prepared pan; bake 10 – 15 minutes, until golden.
- 3) In a small bowl, with electric mixer on high speed, beat cream cheese and sugar until fluffy. Add egg substitute, zest and vanilla; beat until smooth. Pour cream cheese mixture over crust; sprinkle evenly with blueberries. Bake for 25 – 30 minutes, until set. Cool completely on wire rack before cutting into 12 equal bars.
- Serving size: 1 Bar
- Calories per serving: 267, Fat: 9g, Cholesterol: 9mg, Sodium: 182mg, Carbohydrate: 27g

63. Cafe Ole Rice Crispy Bars Recipe

Serving: 10 | Prep: | Cook: 5mins | Ready in:

Ingredients

- 6 cups of cocoa Krispies cereal (You can use the regular cereal)
- 1 package of mini marshmallows
- 3 TB instant coffee grains
- 3 TB salted butter
- Optional Toppings:
- 2 cups bittersweet chocolate chips, white chocolate chips, peanut butter chips or milk chocolate chips
- 1 cup finely chopped walnuts, toasted pecans, toasted almonds, mini chocolate chips (great with the white chocolate), toasted coconut or untoasted sweetened coconut
- 1 TB butter

Direction

- In a glass bowl, melt the butter in the microwave for 30 seconds.
- Add marshmallows and melt for one minute in microwave.
- Mix butter and marshmallows well until smooth.
- Add the instant coffee.
- Stir again until well-combined.
- Add cereal and fold into the marshmallow mix.
- Pour this into a well-buttered 8 inch pan and press lightly with buttered hands.
- Cut into squares or bars and serve.
- *If you wish to dip your bars, cut your bars into finger-length bars and place on waxed paper or silicone baking sheet (Or release aluminum foil)
- Melt your choice of chips with the 1 TB of butter for one minute in the microwave, stirring well for a smooth dipping substance. Dip either one side of the bar or the middle to the end of each bar into the "dip" then dip into your choice of nuts, coconut or mini-chips.

64. Cake Bars Recipe

Serving: 16 | Prep: | Cook: 45mins | Ready in:

Ingredients

- 1 yellow cake mix
- 2 eggs
- 1 stick margarine
- 3 eggs
- 2 (8 oz.) cream cheese
- 1 box powdered sugar
- 2 C. coconut
- 1 C. chopped pecans

Direction

- Preheat oven to 300°
- Put cake mix, 2 eggs, and 1 stick margarine in greased 9 x 13 oblong pan.
- Cream 3 eggs, cream cheese and powdered sugar; spread over other layer.
- Place coconut and pecans over top.
- Bake for 45 minutes
- Cool.
- Cut into bars.

65. Canadian Three Layer Bars Recipe

Serving: 18 | Prep: | Cook: | Ready in:

Ingredients

- First layer:
- ½ cup butter, softened
- 5 tablespoons white sugar
- 4 tablespoons baking cocoa
- 1 egg
- 1 teaspoon vanilla extract
- 2 cups graham cracker crumbs
- 1 cup coconut
- Second layer:
- 4 tablespoons butter, softened
- 2 tablespoons cook and serve vanilla pudding mix (NOT instant pudding mix)
- 3 tablespoons milk
- 2 cups powdered sugar
- Chocolate Frosting:
- 6 tablespoons milk
- 6 tablespoons butter
- 1½ cups white sugar
- ½ cup milk chocolate or sem-sweet chocolate chips

Direction

- For first layer, hand mix ½ cup butter, white sugar, cocoa, egg and extract until fluffy.
- Stir in graham cracker crumbs and coconut.
- Press into an ungreased 7x11 pan; cover and refrigerate 1 hour.
- For second layer, mix 4 tablespoons butter, the dry pudding mix, milk, and powdered sugar until fluffy; spread over chilled crust and refrigerate 1 hour.
- To make the frosting, bring milk, butter and sugar to a gentle boil in a medium saucepan; boil an additional 30 seconds.
- Remove pan from heat and stir in chips; stir vigorously until chips melt and frosting becomes shiny.
- Cool frosting to room temperature; pour over second layer.
- Chill well before cutting; keep refrigerated.

66. Candy Bar Brownies Recipe

Serving: 12 | Prep: | Cook: 30mins | Ready in:

Ingredients

- 4 eggs, lightly beat lightly
- 2 cups sugar
- 3/4 cup melted butter
- 2 tsp vanilla

- 1-1/2 cups flour
- 1/2 tsp baking powder
- 1/3 cup cocoa
- 4 snicker candy bars
- 4 hershey's milk chocolate candy bars

Direction

- Combine eggs, sugar, butter and vanilla.
- Combine flour, baking powder and cocoa.
- Stir into sugar mixture.
- Cut snicker bars into small pieces, shake in flour so they won't sink to the bottom of the pan while baking.
- Fold into sugar mixture.
- Put in 9X13" pan. Sprinkle broken up Hershey bars on top of brownies. Bake at 350 for 30 minutes.

67. Candy Bar Cake Recipe

Serving: 8 | Prep: | Cook: 70mins | Ready in:

Ingredients

- 2 sticks butter
- 2 cups granulated sugar
- 4 eggs
- 1 large plain chocolate candy bar
- 1/4 teaspoon baking soda
- 1 cup buttermilk
- 2-1/2 cups sifted flour
- 2 teaspoons pure vanilla
- 1/8 teaspoon salt
- 1 cup finely chopped pecans
- Frosting:
- 1/3 cup evaporated milk
- 1 cup granulated sugar
- 1 stick oleo
- 1/2 cup chocolate chips

Direction

- Cream butter and sugar then add eggs one at a time beating after each.
- Melt candy bar in double boiler then add to egg mixture.
- Add soda to buttermilk then fold in buttermilk alternatively with flour.
- Stir in vanilla, salt and nuts then pour into greased floured tube pan.
- Bake at 325 for 70 minutes then allow cool slightly before pouring frosting over top.
- For frosting combine milk, sugar and oleo in saucepan and cook 2 minutes.
- After mixture begins to bubble remove from heat and stir in chips then beat until melted.
- Cool slightly then pour over warm cake.

68. Candy Bar Filled Cookies Recipe

Serving: 48 | Prep: | Cook: 30mins | Ready in:

Ingredients

- 1 tube refrigerated sugar cookie dough, softened
- ½ cup all-purpose flour
- 48 miniature Snickers candy bars, or whatever other miniature candy bar or mint you want to experiment with (or cut full-size candy bars into mini pieces)
- Red and green colored sugar

Direction

- In a small bowl, beat cookie dough and flour until combined.
- Shape about 2 teaspoonfuls of dough around each candy bar; roll in colored sugar.
- Place 2" apart on parchment paper-lined baking sheets.
- Bake cookies at 350° for 10 to12 minutes or until edges are golden brown.
- Remove to wire racks to cool.

69. Candy Bar Pie Recipe

Serving: 8 | Prep: | Cook: 10mins | Ready in:

Ingredients

- 2 cups cold milk
- 2 packages chocolate flavor instant pudding
- 8 ounces frozen whipped topping thawed and divided
- 2 milk chocolate toffee candy bars chopped and divided
- 1 chocolate pie crust
- 1 square semisweet baking chocolate melted

Direction

- Beat milk and dry pudding mixes with whisk for 2 minutes or until well blended.
- Gently stir in half of the whipped topping and all but 3 tablespoons of the candy.
- Spoon into trust then top with remaining whipped topping and candy.
- Drizzle with chocolate then serve immediately.

70. Cant Leave Alone Bars Recipe

Serving: 36 | Prep: | Cook: 20mins | Ready in:

Ingredients

- 1 package (18-1/4 ounces) white cake mix
- 2 eggs
- 1/3 cup vegetable oil
- 1 can (14 ounces) sweetened condensed milk
- 1 cup (6 ounces) semisweet chocolate chips
- 1/4 cup butter, cubed

Direction

- In a large bowl, combine the dry cake mix, eggs and oil. With floured hands, press two-thirds of the mixture into a greased 13-in. x 9-in. baking pan. Set remaining cake mixture aside.
- In a microwave-safe bowl, combine the milk, chocolate chips and butter. Microwave, uncovered, on high for 30 seconds; stir. Microwave 30-45 seconds longer or until chips and butter are melted; stir until smooth. Pour over crust.
- Drop by teaspoonfuls of remaining cake mixture over top. Bake at 350° for 20-25 minutes or until lightly browned. Cool before cutting. Yield: 3 dozen.

71. Cappuccino Nanaimo Bars Recipe

Serving: 24 | Prep: | Cook: 90mins | Ready in:

Ingredients

- ---CRUST---
- 1/2 cup unsalted butter
- 1/3 cup unsweetened cocoa powder
- 1/4 cup Granulated sugar
- 1 egg, lightly beaten
- 1 1/2 cups graham cracker crumbs
- 1 cup coconut, shredded
- 1/2 cup walnuts, finely chopped
- ----FILLING----
- 2 tablespoons milk
- 3 tablespoons unsalted butter
- 2 teaspoons instant espresso or coffee granules
- 1/2 teaspoon vanilla
- 2 cups icing sugar
- ---TOPPING----
- 4-5 ounces white chocolate, coarsely chopped
- 1 Tablespoon unsalted butter
- 1-2 ounces semisweet chocolate, coarsely chopped
- 1 tspn unsalted butter

Direction

- In heavy saucepan, combine butter, cocoa, sugar and egg; cook over low heat, stirring, until butter has melted. Remove from heat; stir in graham cracker crumbs, coconut and walnuts. Pat evenly into greased 9-inch square cake pan. Bake in 350F (180C) oven for 10-12 minutes or until just firm. Let cool completely on rack.

- Filling: In small saucepan, heat milk, butter, espresso powder and vanilla over low heat until butter has melted and espresso powder has dissolved. Transfer to mixing bowl; let cool. Beat in sugar until thickened and smooth; spread evenly over cooled base. Refrigerate for about 45 minutes or until firm.
- Topping: Meanwhile, in top of double boiler over hot (not boiling) water, melt together chocolate and butter; spread over filling. Swirl in the melted semisweet chocolate for a little decoration. With sharp knife, score through topping of bars only. You can also decorate each serving by placing a couple of chocolate covered espresso beans while topping is still soft. Refrigerate until topping is set. Cut into bars.
- Bars can be covered and refrigerated for up to 5 days or frozen in airtight container for up to 1 month.

72. Cappuccino Bars Recipe

Serving: 24 | Prep: | Cook: 37mins | Ready in:

Ingredients

- 1 tsp cocoa powder, plus extra for dusting
- 2 rounded tbsp coffee granules
- 225g/8oz butter, softened
- 225g/8oz caster sugar
- 4 eggs
- 225g/8oz self-raising flour
- 1tsp baking powder
- FOR THE WHITE chocolate frosting
- 100g/4oz white chocolate, broken into pieces
- 50g/2oz butter, softened
- 3tbsp milk
- 175g/6oz icing sugar

Direction

- Preheat the oven to 180*C/gas 4/fan oven 160. Butter and line the bottom of a shallow 28 x 18cm/ x 7in oblong tin. Mix the cocoa and coffee into 2 tablespoons warm water. Put in a large bowl with the other cake ingredients.
- Whisk for about 2 minutes with an electric hand blender to combine, then tip into the tin and level out. Bake for 35-40 minutes until risen and firm to the touch. Cool in the tin for 10 minutes, then cool on the rack. Peel off the paper.
- For the frosting, melt the chocolate, butter and milk in a bowl over a pan of simmering water. Remove the bowl and sift in the icing sugar. Beat until smooth, then spread over the cake. Finish with dusting of cocoa powder. Cut into 24 bars

73. Caramel Apple Bars Recipe

Serving: 36 | Prep: | Cook: 20mins | Ready in:

Ingredients

- 1/2 cup cold butter
- 1 pouch (1 lb 1.5 oz) Betty Crocker® oatmeal cookie mix
- 1 egg
- 1 cup finely chopped peeled apple
- 3/4 cup caramel topping
- 1/4 cup Gold Medal® all-purpose flour

Direction

- Heat oven to 350°F. Spray bottom of 13x9-inch pan with cooking spray.
- In large bowl, cut butter into cookie mix using fork or pastry blender. Stir in egg until mixture is crumbly.
- Reserve 1 1/2 cups cookie mixture. Press remaining cookie mixture into bottom of pan. Bake 15 minutes. Sprinkle apple evenly over crust. In small bowl, mix caramel topping and

flour; drizzle over apples. Sprinkle reserved cookie mixture over apples.
- Bake 20 to 25 minutes or until golden brown. Cool completely, about 2 hours. For bars, cut into 9 rows by 4 rows.

74. Caramel Bars Recipe

Serving: 24 | Prep: | Cook: 20mins | Ready in:

Ingredients

- 1 package caramel~wrappers removed
- 1 5oz can evaporated milk, divided 1/3 cup + 1/4 cup
- 1/2 cup butter melted
- 1 package German chocolate cake mix
- 1 package chocolate chips

Direction

- 1. In double boiler combine caramel and 1/3 cups evaporated milk, and melt until smooth.
- 2. Pre-heat oven to 350. Meanwhile, take the melted butter and combine with cake mix and 1/4 cup evaporated milk and mix. Spread half of the mixture on bottom of 13 x 9 cake pan. Bake about 6 minutes.
- 3. Take out and add the bag of chocolate chips and then pour caramel over the mixture. Crumble the rest of the mixture over the top. Return to oven and bake another 12-14 minutes.
- 4. Let cool and cut into squares. Enjoy!

75. Caramel Candy Bars Recipe

Serving: 54 | Prep: | Cook: 22mins | Ready in:

Ingredients

- 14 oz. pkg. caramel candies
- 1/3 cup milk
- 2 cups flour
- 2 cups quick-cooking or regular oats
- 1 1/2 cup packed brown sugar
- 1 t. soda
- 1/2 t. salt
- 1 egg
- 1 cup margarine, softened
- 6 oz. pkg. semi-sweet chololate chips
- 1 cup chopped walnuts or dry roasted peanuts

Direction

- Heat oven to 350*.
- Grease rectangular pan (13x9x2).
- Heat candies and milk in a 2 qt. saucepan over low heat, stirring frequently until smooth; remove from heat.
- Mix flour, oats, brown sugar, baking soda, salt and egg in a large bowl.
- Stir in margarine with fork until mixture is crumbly.
- Press half of the crumbly mixture in pan.
- Bake for 10 min.
- Take out of the oven.
- Sprinkle with chocolate chips and walnuts; drizzle with caramel mixture.
- Sprinkle remaining crumbly mixture over top.
- Bake until golden brown, 20-25 min.
- Cool for 30 min.
- Loosen edges from sides of pan, cool completely. (You may want to loosen your waistband on your pants too)
- Cut into bars about 2"x1".

76. Caramel Cashew Bars Recipe

Serving: 36 | Prep: | Cook: 16mins | Ready in:

Ingredients

- 1 roll (16.5 oz) Pillsbury® Create 'n Bake® refrigerated chocolate chip cookies
- 1 bag (11.5 oz) milk chocolate chips (2 cups)
- 1 container (18 oz) caramel apple dip (1 1/2 cups)

- 3 cups crisp rice cereal
- 1 1/4 cups chopped cashews

Direction

- Heat oven to 350°F. In ungreased 13x9-inch pan, break up cookie dough. With floured fingers, press dough evenly in bottom of pan to form crust.
- Bake 15 to 18 minutes or until light golden brown. Cool 15 minutes.
- Meanwhile, in 3- to 4-quart saucepan, cook 1 cup of the chocolate chips and 1 cup of the dip over medium heat, stirring constantly, until melted and smooth. Remove from heat. Stir in cereal and cashews.
- Spread cereal mixture over crust. In 1-quart saucepan, heat remaining chocolate chips and dip over medium heat, stirring constantly, until melted and smooth. Spread over cereal mixture. Refrigerate until chocolate mixture is set, about 30 minutes. For bars, cut into 6 by 6 rows.
- High Altitude (3500-6500 ft.): Bake crust 16 to 19 minutes.

77. Caramel Cashew Crispy Bars Recipe

Serving: 36 | Prep: | Cook: 15mins | Ready in:

Ingredients

- 1 roll (16.5 oz) refrigerated chocolate chip cookies
- 1 bag (11.5 oz) milk chocolate chips (2 cups)
- 1 container (18 oz) caramel apple dip (1 1/2 cups)
- 3 cups crisp rice cereal
- 1 1/4 cups chopped cashews

Direction

- Heat oven to 350°F.
- In ungreased 13x9-inch pan, break up cookie dough. With floured fingers, press dough evenly in bottom of pan to form crust.
- Bake 15 to 18 minutes or until light golden brown. Cool 15 minutes.
- Meanwhile, in 3- to 4-quart saucepan, cook 1 cup of the chocolate chips and 1 cup of the dip over medium heat, stirring constantly, until melted and smooth.
- Remove from heat.
- Stir in cereal and cashews.
- Spread cereal mixture over crust. In 1-quart saucepan, heat remaining chocolate chips and dip over medium heat, stirring constantly, until melted and smooth.
- Spread over cereal mixture.
- Refrigerate until chocolate mixture is set, about 30 minutes.
- For bars, cut into 6 by 6 rows.

78. Caramel Cheesecake Bars Recipe

Serving: 16 | Prep: | Cook: 45mins | Ready in:

Ingredients

- 1-1/2 cups crushed vanilla wafers
- 1/4 cup chopped pecans
- 3 tablespoons butter softened
- 32 ounces cream cheese softened
- 1 cup granulated sugar
- 8 ounces sour cream
- 3 tablespoons unbleached flour
- 1 tablespoon pure vanilla extract
- 4 eggs
- 1/4 cup caramel topping
- 1/4 cup chopped pecans

Direction

- Preheat oven to 325. Prepare a rectangular cake pan with cooking spray then set aside. Combine wafers, 1/4 cup pecans and butter then mix until crumbly then press mixture onto bottom of prepared pans then set aside. In another mixing bowl combine cream cheese, sugar, sour cream, flour, vanilla extract and eggs then mix until smooth then pour over crust in pan. Bake for 45 minutes then cool and refrigerate for hours. Drizzle top with caramel topping and sprinkle with remaining pecans.

79. Caramel Crunch Bars Recipe

Serving: 810 | Prep: | Cook: 21mins | Ready in:

Ingredients

- caramel Crunch Bars
- From Baking From My Home to Yours by Dorie Greenspan
- For the base: 1 ½ cup all-purpose flour
- 1 tsp. instant espresso powder or finely ground instant coffee
- ½ tsp salt
- ¼ tsp ground cinnamon
- 2 sticks (8oz) unsalted butter, at room temperature
- ½ cup light brown sugar
- ¼ cup sugar
- 1 tsp pure vanilla extract
- 3 oz. bittersweet or premium milk chocolate, finely chopped
- For the topping:
- 6 oz. bittersweet or premium milk chocolate, finely chopped
- ¾ cup Heath toffee bits

Direction

- Getting Ready: Center a rack in the oven and preheat the oven to 375 degrees F. Lightly butter a 9x13 inch baking pan, line the pan with foil and butter the foil. Put the pan on a baking sheet.
- To make the base: Whisk together the flour, coffee, salt and cinnamon.
- Working with a stand mixer, preferably fitted with a paddle attachment, or a hand mixer in a large bowl, beat the butter at medium speed until smooth, about 3 minutes. Add the sugars and beat for another three minutes or until the mixture is light and creamy. Beat in the vanilla and turn off the mixer. Add all the dry ingredients, cover the stand mixer with a kitchen towel (so you and your kitchen don't get showered in flour) and pulse the mixer on and off at low speed about 5 times- at which point a peek at the bowl should reveal that it's safe to turn the mixer to low and mix, uncovered, just until the dry ingredients are almost incorporated. Add the chopped chocolate and mix only until the dry ingredients disappear. If the chocolate isn't evenly mixed, finish the job by hand with a spatula. You'll have a very heavy, very sticky dough. Scrape the dough into the buttered pan and, with the spatula and your fingertips, cajole it into a thin, even layer.
- Bake for 20 to 22 minutes, or until the base is bubbly – so bubbly that you can almost hear it percolating – and puckery. It will look as though it is struggling to pull away from the side of the pan. Transfer the pan to a rack and turn off the oven.
- To make the topping: Scatter the chocolate evenly over the top of the hot base and pop the pan back into the oven for 2 to 3 minutes, until the chocolate is soft.. Remove from oven and immediately spread chocolate over bars, using offset spatula or the back of a spoon. Sprinkle the toffee bits over the chocolate and press them down lightly with your fingertips. Place the baking pan on a rack to cool to room temperature.
- If, by the time the bars are cool, the chocolate has not set, refrigerate them briefly to firm the chocolate.
- Carefully lift out of the pan, using foil edges as handles, and transfer to a cutting board. Trim the edges if they seem a bit thick. Cut about 54 bars, each about 2 inches by 1 inch, taking care not to cut through the foil.

80. Caramel Krispy Bars Recipe

Serving: 32 | Prep: | Cook: 5mins | Ready in:

Ingredients

- 4 c crisp rice cereal
- 1 bag caramels
- 3 T water
- 1 c peanuts
- 1 small bag butterscotch chips
- 1 small bag semi-sweet chips

Direction

- Combine cereal and peanuts in large mixing bowl and set aside.
- Melt caramels in saucepan with water.
- When smooth, quickly but gently stir in to cereal mixture.
- Spread into buttered 9x13 pan.
- Sprinkle chips on top.
- Bake at 250-300 until chips are soft and shiny.
- Spread chips to form icing.
- Allow to cool until icing forms a semi-hard candy shell.

81. Caramel Peanut Butter Bars Recipe

Serving: 25 | Prep: | Cook: 25mins | Ready in:

Ingredients

- cookie Base:
- 1 pouch (1 lb 1.5 oz) Betty Crocker sugar cookie mix
- 1/2 cup butter or margarine, softened
- 1 egg
- 15 miniature chocolate-covered peanut butter cup candies, coarsely chopped
- Filling
- 36 caramels (from 14-oz bag), unwrapped
- 1 can (14 oz) sweetened condensed milk (not evaporated)
- 1/4 cup creamy peanut butter
- 1/2 cup peanuts
- Topping:
- 1 container (1 lb) Betty Crocker Rich & Creamy milk chocolate frosting
- 1/2 cup peanuts, chopped

Direction

- Heat oven to 350°F. Spray bottom and sides of 13x9-inch pan with cooking spray.
- In large bowl, stir cookie mix, butter and egg until soft dough forms. Stir in candies. Press dough in bottom of pan. Bake 18 to 20 minutes or until light golden brown.
- Meanwhile, in 2-quart saucepan, heat caramels and milk over medium heat, stirring constantly, until caramels are melted. Stir in peanut butter. Heat to boiling. Cook 2 minutes, stirring frequently. Remove from heat; stir in 1/2 cup peanuts. Spread over warm cookie base. Cool completely, about 2 hours.
- Spread frosting evenly over filling. Sprinkle with chopped peanuts. Refrigerate about 2 hours or until chilled. Cut into bars. Store covered in refrigerator.

82. Caramel Squares Recipe

Serving: 5 | Prep: | Cook: 30mins | Ready in:

Ingredients

- BASE :
- 3/4 C flour
- 3/4 tbsp caster sugar
- 50 g butter
- 2 tsp water
- 1 small egg
- FILLING :
- 200 g condensed milk
- 10 g butter
- 1 tbsp golden syrup or honey
- TOPPING :

- 60 g dark baking chocolate
- 20 g butter

Direction

- Pre heat oven 210 deg.
- Grease a pan.
- For the base, with the hand or processor mix all the ingredients until it resembles breadcrumbs.
- Add the egg and the water.
- Roll lightly on floured surface and cover with a wrap and chill until set.
- Now press in the lined tin until all base covered.
- Line it with baking paper, spread with some pulses and bake for 10 mins.
- Remove the paper and the pulses and bake 10 more mins until lightly golden.
- Reduce the oven to 180 deg.
- Caramelise all the ingredients over low heat until it melts, boils and thickens.
- Spread over the base and bake for 10 mins.
- Cool it.
- For the topping, double boil the chocolate and butter until melted.
- Cool a bit and spread over the filling.
- Cool until set and cut into squares.

83. Carmel Fudge Squares Recipe

Serving: 0 | Prep: | Cook: | Ready in:

Ingredients

- 1 1/3 stick butter
- 2 c. medium brown sugar
- 1 c. sifted flour
- 2 tsp. vanilla
- 1 tsp. baking powder
- 2 unbeaten eggs
- 1 c. pecans

Direction

- Melt butter and mix with sugar, add the remaining ingredients.
- Put in greased and floured 8 or 9 inch pan.
- Bake at 300 degree oven for 1 hour and 20 minutes.
- Cool in pan and cut into squares and roll in powdered sugar.

84. Carrot Bars W Cream Cheese Frosting Recipe

Serving: 24 | Prep: | Cook: 40mins | Ready in:

Ingredients

- 2 cups sugar
- 4 eggs (jumbo)
- 1 1/2 cups oil (I use canola)
- 2 cups flour
- 2 teaspoons baking soda
- 1 teaspoon salt
- 2 teaspoons cinnamon
- 3 small jars or containers of baby food carrots
- Frosting:
- Beat until smooth,
- 1/2 cup butter
- 8 ounce cream cheese
- 1/2 teaspoon real vanilla
- then add 1 1/2 to 2 cups of powdered sugar and mix til frosting is to your liking.
- Crushed walnuts (optional)

Direction

- Cream together sugar, eggs and oil.
- Add your flour, baking soda, salt, cinnamon and carrots.
- Pour into a greased and floured 14 1/2 X 11 pan (I use a lasagna pan).
- Bake at 350 degrees for 35-40 minutes.
- Let cool completely.
- Frost and top with crushed walnuts (optional)
- Refrigerate
- Enjoy

85. Carrot Cake Bars Recipe

Serving: 24 | Prep: | Cook: 23mins | Ready in:

Ingredients

- 3 large eggs
- 3.5 ounce jar of carrot baby food
- 3/4 cup brown sugar
- 1/2 cup canola oil
- 1 teaspoon vanilla extract
- 2 teaspoons baking powder
- 2 teaspoons cinnamon
- 1/2 teaspoon allspice
- 1/4 teaspoon salt
- 1 3/4 cups all-purpose flour
- 2 cups grated carrot
- 1/2 cup raisins
- 1/2 cup pecans, chopped

Direction

- Line a 13x9x2 pan with aluminum foil, extending foil past sides of pan.
- Spray with non-stick cooking spray.
- Preheat oven to 350 degrees F.
- Beat together the eggs, baby food, brown sugar, canola oil, vanilla extract, baking powder, cinnamon, allspice and salt.
- On low speed, beat in the flour until blended.
- Stir in carrots, raisins and pecans.
- Spread batter in pan evenly.
- Bake 22 to 24 minutes.
- Remove from oven.
- Cool completely.
- Cut into bars.

86. Carrot Cake WannaBe Bars Recipe

Serving: 24 | Prep: | Cook: 25mins | Ready in:

Ingredients

- 2c sugar
- 2c flour
- 1c nuts chopped(optional-we like pecans or walnuts)
- 4 lg eggs
- 1 1/4c canola oil
- 3c grated carrots
- 4tsp cinnamon
- 1/2tsp salt
- 3 tsp baking powder

Direction

- Preheat oven to 350F.
- Mix all dry ingredients (and nuts if using) in a bowl.
- Put all others into a medium bowl and beat until combined.
- Slowly add dry mixture, beating with mixer until just combined.
- Don't overbeat.
- Pour into greased and floured jelly roll pan 12 x 15.
- Bake for 20-30min until toothpick comes out clean.
- Cool
- Now frost with my Speedy Quick Cream Cheese Frosting
- Enjoy!

87. Cashew Caramel Crunch Squares Recipe

Serving: 24 | Prep: | Cook: 18mins | Ready in:

Ingredients

- 1 (14 ounce) bag of caramels
- 2 tablespoons butter
- 2 tablespoons water
- 6 cups cocoa krispies cereal
- 1 cup cashew nuts
- 1 cup white chocolate chips

Direction

- Grease a 13 x 9 inch pan.
- Put the caramels, butter and water into a large saucepan.
- Place over medium low heat and cook 18 minutes, stirring occasionally until caramels melt and mixture is smooth.
- Stir in cereal and nuts.
- Let cool 1 minute, then stir in white chocolate chips.
- Press into prepared pan and let cool.
- Invert onto cutting board.
- Cut in 2 inch squares.
- Makes 24

88. Channel Lemon Squares Recipe

Serving: 24 | Prep: | Cook: 30mins | Ready in:

Ingredients

- CRUST:
- 1/2 cup (1 stick) (113 grams) unsalted butter, room temperature
- 1/4 cup (25 grams) confectioner's (powdered or icing) sugar
- 1 cup (140 grams) all purpose flour
- 1/8 teaspoon salt
- FILLING:
- 140 grams cream cheese, room temperature
- 100 grams granulated white sugar
- 1/2 cup fresh lemon juice
- 2 large eggs
- 1 tablespoon grated lemon zest
- Topping:
- Channel logo :)
- powder sugar

Direction

- Preheat oven to 350 degrees F and place rack in center of oven. Cover with foil and grease with butter an 8 x 8 inch (20 x 28 cm) pan.
- For crust
- In the bowl of your electric mixer, or with a hand mixer, cream the butter and sugar until light and fluffy. Add the flour and salt and beat until the dough just comes together. Press into the bottom of your greased pan and bake for about 20 minutes, or until lightly browned. Remove from oven and place on a wire rack to cool while you make the filling.
- Filling:
- Preheat oven to 375F.
- Beat the cream cheese until smooth. Add sugar and beat until incorporated. Add eggs, one at a time, and beat until combined. Add remaining ingredients and process until well blended and smooth. Pour filling over baked crust and bake for approximately 25 - 30 minutes or until filling is set. Transfer to a wire rack to cool and then cover and refrigerate until well chilled, at least an hour.
- Take it out from the pan and place on a cutting board and cut into squares.
- I found some rubber letters and numbers that belong to my little kid. I spotted the O letter into half lengthwise and then inverted them and used an UHU to stick them together to form the channel logo. I placed the logo over each square and sprinkle some powder sugar over and then left the logo. I had to deliver the samples the second day and that was the only way available in such short time.

89. Cheerio Bars Recipe

Serving: 15 | Prep: | Cook: 5mins | Ready in:

Ingredients

- 1 C. peanut butter
- 1 C. sugar
- 1 C. honey or light corn syrup
- 6 C. cheerios
- 1 C. salted peanuts

Direction

- Mix Cheerios and peanuts together in a large bowl.
- Bring sugar and honey or syrup to a boil in 2 qt. saucepan.
- Remove from heat, stir in peanut butter until blended.
- Pour over Cheerios and mix until well coated.
- Spread in buttered 9 x 13 pan and let cool.
- Cut in squares.

90. Cheescake Bars Recipe

Serving: 40 | Prep: | Cook: 120mins | Ready in:

Ingredients

- 1 1/4 cups flour
- 1/2 cup brown sugar
- 1/2 cup finley chopped almonds or other nuts if u want
- 1/2 cup butter flavored shortening or scince i dont really like shortening use butter
- 2 8-once packs of cream cheese
- 2/3 cup of sugar
- 2 eggs
- 3/4 teaspoon almond extract
- fruits such as strawberrys blueberrys rasberrys to put on top
- 1/2 cup sliced almonds

Direction

- Combine flour, brown sugar, and 1/2 cup finely chopped almonds.
- Mix in or using pastry blender cut shortening until mixture resembles fine crumbs.
- Set aside about 1/2 cup of mixture.
- Press remaining mixture down on ungreased 13 by 9 by 2 in baking pan.
- Bake crust for 10 to 15 minutes.
- MEANWHILE in another bowl beat sugar cream cheese eggs and almond extract spread mixture over hot crust.
- Bake for another 15 minutes.
- Stir preserves and spread over cheese cake bars also put remaining 1/2 cup of topping sprinkled over preserves.
- Bake yet another 10 to 8 minutes cool pan.
- Chill for AT LEAST 3 hrs. before cutting into bars.
- Top with whatever fruit desired.
- ENJOY.

91. Cheesecake Squared Recipe

Serving: 18 | Prep: | Cook: 50mins | Ready in:

Ingredients

- Base:
- 1 pkg. German chocolate cake mix
- 1/2 cup of coconut
- 1/2 cup of butter
- 1 egg
- Filling:
- 3 8 oz. packages of cream cheese softened
- 3/4 cup of sugar
- 1 tsp of vanila extract
- 1 Tbsp of lemon juice
- 5 eggs
- Topping:
- 2 cups of sour cream
- 2 Tbsp of sugar
- 1/2 vanilla
- 1/2 tsp of lemon juice

Direction

- Base: Blend ingredients: press into 13 x 9 x 2 pan.
- Filling: Combine ingredients; spread over base.
- Bake at 350 degrees for 35 minutes.
- Topping: Mix topping, spread over cheesecake, return to oven and bake another 8 minutes.
- Garnish with toasted coconut and/or 1/3 cup of chopped pecans.
- Chill for 8 hours.

- Serves 18.

92. Cherry Bars Recipe

Serving: 16 | Prep: | Cook: 45mins | Ready in:

Ingredients

- 1 3/4 cup of sugar
- 1 cup of butter
- 1 tsp of vanilla
- 21 ounce can of cherry pie filling
- 4 eggs
- 3 cups of flour
- 1 1/2 tsp of baking powder
- icing:
- 1 cup powdered sugar
- 1/2 tsp of almond extract
- 1 to 2 tbsp of milk

Direction

- Cream together sugar, butter and vanilla.
- Add eggs one at a time.
- Add flour gradually.
- Pour 2/3 of the batter in greased 11 x 15 jelly roll pan.
- Spread cherry filling over batter.
- Add remaining batter by dropping spoonfuls on top of the cherry mixture.
- Bake at 350. for 25-35 minutes.
- Make icing by mixing the icing ingredients well.
- Drizzle over cooled baked cherry bars.

93. Cherry Oatmeal Bars Recipe

Serving: 1 | Prep: | Cook: 40mins | Ready in:

Ingredients

- 1 cup shortening
- 2 1/4 cups brown sugar
- 4 1/2 cups rolled oats, uncooked
- 2 cups flour
- 2 teaspoons baking soda
- 2 21 ounce cans tart cherry pie filling
- 2 1/2 cups coconut

Direction

- Cream shortening and sugar for 10 minutes. Combine dry ingredients. Add to creamed mixture. Mix at low speed until crumbly.
- Spread 2/3 of dough in greased 9 x 13 pan. Spread tart cherry pie filling mixed with coconut evenly over entire surface. Cover with remainder of dough.
- Bake in 325F oven for 40 minutes. Cut into 2 inch bars.

94. Cherry Pie Crumb Bars Recipe

Serving: 1 | Prep: | Cook: 30mins | Ready in:

Ingredients

- 1 pkg. white (or yellow) cake mix
- 1 1/4 cups rolled quick oats, divided
- 1/2 cup (8 tablespoons) margarine or butter, room temperature, divided
- 1 egg
- 1 (21 oz.) can cherry pie filling
- 1/4 cup brown sugar
- 1/2 cup chopped pecans

Direction

- Heat oven to 350 degrees. Grease and flour a 13x9-inch pan.
- Combine cake mix, 6 tablespoons butter and 1 cup rolled oats.
- Reserve 1 cup of this mixture for crumb topping. To remaining mixture, add egg; mix well. Press into pan. Pour cherry filling over crust; spread to cover.
- In large bowl add remaining 1 cup crumb mixture, 1/4 cup oats, 2 tablespoons butter,

nuts, and brown sugar. Mix well. Sprinkle over cherries. Bake 30-40 minutes.

95. Cherry Squares Recipe

Serving: 10 | Prep: | Cook: 45mins | Ready in:

Ingredients

- 1/2 cup butter
- 1/2 cup margarine
- 1-3/4 cups sugar
- 4 eggs
- 1 tsp. vanilla
- 1/2 tsp. almond flavouring
- 1/2 tsp. soda
- 1-1/2 tsp. baking powder
- 3 cups flour
- 1/2 tsp. salt
- 1 can cherry pie filling

Direction

- Cream the shortening and sugar.
- Beat well.
- Add eggs, one at a time.
- Add vanilla and almond flavouring.
- Sift the dry ingredients together and add gradually to creamed mixture.
- Save back a little more than one cup of batter.
- Spread the rest in an 11 x 17 inch greased pan.
- Spread the pie filling over the batter.
- Spoon the remaining one cup of batter in small islands over the cherry layer.
- Bake at 350 degrees F for 40-45 minutes.
- Sprinkle top with powdered sugar.
- Cut into squares when cool.

96. Chips Ahoy Peanut Butter Cheesecake Squares Recipe

Serving: 1 | Prep: | Cook: 35mins | Ready in:

Ingredients

- 20 peanut butter chips Ahoy chocolate chip cookies, finely crushed
- 3 Tbsp. margarine or butter, melted
- 2 pkg. (8 oz. each) cream cheese, softened
- 1/2 cup sugar
- 1/2 tsp. vanilla
- 2 eggs
- 1/4 cup creamy peanut butter

Direction

- Preheat oven to 350°F.
- Mix crumbs and margarine; press firmly onto bottom of 9-inch square baking pan.
- Beat cream cheese, sugar and vanilla in large bowl with electric mixer on medium speed until well blended. Add eggs, 1 at a time, mixing on low speed after each addition just until blended. Remove 1/2 cup of the batter; set aside.
- Spread remaining batter over crust.
- Stir peanut butter into reserved 1/2 cup batter. Spoon over cheesecake. Cut through batter with knife several times for marble effect.
- Bake 35 to 40 min. or until center is almost set. Cool completely on wire rack. Cover.
- Refrigerate 3 hours or overnight. Cut into 25 squares. Store in airtight container in refrigerator

97. Chock Full Blondie Squares Recipe

Serving: 10 | Prep: | Cook: 25mins | Ready in:

Ingredients

- 1 cup boiling-hot water
- 1 cup dried cranberries (5 oz)
- 1 cup dried tart cherries (5 oz)
- 1 cup golden raisins (5 oz)
- 2 1/2 cups all-purpose flour
- 1 1/2 teaspoons baking soda

- 1 teaspoon salt
- 3/4 teaspoon cinnamon
- 2 sticks (1 cup) unsalted butter, melted and cooled
- 2 cups sugar
- 3 large eggs
- 1 1/2 teaspoons vanilla
- 1 cup whole almonds with skins (6 oz), toasted and very coarsely chopped
- 8 oz fine-quality bittersweet chocolate (not unsweetened; preferably 60 to 70% cacao), coarsely chopped
- Special equipment: a 17- by 12-inch shallow baking pan (1 inch deep)

Direction

- Put oven rack in middle position and preheat oven to 325°F. Butter and flour baking pan, knocking out excess flour.
- Pour boiling-hot water over dried fruit in a small bowl and soak 20 minutes, then drain well in a sieve.
- Stir together flour, baking soda, salt, and cinnamon in another bowl.
- Beat together melted butter, sugar, eggs, and vanilla in a large bowl with an electric mixer at high speed until creamy, about 1 minute. Reduce speed to low, then add flour mixture and mix until just combined. Mix in dried fruit, almonds, and chocolate.
- Spread batter evenly in baking pan and bake until golden brown and a wooden pick or skewer inserted in center comes out clean, 25 to 30 minutes. Cool completely in pan on a rack. Run a thin knife around edges of pan to loosen blondie, then cut blondie into roughly 3-inch squares.
- Cooks' note: Blondie can be baked (but not cut into squares) 2 days ahead and cooled completely, then kept, wrapped well in plastic wrap, at room temperature.

98. Chocolate And Peanut Butter Dream Bars Recipe

Serving: 24 | Prep: | Cook: 20mins | Ready in:

Ingredients

- Crust:
- ½ cup brown sugar
- ½ cup softened butter
- 1 cup flour
- Filling:
- 2 eggs
- 1 cup brown sugar
- 1 teaspoon vanilla extract
- 2 tablespoons flour
- 1 teaspoon baking powder
- ½ teaspoon salt
- ½ cup milk chocolate chips
- ½ cup peanut butter chips
- NOTE: These can also be made with chocolate chips and butterscotch chips, or all chocolate chips – whatever combination you like...I'm sure milk or dark chocolate and white chocolate would be another good combination, or perhaps part chips and part toffee bits - lots of variations possible with these.
- Frosting:
- 2 tablespoons baking cocoa
- 2 tablespoons butter
- 3 tablespoons boiling water
- 1 cup powdered sugar

Direction

- For crust, cream together sugar and butter until smooth, then stir in flour until well blended.
- Press crust into lightly sprayed 9x13 pan.
- Bake at 350 degrees for 10 minutes; remove from oven and top immediately with the filling.
- While crust is baking, prepare filling by mixing together eggs, brown sugar and extract.
- Stir in flour, baking powder and salt until well blended.

- Stir in chips and incorporate into batter thoroughly.
- Pour filling over partially baked crust, then return pan to oven and bake an additional 15 to 20 minutes, until done.
- Drizzle glaze over filling while it is still a bit warm.
- For glaze, mix cocoa, butter and boiling water in a small saucepan, cooking over low heat until mixture is thick and smooth.
- Remove pan from heat and stir in powdered sugar; add a little milk or water if too thick to drizzle.
- Drizzle frosting over slightly warm bars.
- Cool bars completely before cutting into squares and storing in tightly covered container.

99. Chocolate Bar Nut Brownies Recipe

Serving: 24 | Prep: | Cook: 35mins | Ready in:

Ingredients

- 1 (17 5/8 ounce) package walnut brownie mix (Duncan Hines)
- vegetable oil
- water
- eggs
- 3 (8 Oz) Symphony chocolate bars with almond and Toffee (a must)
- 1/2 Cup Chopped walnuts (optional)

Direction

- Prepare the brownie mix according to package directions.
- Add the Chopped Walnuts to the mix.
- Line a 13 by 9-inch cake pan with aluminum foil and spray with vegetable oil cooking spray. Spoon in half of the brownie batter and smooth with a spatula or the back of a spoon. Place the candy bars side by side on top of the batter. (Do not break) Cover with the remaining batter.
- Bake according to package directions. Let cool completely, then lift from the pan using the edges of the foil. This makes it easy to cut the brownies into squares.

100. Chocolate Bottom Banana Squares Recipe

Serving: 12 | Prep: | Cook: 35mins | Ready in:

Ingredients

- 1/2 cup butter softened
- 1 cup granulated sugar
- 1 large egg
- 1 teaspoon vanilla
- 1-1/2 cups mashed ripe bananas
- 1-1/2 cups all-purpose flour
- 1 teaspoon baking powder
- 1 teaspoon baking soda
- 1/2 teaspoon salt
- 1/4 cup baking cocoa

Direction

- Preheat oven to 350 then grease a rectangular baking pan and set aside.
- In mixing bowl cream butter and sugar then add egg and vanilla and beat thoroughly.
- Blend in bananas. Combine flour, baking powder, baking soda and salt.
- Add to creamed mixture and stir to just mix.
- Divide batter in half then add cocoa to half the batter and spread into prepared pan.
- Spoon remaining batter on top and swirl with a spatula or knife.
- Bake for 25 minutes then cool.

101. Chocolate Cake Squares With Eggnog Sauce Recipe

Serving: 15 | Prep: | Cook: 45mins | Ready in:

Ingredients

- For Cake:
- 1-1/2 teaspoons baking soda
- 1 cup buttermilk or sour milk*
- 3/4 cup cocoa
- 3/4 cup boiling water
- 1/4 cup (1/2 stick) butter or margarine, softened
- 1/4 cup shortening
- 2 cups sugar
- 2 eggs
- 1 teaspoon vanilla extract
- 1/8 teaspoon salt
- 1-3/4 cups all-purpose flour
- eggnog Sauce (recipe follows)
- *To sour milk: Use 1 tablespoon white vinegar plus milk to equal 1 cup.
- eggnog Sauce:
- 1 tablespoon cornstarch
- 2 tablespoons cold water
- 1-1/3 cups milk
- 1/4 cup sugar
- 3 egg yolks, beaten
- 1/4 teaspoon each brandy and vanilla extracts
- Several dashes ground nutmeg

Direction

- Cake:
- Heat oven to 350°F. Grease and flour 13×9×2-inch baking pan.
- 2. Stir baking soda into buttermilk in medium bowl; set aside. Stir together cocoa and water until smooth; set aside.
- 3. Beat butter, shortening and sugar in large bowl until creamy. Add eggs, vanilla and salt; beat well. Add buttermilk mixture alternately with flour to butter mixture, beating until blended. Add cocoa mixture; blend thoroughly. Pour batter into prepared pan.
- 4. Bake 40 to 45 minutes or until wooden pick inserted in center comes out clean. Cool completely. Serve with Eggnog Sauce.
- Eggnog Sauce:
- Stir cornstarch and water in saucepan until smooth. Add milk, sugar and egg yolks. Beat with whisk until well blended. Cook over medium heat, stirring constantly, until thickened. Remove from heat. Stir in extracts. Cool completely. Sprinkle nutmeg over top. Cover; refrigerate leftover sauce.

102. Chocolate Caramel Cashew Squares Recipe

Serving: 1 | Prep: | Cook: 18mins | Ready in:

Ingredients

- 1 Cups All Purpose flour
- 1 Cup brown sugar firmly packed
- 1 Confectioners sugar optional
- 1 egg
- 1 Cup cashews coarsely chopped
- 1 Cup chocolate morsels
- 12 Ounces caramel ice cream topping
- 1 Cup milk chocolate morsels
- 1 Cup margarine

Direction

- Preheat oven to 350F.
- Combine flour and brown sugar in large bowl. Cut in margarine with pastry blender or 2 knives until mixture resembles coarse crumbs.
- Stir in 1/2 cup chocolate morsels; press firmly onto bottom of ungreased 13x9-inch baking pan. Bake 15 minutes.
- Beat egg and ice cream topping in medium bowl with wire whisk until well blended. Stir in remaining 1/2 cup chocolate morsels and the cashews; spread evenly over crust.
- Bake 18 to 20 minutes, or until golden brown. Cool completely. Cut into 24 squares. Sprinkle with confectioners' sugar, if desired.

- Yield: 24 servings (1 square each)

103. Chocolate Caramel Layer Squares Recipe

Serving: 48 | Prep: | Cook: 25mins | Ready in:

Ingredients

- 1 (14 oz) bag of Kraft caramels
- 2/3 cup evaporated milk
- 1 pkg German chocolate cake mix
- 3/4 cup melted margarine
- 1 cup chopped nuts
- 1 (6 oz) bag chocolate chips

Direction

- Combine caramels and 1/2 cup evaporated milk in the top of a double boiler. Cook until caramels are melted. Stir often. Remove from heat.
- Combine dry cake mix, remaining milk and margarine.
- Mix with an electric mixer until dough holds together.
- Stir in nuts.
- Press 1/2 cake mixture into greased 9"x12" pan.
- Bake at 350 degrees for 6 minutes.
- Remove from oven and sprinkle with chocolate chips over crust.
- Pour caramel mixture over chocolate chips and spread evenly.
- Crumble remaining cake mixture over caramel and return to oven for 15 to 18 minutes.
- Cool on rack and chill for 30 minutes.
- Cut into squares.

104. Chocolate Cheesecake Candy Cane Bars Recipe

Serving: 16 | Prep: | Cook: 45mins | Ready in:

Ingredients

- Crust:
- 20 chocolate wafer cookies
- 3 tablespoons unsalted butter, melted
- 1 tablespoon sugar
- 1/2 teaspoon ground coffee beans
- 1/4 teaspoon fine salt
- Filling:
- 8 ounces semisweet chocolate, finely chopped
- 8 ounces cream cheese, room temperature
- 2/3 cup sugar
- 1/2 cup sour cream
- 2 large eggs, room temperature
- Glaze:
- 4 ounces bittersweet chocolate, chopped
- 2 tablespoons unsalted butter
- 1 teaspoon light or dark corn syrup
- 2 tablespoons sour cream, room temperature
- 1/2 cup crushed candy canes (see Cooks Note)

Direction

- Preheat oven to 350 degrees F. Line an 8-inch square baking dish with foil.
- For the crust: Process the chocolate wafers in a food processor with the butter, sugar, coffee, and salt until fine. Evenly press the crust into the prepared dish covering the bottom completely. Bake until the crust sets, about 15 minutes.
- Meanwhile, make the filling: Put the chocolate in a medium microwave-safe bowl; heat at 75 percent power until softened, about 2 minutes. Stir, and continue to microwave until completely melted, up to 2 minutes more. (Alternatively put the chocolate in a heatproof bowl. Bring a saucepan filled with an inch or so of water to a very slow simmer; set the bowl over, but not touching, the water, and stir occasionally until melted and smooth.)

- Blend the cream cheese, sugar, and sour cream together in the food processor until smooth. Scrape down the sides, as needed. Add the eggs and pulse until just incorporated. With the food processor running, pour the chocolate into the wet ingredients and mix until smooth.
- Pour the filling evenly over the crust. Bake until filling puffs slightly around the edges, but is still a bit wobbly in the centre, about 25 to 30 minutes. Cool on a rack.
- For the Glaze: Put the chocolate, butter and corn syrup in microwave safe bowl. Heat glaze in the microwave at 75 percent power until melted, about 2 minutes. Stir the ingredients together until smooth; add the sour cream. Spread glaze evenly over the warm cake and scatter the crushed candy canes over top. Cool completely, then refrigerate overnight.
- Cut into small bars or squares. Serve chilled or room temperature.
- Store cookies covered in the refrigerator for up to 5 days.
- Cook's Note: To crush the candy canes, remove wrappers and place in a resealable plastic bag. Use a rolling pin to roll and break the candy up into small pieces, about 1/4 inch or so.

105. Chocolate Cheesecake Squares Recipe

Serving: 9 | Prep: | Cook: 135mins | Ready in:

Ingredients

- nonstick cooking spray
- 8 chocolate wafer cookies
- 1 bar (8 ounces) reduced-fat cream cheese
- 1 cup reduced-fat sour cream
- 1/3 cup unsweetened cocoa powder
- 2 tablespoons cornstarch
- 3/4 cup sugar
- 1 large whole egg plus 1 large egg white
- 1/3 cup semisweet chocolate chips

Direction

- 1. Preheat oven to 325°. Coat an 8-inch square baking pan with cooking spray. Line with two crisscrossed pieces of parchment or wax paper, spraying between sheets. Spray lined pan; set aside.
- 2. Process cookies in a food processor until finely ground. Gently press crumbs into bottom of prepared pan (do not rinse processor bowl).
- 3. Blend cream cheese and sour cream in food processor until smooth, scraping down sides of bowl as needed. Add cocoa, cornstarch, sugar, egg, and egg white; process until smooth. Pour into pan; sprinkle with chocolate chips.
- 4. Bake until just set, 35 to 40 minutes; cool completely in pan. Refrigerate at least 1 hour. Invert onto a tray; peel off paper, and reinvert crust side down. Cut into 9 squares.

106. Chocolate Chip Cheese Bars

Serving: 36 | Prep: | Cook: 15mins | Ready in:

Ingredients

- 1 tube (18 ounces) refrigerated chocolate chip cookie dough
- 1 package (8 ounces) cream cheese, softened
- 1/2 cup sugar
- 1 egg

Direction

- Cut cookie dough in half. For crust, press half of the dough onto the bottom of a greased 8-in. square baking pan.
- In a large bowl, beat the cream cheese, sugar and egg until smooth. Spread over crust. Crumble remaining dough over top.
- Bake at 350° for 35-40 minutes or until a toothpick inserted in the center comes out

clean. Cool on a wire rack. Refrigerate leftovers.
- \Note: 2 cups of your favorite chocolate chip cookie dough can be substituted for the refrigerated dough.
- Nutrition Facts
- 1 piece: 220 calories, 12g fat (5g saturated fat), 37mg cholesterol, 113mg sodium, 26g carbohydrate (19g sugars, 0 fiber), 3g protein.

107. Chocolate Chip Cheese Bars Recipe

Serving: 1 | Prep: | Cook: 35mins | Ready in:

Ingredients

- 1 (18 oz) tube refrigerated chocolate chip cookie dough
- 1 (8 oz) pkg. cream cheese softened
- 1/2 C. sugar
- 1 egg

Direction

- Cut cookie dough in half. For crust, press half of the dough onto the bottom of a greased 8" square baking pan.
- In a mixing bowl, beat cream cheese, sugar and egg until smooth. Spread over crust. Crumble remaining dough over top.
- Bake at 350 for 35-40 minutes or until a toothpick inserted in center comes out clean. Cool on a wire rack. Refrigerate leftovers.

108. Chocolate Chip Cheesecake Bars Recipe

Serving: 12 | Prep: | Cook: 35mins | Ready in:

Ingredients

- 2 rolls refrigerated chocolate chip cookie dough.
- 16 oz cream cheese
- 2 eggs
- 1/3 cup sugar
- 1 teaspoon vanilla

Direction

- Unwrap cookie dough n place in freezer for a short bit to help with slicing.
- Mix cream cheese, eggs sugar and vanilla, beat well.
- Spray o lightly grease a 13x9" cake pan.
- Slice one roll of cookie dough into 1/4" slices and cover bottom of pan, don't press together.
- Pour cream cheese batter over them.
- Slice other roll of cookie dough and place on top of batter.
- Bake in preheated 350 degree oven for about 35 minutes.
- Cool n chill.
- Cut into bars.

109. Chocolate Chip Cookie Bars Recipe

Serving: 36 | Prep: | Cook: 20mins | Ready in:

Ingredients

- 3/4 cups butter flavored Crisco
- 1 1/2 cups dark brown sugar (can use light but I like the flavor better this way)
- 2 tbsp milk
- 1 tbsp vanilla
- 1 egg
- 1 3/4 cup AP flour (can add part whole wheat if you like 3/4)
- 1 tsp salt
- 3/4 tsp baking soda
- 1 1/2 cups chocolate chips (or 1 cup chips and 1 cup nuts)

Direction

- Preheat oven to 350oF.
- Cream together Crisco and sugar; add milk, vanilla and egg, mix until well combined.
- Mix together flour, salt and soda.
- Add flour mixture to sugar mixture, mix well.
- Add chips (and nuts).
- Butter and flour 9x13" baking pan (I use baker's joy). Press dough evenly into pan.
- Bake for 20 to 25 minutes until lightly browned and firm.
- Cool on wire rack and cut into bars.

110. Chocolate Chip Cream Cheese Bars Recipe

Serving: 24 | Prep: | Cook: 32mins | Ready in:

Ingredients

- 2 8 oz pkgs cream cheese
- 1/2 cup sugar
- 2 1/2 tsp. vanilla
- 2 eggs
- 2 20 oz. pkgs of prepared chocolate chip cookie dough, in rolls

Direction

- Freeze cookie dough for about 1/2 hr. before using.
- Preheat oven to 350.
- Combine cream cheese, sugar, eggs, and vanilla till well blended.
- Slice and press 1 roll of dough into an ungreased 13 x 9 pan.
- Pour the cream cheese mixture over the dough.
- Slice remaining roll of cookie dough into slices, flattening as much as possible with your hands.
- Lay the flattened slices over the filling, covering as much as you can.
- Bake for 30 to 35 minutes until golden brown.
- Cool completely, sprinkle with powdered sugar if desired.
- Refrigerate at least an hour before cutting.

111. Chocolate Coconut Bars Recipe

Serving: 0 | Prep: | Cook: 15mins | Ready in:

Ingredients

- 2 cups graham cracker crumbs
- 1/2 cup butter, melted
- 1/4 cup sugar
- 2 cups flaked coconut
- 1 can (14 oz) sweetened condensed milk
- 1/2 cup chopped pecans
- 1 plain chocolate candy bar (7 oz.)
- 2 tbsp creamy peanut butter

Direction

- Combine the crumbs, butter, and sugar.
- Press into a greased 13 x 9 inch baking pan.
- Bake at 350 F for 10 minutes.
- Meanwhile, in a bowl, combine the coconut, milk, and pecans.
- Spread over the crust.
- Bake at 350 F for 15 minutes.
- Cool in the pan on a wire rack.
- In a small saucepan, melt the candy bar and peanut butter over low heat.
- Spread over cooled bars.
- Let stand until frosting is set.
- Cut into bars.

112. Chocolate Dulce De Leche Bars Recipe

Serving: 8 | Prep: | Cook: 25mins | Ready in:

Ingredients

- For shortbread crust:

- 1 stick butter, softened
- 1/3 cup packed dark brown sugar
- 1/2 teaspoon pure vanilla extract
- 1/2 teaspoon kosher salt
- 1 cup all-purpose flour
- For chocolate dulce de leche:
- 1 cup heavy cream
- 1 cup dulce de leche
- 4 large egg yolks
- 5 ounces 60% cacao bittersweet chocolate, finely chopped

Direction

- Prep time does not include chilling of bars.
- Make shortbread crust by preheating oven to 375F degrees.
- Butter shallow 9x9.5 inch square baking pan.
- Line bottom and 2 sides with parchment paper, leaving overhang.
- Butter parchment.
- Blend together butter, brown sugar, vanilla and salt in bowl with fork.
- Sift in flour and blend with fork until soft dough forms.
- Spread dough evenly in baking pan using spatula, then prick all over with fork.
- Bake until golden, 15 to 20 minutes, then cool completely in pan (about 30 minutes).
- To make chocolate Dulce de Leche, bring cream and Dulce de Leche to a simmer in small heavy saucepan, stirring with wooden spoon until dissolved.
- Whisk together yolks in bowl, then slowly whisk in hot cream mixture.
- Return to pan and cook over medium heat, stirring constantly, until thermometer registers 170F degrees.
- Remove from heat and whisk in chocolate until melted.
- Pour chocolate mixture over cooled shortbread and chill, uncovered, until set (about 2 hours).
- Run a small knife around edges to loosen, then transfer to cutting board.
- Cut with hot clean knife into bars.
- Chill until ready to serve.

113. Chocolate Macaroon Squares Recipe

Serving: 20 | Prep: | Cook: 30mins | Ready in:

Ingredients

- 1 (18.25 ounce) box chocolate cake mix
- 1/3 cup butter or margarine, softened
- 1 large egg, lightly beaten
- 1 1/4 cups (14 ounce can) sweetened condensed milk
- 1 large egg
- 1 teaspoon vanilla extract
- 1 1/3 cups flaked sweetened coconut, divided
- 1 cup chopped pecans
- 1 cup (6 ounces) semisweet chocolate chips

Direction

- Heat oven to 350 degrees F.
- Combine cake mix, butter and egg in large bowl; mix with fork until crumbly.
- Press onto bottom of ungreased 13 x 9-inch baking pan.
- Combine sweetened condensed milk, egg and vanilla extract in medium bowl; beat until well blended.
- Stir in 1 cup coconut, nuts and chocolate chips.
- Spread mixture evenly over base; sprinkle with remaining coconut.
- Bake for 28 to 30 minutes or until center is almost set (center will firm when cool).
- Cool in pan on wire rack.

114. Chocolate Mint Bars Recipe

Serving: 20 | Prep: | Cook: 23mins | Ready in:

Ingredients

- Bottom layer

- 1 cup all purpose flour(4 1/2 oz)
- 1/2 tsp salt
- 1 cup granulate sugar
- 1/2 cup egg substitute
- 1/4 cup butter,melted
- 2 tblsp water
- 1 tsp vanilla extract
- 2 large eggs,beaten
- 1 16 oz can chocolate syrup
- cooking spray
- mint LAYER
- 2 cups powdered sugar
- 1/4 cup butter,melted
- 2 tblsp fat free milk
- 1/2 tsp peppermint extract
- 2 drops green food coloring
- glaze
- 3/4 cup semi sweet chocolate chips
- 3 tblsp butter.

Direction

- Preheat oven to 350.
- To prepare bottom layer, lightly spoon flour into a measuring cup: level with a knife, combine flour and salt: stir with a whisk.
- Combine granulated sugar, egg substitute, 3/4cup melted butter, 2 tbsp. water, vanilla, eggs and chocolate syrup in a medium bowl; until smooth.
- Add flour mixture to chocolate mixture, stirring until blended.
- Pour batter into a 13 x9 baking pan coated with cooking spray.
- Bake at 350 for 23 min or until a wooden pick inserted comes out clean.
- Cool completely in pan on a wire rack.
- To prepare the mint layer:
- Combine powdered sugar, 1/4 cup melted butter, milk, peppermint extract, food coloring.
- In medium bowl; beat with a mixer until smooth.
- Spread mixture over cooled cake.
- To prepare the Glaze:
- Combine the chocolate chips and three tbsp. butter in a medium microwave safe bowl.
- Microwave high for 1 min or until melted, stirring after 30 sec.
- Let stand 2 min.
- Spread chocolate mixture evenly over top.
- Cover and refrigerate until ready to serve. Cut into 20 pieces.

115. Chocolate Nougat Squares Recipe

Serving: 16 | Prep: | Cook: 40mins |Ready in:

Ingredients

- 4- chocolate covered candy bars (such as milky way or midnight bars)cut into ½ inch chunks
- 1 1/4-- cups unsifted bleached cake flour
- 1/4-- cup unsweetened cocoa powder
- 1/4-- teaspoon baking powder
- 1/8- teaspoon salt
- 1/2- pound (16 tablespoons or 2 sticks) unsalted butter melted and cooled to tepid…..
- 4- ounces unsweetened chocolate , melted and cooled to tepid
- 4- large eggs
- 2- cups granulated sugar
- 2 1/2 - teaspoons vanilla extract

Direction

- Preheat the oven to 325 degrees F.
- Film the inside of a 9x9 by 2 inch baking pan with non-stick cooking spray.
- Chill the candy…..refrigerate the chunks of chocolate candy for 20 minutes.
- Refrigerating the candy helps to keep its shape intact as it's incorporated into the batter.
- Mix the batter, sift the flour, cocoa powder, baking powder, and salt onto a sheet of waxed paper.
- In a medium -sized mixing bowl, whisk the melted butter and chocolate until smooth.
- In a large mixing bowl, whisk until combined, about 30 seconds.

- Blend in the vanilla extract and melted butter-chocolate mixture.
- Sift the flour mixture over and stir to form a batter, mixing thoroughly until the particles of flour are absorbed, using a whisk or flat wooden paddle.
- Carefully stir in the chunks of candy.
- Scrape the batter into the prepared pan and spread evenly.
- Smooth the top with a rubber spatula.
- Bake, the brownies in the preheated oven for 35- 40 minutes, or until set.
- Let the brownies stand in pan on a cooling rack for 2 hours.
- Refrigerate for 1 hour.
- With a small sharp knife, cut them into quarters then cut each quarter into 4 squares.
- Remove the squares from the baking pan, using a small spatula.
- Store in airtight container.
- Makes 16 squares.

116. Chocolate Peanut Butter Bars Iv From Allrecipes Recipe

Serving: 36 | Prep: | Cook: | Ready in:

Ingredients

- 2 1/2 cups graham cracker crumbs
- 1 cup peanut butter
- 1 cup butter, melted
- 2 cups semisweet chocolate chips
- 2 3/4 cups confectioners' sugar

Direction

- In a medium bowl, stir together graham cracker crumbs, confectioners' sugar, peanut butter and melted butter. Press firmly into the bottom of a 9x13 inch pan. Melt chocolate chips over a double boiler or in the microwave, stirring occasionally. Spread melted chocolate over the crumb crust. Chill for about 5 minutes, then cut into bars before the chocolate is completely set, then chill until ready to serve.

117. Chocolate Peanut Butter Bars Recipe

Serving: 36 | Prep: | Cook: 8mins | Ready in:

Ingredients

- ⅔ cup butter
- 1 cup brown sugar
- 3 cups of quick-cooking oats
- 1 tablespoon vanilla extract
- ¼ teaspoon salt
- 1 package milk chocolate chips
- 1 cup creamy or chunky peanut butter

Direction

- Melt the butter and mix with sugar, oatmeal, vanilla and salt.
- Press into a 9x13 pan and bake at 400 degrees for 8 minutes.
- Cool completely.
- In a microwavable bowl, melt chocolate chips in the microwave.
- Stir in peanut butter and blend together well.
- Pour over cooled oatmeal bars.
- Allow chocolate mixture to cool (or refrigerate until it sets).
- Cut into bars and store in covered container.
- In hot, humid weather, store in refrigerator.

118. Chocolate Peanut Butter Dream Bars Recipe

Serving: 24 | Prep: | Cook: | Ready in:

Ingredients

- cookiE BASE:

- 1 pouch (1 lb. 1.5-oz.) Betty Crocker double chocolate chunk cookie mix
- 1/4 cup vegetable oil
- 2 Tbsp. cold strong brewed coffee
- 1 egg
- FILLING:
- 1 pkg. (8-oz.) cream cheese, softened
- 1/4 cup sugar
- 1 container (8-oz.) frozen whipped topping, thawed
- 1 bag (9- oz.) miniature chocolate-covered peanut butter cup candies, chopped
- TOPPING:
- 1/4 cup creamy peanut butter
- 1/4 cup milk
- 2 Tbsp. sugar
- 3 oz. bittersweet baking chocolate, melted
- 1 cup dry-roasted peanuts

Direction

- Preheat the oven to 350*F.
- In a large bowl stir cookie base ingredients until soft dough forms.
- Spread dough in bottom of an ungreased 13x9" pan.
- Bake 12-15 minutes or until just set.
- Cool completely about 30 minutes.
- In a large bowl, beat cream cheese and 1/4 cup sugar with an electric mixer on medium speed until smooth.
- Fold in whipped topping and candies.
- Spread over cooled cookie base.
- In a small bowl microwaveable bowl, beat peanut butter, milk and 2 Tbsp. sugar with a wire whisk until smooth.
- Microwave uncovered on HIGH 30 to 60 seconds, too thin for drizzling.
- Drizzle mixture over filling.
- Drizzle with melted chocolate.
- Sprinkle with peanuts.
- Refrigerate about 2 hours or until set.
- For bars cut into 6 rows by 4 rows.
- Store covered in refrigerator.

119. Chocolate Peanut Butter Oat Bars Recipe

Serving: 48 | Prep: | Cook: 20mins | Ready in:

Ingredients

- 3/4 cup butter, softened
- 3/4 cup peanut butter (creamy or crunchy)
- 3/4 cup sugar
- 3/4 cup packed brown sugar
- 2 teaspoons water
- 2 eggs
- 1 1/2 teaspoons vanilla
- 1 1/2 cups all-purpose flour
- 1 1/2 cups quick-cooking oats
- 3/4 teaspoon baking soda
- 1/2 teaspoon salt
- Glaze:
- 1 1/2 cups milk chocolate chips
- 1/2 cup butterscotch chips
- 1/2 cup creamy peanut butter(Yum!!)

Direction

- Heat oven to 325 degrees F.
- Grease a 15 x 10 x 1 inch baking pan.
- In a large mixing bowl, cream butter, peanut butter, sugars and water.
- Beat in eggs and vanilla
- Combine flour, oats, soda and salt in separate bowl.
- Gradually add to creamed mixture.
- Spread into prepared pan and bake 18 - 22 minutes or until lightly browned
- In a microwave-safe bowl, melt chips and peanut butter.
- Pour over warm bars and spread evenly
- Cool completely on a wire rack before cutting
- Makes 4 dozen
- ***
- -In the will of God, there is no higher, holier calling than to be a wife and mother (Titus 2:4-5)

120. Chocolate Peanut Fudge Bars Recipe

Serving: 30 | Prep: | Cook: 240mins | Ready in:

Ingredients

- Crust
- 2 c chocolate cookie crumbs
- 1/2 c butter, melted
- Filling
- 1 package cream cheese
- 1 c powdered sugar
- 1/2 c creamy peanut butter
- 2 tbsps milk
- Topping
- 2 c semi-sweet chocolate chips
- 1/2 c creamy peanut butter
- 1 c peanuts, coarsely chopped

Direction

- In medium bowl, mix crust ingredients & mix well.
- Press firmly on bottom of 9x13 pan.
- Refrigerate at least 30 mins.
- In medium mixer bowl, mix filling ingredients, mix at low-ish speed 30 seconds.
- Beat at medium high speed 2 mins or until light & fluffy.
- Spread over crust.
- In medium saucepan melt chocolate chips over low heat/flame stirring constantly, until smooth.
- Stir in peanut butter, mix well.
- Stir in peanuts.
- Spread over filling.
- Refrigerate at least 4 hrs.

121. Chocolate Pecan Pumpkin Bars Recipe

Serving: 15 | Prep: | Cook: 30mins | Ready in:

Ingredients

- 1 cup white flour
- 1 cup whole wheat flour
- 3/4 cup granulated sugar
- 1 cup pecans very finely chopped
- 2 teaspoons baking powder
- 1 teaspoon ground cinnamon
- 1/2 teaspoon baking soda
- 1/2 teaspoon salt
- 4 large eggs beaten
- 1 teaspoon vanilla
- 15 ounce can pure pumpkin
- 1/2 cup canola oil
- 1/4 cup milk
- 1/2 cup miniature chocolate chips

Direction

- Preheat oven to 350.
- Lightly oil or coat a jelly roll pan with non-stick cooking spray and set aside.
- Whisk together flours, sugar, pecans, baking powder, cinnamon, baking soda and salt.
- In separate bowl combine eggs, pumpkin, canola oil, vanilla and milk.
- Add to dry mixture along with chocolate chips then stir to combine.
- Spread batter evenly in the prepared pan and bake for 25 minutes then cool on wire rack.

122. Chocolate Raspberry Cheesecake Bars Recipe

Serving: 12 | Prep: | Cook: 17mins | Ready in:

Ingredients

- Crust
- 1 Cup flour
- ¼ Cup powdered sugar
- ½ Cup margarine
- Filling
- ½ Cup raspberry jam
- 3 oz pkg cream cheese (softened)

- 2 Tbl milk
- 1 Cup (6oz) white chocolate chips
- glaze
- 2 oz (2 squares) semisweet baking chocolate
- 1 Tbl shortening

Direction

- Oven 375
- Blend flour and powdered sugar, cut in margarine until crumbly.
- Press mixture into 9 inch square pan
- Bake 15 to 17 minutes or until lightly browned
- Spread jam evenly over baked crust.
- In small bowl, beat cream cheese and milk until smooth.
- Add melted chips to cream cheese mixture; beat until smooth.
- Drop cream cheese mixture by spoonfuls onto jam, spread evenly with a light hand
- Chill until set
- In small saucepan over low heat melt chocolate with shortening, stirring constantly.
- Spread over white chocolate layer. Chill completely, cut into bars.
- Cover and refrigerate

123. Chocolate Snicker Bar Brownies Recipe

Serving: 12 | Prep: | Cook: 35mins | Ready in:

Ingredients

- 4 lg eggs, slightly beaten
- 2 cups sugar
- 3/4 cup butter, melted
- 2 tsp vanilla
- 1 1/2 cups all-purpose flour
- 1/2 tsp baking powder
- 1/4 tsp salt
- 1/3 cup cocoa
- 4 Snickers bars, coarsely chopped
- 3 milk chocolate bars, finely chopped

Direction

- Combine first four ingredients in a large bowl.
- Combine flour and next three ingredients; stir into sugar mixture.
- Fold in chopped Snickers bars.
- Spoon mixture into a greased 13x9 pan; sprinkle with chocolate bars. Bake at 350 degrees for 30 to 35 min.

124. Chocolate Streusel Bars Eagle Brand Recipe

Serving: 15 | Prep: | Cook: 35mins | Ready in:

Ingredients

- 1 3/4 cups all-purpose flour
- 1 cup sugar
- 1/4 cup unsweetened cocoa
- 1/2 cup cold butter or margarine
- 1 egg, beaten
- 1 (14-ounce) can EAGLE BRAND® sweetened condensed milk (NOT evaporated milk)
- 2 cups semi-sweet chocolate chips, divided
- 1 cup chopped nuts

Direction

- Preheat oven to 350°F.
- Combine flour, sugar and cocoa; cut in butter until crumbly.
- Add egg; mix until well blended.
- Reserve 1 1/2 cups crumb mixture.
- Press remainder evenly on bottom of greased 13x9-inch baking pan.
- Bake 10 minutes.
- In heavy saucepan, over low heat, combine EAGLE BRAND® and 1 cup chocolate chips; cook and stir until chips are melted and mixture is smooth.
- Spread evenly over prepared crust.
- To reserved crumb mixture, add nuts and remaining 1 cup chocolate chips; sprinkle evenly over top.

- Bake 25 to 30 minutes or until center is set. Do not overbake.
- Cool. Cut into bars.
- Store leftovers covered at room temperature.

125. Chocolate Toffee Caramel Bars Recipe

Serving: 36 | Prep: | Cook: 35mins | Ready in:

Ingredients

- 32 vanilla caramels, unwrapped
- ½ cup butter
- 1 (14 ounce) can sweetened condensed milk
- 1 package butter Recipe yellow cake mix (my fave is Pillsbury Moist Supreme)
- 1/3 cup vegetable or canola oil
- 2 eggs
- 1 (12 ounce) package milk chocolate chips
- 1 cup white chocolate chips
- 1 cup Heath Toffee Bits (Bits-o-Brickle)

Direction

- I TOLD you, you didn't want to know the fat content of these!!
- Unwrap the caramels and put them in a microwaveable bowl.
- Add the butter and sweetened condensed milk; set aside.
- In a large bowl, combine cake mix, oil and eggs, blending well (batter will be very thick).
- Stir in chocolate chips, white chips and toffee bits.
- Press half of the mixture into the bottom of a greased 9x13 pan.
- Bake at 350 degrees for 10 minutes.
- While crust is baking, melt the caramel mixture in the microwave, stirring frequently until caramels are melted and mixture is smooth.
- Remove crust from oven and slowly pour caramel mixture over hot crust.
- Top with reserved crust mixture - it's really thick, so I just take chunks of the mixture and break it up over the caramel filling.
- Bake an additional 25 minutes or until top is set and edges are a golden brown.
- Cool 20 minutes and then run a sharp knife around edges of the pan to loosen the bars.
- Cool completely; cut into bars.

126. Chocolate Dipped Deluxe Overnight No Bake Power Bar Recipe

Serving: 10 | Prep: | Cook: 25mins | Ready in:

Ingredients

- 1 cup rolled oats
- 1/2 cup sesame seeds, toasted and ground
- 1/2 cup dried apricots; chopped fine
- 1/2 cup raisins; chopped fine
- 1 cup shredded unsweetened dried coconut
- 1 cup almonds; blanched, chopped or slivered
- 1/2 cup nonfat dried milk powder
- 1/2 cup toasted wheat germ
- 2 teaspoon butter or margarine
- 1 cup white corn syrup or 3/4 cup honey
- 3/4 cup sugar
- 1/4 cup chunky peanut butter
- 1 teaspoon orange or lemon extract
- 2 teaspoon grated orange or lemon peel
- 12 oz chocolate chips; 2 cups
- 4 oz paraffin, food grade or 3/4 cup butter

Direction

- Toast the sesame seeds in a frying pan for about 7 minutes, until golden.
- Toast the oats in a 300 degree oven in a 10 inch by 15 inch baking pan for 25 minutes, stirring to prevent scorching.
- Mix the seeds, apricots, raisins, coconut, almonds, dry milk, and wheat germ; mix well. Mix hot oats into dried fruit mixture.

- Butter the hot baking pan; set aside.
- In the frying pan, combine corn syrup or honey and sugar; bring to a rolling boil over medium high heat and quickly stir in the peanut butter, orange extract, and orange peel. At once, pour over the oatmeal mixture and mix well.
- Quickly spread in buttered pan and press into an even layer. Then cover and chill until firm, at least 4 hours or overnight.
- DIPPING FOR CHOCOLATE COATING
- Cut into bars about 1 1/4 by 2 1/2 inches.
- Combine chocolate chips and paraffin in to top of a double boiler. Place over simmering water until melted; stir often. Turn heat to low.
- Using tongs, dip 1 bar at a time into chocolate, hold over pan until it stops dripping, then place on wire racks set above waxed paper.
- With paraffin, the coating firms very quickly, bars with butter in the chocolate coating may need to be chilled. When firm and cool), serve bars, or wrap individually in foil. Store in the refrigerator up to 4 weeks; freeze to store longer.
- Makes about 4 dozen bars, about 1 ounce each.
- Per piece: 188 cal.; 4.4 g protein; 29 g carbo.; 9.8 g fat; 0.6 mg chol.; 40 mg sodium.

127. Chocolate Caramel Layer Bars Recipe

Serving: 36 | Prep: | Cook: 15mins | Ready in:

Ingredients

- 1 roll (16.5 oz) Pillsbury® Create 'n Bake® refrigerated chocolate chip cookies
- 1 bag (11.5 oz) milk chocolate chips (2 cups)
- 1 container (18 oz) caramel apple dip (1 1/2 cups)
- 3 cups Rice Chex® cereal
- 1 cup chopped peanuts

Direction

- Heat oven to 350°F. In ungreased 13x9-inch pan, break up cookie dough. With floured fingers, press dough evenly in bottom of pan to form crust.
- Bake 15 to 18 minutes or until light golden brown. Cool 15 minutes.
- Meanwhile, in 4-quart saucepan, cook 1 cup of the chips and 1 cup of the dip over medium heat, stirring constantly, until melted and smooth. Remove from heat. Stir in cereal and peanuts.
- Spread cereal mixture over cooled crust. In 1-quart saucepan, heat remaining chips and dip over medium heat, stirring constantly, until melted and smooth. Spread over cereal mixture. Refrigerate until chocolate mixture is set, about 30 minutes. For bars, cut into 6 rows by 6 rows. Store tightly covered. Try using semisweet chocolate chips instead of the milk chocolate chips.

128. Chocolate Cherry Bars Recipe

Serving: 24 | Prep: | Cook: 35mins | Ready in:

Ingredients

- 1 cup butter, softened, divided
- 2-1/2 cups packed brown sugar, divided
- 1/2 tsp. baking soda
- 1/4 tsp. salt
- 4 eggs, divided
- 1-1/2 tsp. vanilla, divided
- 2-1/2 cups all-purpose flour, divided
- 1-1/2 cups quick-cooking rolled oats
- 6 oz. bittersweet chocolate, chopped
- 2 cups (10 oz.) fresh sweet cherries (such as Bing or Royal Ann), pitted
- 1/2 cup slivered toasted almonds

Direction

- Preheat oven to 350 degrees F. Line 13x9x2-inch baking pan with foil; set aside. In mixing bowl beat 1/2 cup of the butter on medium to high 30 seconds. Add 1 cup of the brown sugar, the baking soda, and salt. Beat until combined, occasionally scraping bowl. Beat in 1 egg and 1/2 teaspoon of the vanilla. Beat or stir in 1-1/4 cups of the flour. Stir in oats; set aside.

- For filling, in saucepan stir remaining 1-1/2 cups brown sugar and 1/2 cup butter over medium heat until combined; cool slightly. Stir in remaining 3 eggs and 1 teaspoon vanilla; lightly beat with wooden spoon. Stir in remaining 1-1/4 cups flour and the chocolate.
- Set aside 3/4 cup oats mixture; press remaining in pan. Spread filling, top with cherries, dot with reserved oats mixture, and sprinkle nuts. Bake 25 minutes, until top is light brown and filling is moist. Cool on rack 1 hour. Cover and refrigerate at least 2 hours.
- Lift from pan; cut with serrated knife. Store, covered, at room temperature.

129. Chocolate Covered Cherry Bars Recipe

Serving: 48 | Prep: | Cook: 25mins | Ready in:

Ingredients

- 1 10 oz. jar maraschino -cherries without stems
- 1 1/2 c sugar
- 1/2 c butter or margarine melted
- 2 oz unsweetened chocolate, -melted and cooled
- 1 ts vanilla
- 2 eggs
- 1 1/2 c all-purpose flour
- 1/2 ts baking powder
- 1/2 c milk
- 1 6 oz. package (1 cup) semi-sweet chocolate pieces
- (do-not use imitation)
- 1/2 c sweetened condensed milk

Direction

- Drain cherries, reserving 1/3 cup juice. Place cherries in a food processor bowl; cover and process with on/off turns till coarsely chopped, or chop by hand.
- Combine sugar, butter or margarine, unsweetened chocolate, and vanilla in a medium mixing bowl. Add eggs; beat for 1 minute at medium speed.
- Stir together flour, baking powder, and dash salt. Add to chocolate mixture alternately with milk, mixing well after each addition. Spread batter in a greased and floured 15x10x1 inch baking pan. Sprinkle with chopped cherries.
- Combine chocolate pieces and sweetened condensed milk in a small heavy saucepan. Stir over low heat till chocolate is melted. Stir in reserved cherry juice.
- Use a spoon to drizzle evenly over batter.
- Bake in a 350*F for 25 to 30 minutes or till a wooden toothpick comes out clean. Cool on wire rack.
- Spray a thin knife with non-stick spray coating; wipe off excess. Use knife to cut chocolate mixture into squares.

130. Chocolate Glazed Almond Bars Recipe

Serving: 40 | Prep: | Cook: 20mins | Ready in:

Ingredients

- 2c. all-purpose flour
- 1/2c packed brown sugar
- 1/2tsp. salt
- 3/4c cold butter
- 3 egg whites
- 1c sugar
- 1 can(121/2oz.) almond filling
- 2c sliced almonds
- 4 squares(1oz.ea. bittersweet chocolate,melted

Direction

- In a large bowl, combine flour, brown sugar and salt. Cut in butter until mixture resembles coarse crumbs. Pat into a 13x9x2" baking pan coated with cooking spray. Bake at 350 for 18-22 mins. or till edges are lightly browned.
- Meanwhile, in a large bowl, whisk the egg whites, sugar and almond filling until blended. Stir in almonds. Pour over crust. Bake for 20-25 mins or until set. Cool completely on wire rack
- Drizzle with chocolate. Cut into bars. .store in an airtight container in the refrigerator.

131. Chocolate Peanut Butter Dream Bars Recipe

Serving: 24 | Prep: | Cook: 12mins | Ready in:

Ingredients

- 1 pouch (1 lb 1.5 oz) Betty Crocker® double chocolate chunk cookie mix
- 1/4 cup vegetable oil
- 2 tablespoons cold strong brewed coffee or water
- 1 egg
- Filling
- 1 package (8 oz) cream cheese, softened
- 1/4 cup sugar
- 1 container (8 oz) frozen whipped topping, thawed
- 1 bag (9 oz) miniature chocolate-covered peanut butter cup candies, chopped
- Topping
- 1/4 cup creamy peanut butter
- 1/4 cup milk
- 2 tablespoons sugar
- 3 oz bittersweet baking chocolate, melted
- 1 cup unsalted dry-roasted peanuts

Direction

- 1. Heat oven to 350°F. In large bowl, stir cookie base ingredients until soft dough forms. Spread dough in bottom of ungreased 13x9-inch pan. Bake 12 to 15 minutes or just until set. Cool completely, about 30 minutes.
- 2. In large bowl, beat cream cheese and 1/4 cup sugar with electric mixer on medium speed until smooth. Fold in whipped topping and candies. Spread over cooled cookie base.
- 3. In small microwavable bowl, beat peanut butter, milk and 2 tablespoons sugar with wire whisk until smooth. Microwave uncovered on High 30 to 60 seconds, stirring after 30 seconds, to thin for drizzling. Drizzle mixture over filling. Drizzle with melted chocolate. Sprinkle with peanuts. Refrigerate about 1 hour or until set. For bars, cut into 6 rows by 4 rows. Store covered in refrigerator.

132. Chocolatey Peanut Buttery Bars Recipe

Serving: 24 | Prep: | Cook: 30mins | Ready in:

Ingredients

- 2 cups chocolate cookie crumbs, finely ground
- 1/2 cup plus 2 Tbsp. butter
- 1 pound cream cheese
- 2/3 cup sugar
- 2 large eggs
- 3/4 cup smooth peanut butter
- 1/2 cup heavy cream
- 3-1/2 ounces semisweet or bittersweet chocolate, finely chopped

Direction

- Preheat oven to 325 Degrees F.
- Spray a 13 x 9 inch pan with PAM or other cooking spray.
- In a medium saucepan over a low heat melt butter and stir in cookie crumbs until combined.
- With your fingers press the mixture evenly into the bottom of the pan. Bake on the middle rack for 15 minutes or until it appears dry.
- Remove from oven and set aside.

- Using an electric mixer, beat together cream cheese and sugar till smooth.
- Beat in eggs and then stir in peanut butter until creamy.
- With a rubber spatula spread the peanut butter mixture evenly over the baked crust.
- Bake on a middle oven rack for 10-15 minutes until set.
- Allow pan to cool on a wire rack to room temperature.
- Bring the cream to a boil then remove from heat and add the chopped chocolate.
- Using a wire whisk, beat until smooth.
- With a rubber spatula, spread your chocolate mixture over the peanut butter mixture evenly.
- Refrigerate until firm.
- Using a large and sharp knife, cut into bars wiping the knife clean with a damp paper towel each time you slice.
- These can be stored in an airtight container in the refrigerator for 3 days or frozen up to 1 month.
- Note: The number of squares depends on the size they are cut.

133. Chunky Love Bars Recipe

Serving: 16 | Prep: | Cook: 15mins | Ready in:

Ingredients

- 1 stick unsalted butter
- 3/4 cup flour
- 2 tablespoons unsweetened baking cocoa
- 1/2 cup graham cracker crumbs
- 1/3 cup sugar, plus 2 tablespoons
- 1 tablespoon brown sugar
- 4 oz dark chocolate chunks
- 1/2 cup salted peanuts
- 1 banana, chopped to 1/2" pieces
- 1 tablespoon heavy cream

Direction

- Preheat oven to 350 degrees.
- Generously grease and lightly flour a 9" square casserole.
- In a medium sized bowl, combine 6 tablespoons of the butter, softened, with 1/2 cup of the sugar and the baking cocoa.
- Cut flour and graham cracker crumbs into the mixture until the dough just comes together.
- Press dough into the bottom of the casserole in an even layer.
- Bake for about 15 minutes, until slightly golden.
- Remove from heat and turn off oven.
- While crust is still hot, sprinkle the chocolate, peanuts and banana pieces evenly across the top.
- In a heavy-bottomed skillet, heat up the remaining 2 tablespoons of the butter with the remaining 2 tablespoons sugar, 1 tablespoon brown sugar and the heavy cream.
- Bring to a boil, stirring with a spatula, and let bubble for about 1 minute, until the fats and sugar are congealed and no longer separate.
- Turn off heat.
- Carefully lift pan and drizzle caramel evenly over the casserole.
- There should be enough to just cover any crust surface.
- Refrigerate casserole for 20 minutes or until completely cool and hardened.
- Cut into cubes and serve.

134. Citrus Bars Recipe

Serving: 24 | Prep: | Cook: 52mins | Ready in:

Ingredients

- Crust:
- 1 cup butter, softened
- 2 1/4 cups all-purpose flour, divided
- 1/2 cup powdered sugar
- ****
- 1 3/4 cups granulated sugar

- 1/3 cup fresh lemon juice
- 1/3 cup fresh orange juice
- 1 teaspoon finely grated orange rind
- 4 large eggs, beaten
- 1 teaspoon baking powder
- 1/4 teaspoon salt
- 1 tablespoon powdered sugar
- Garnish: orange and lemon rind strips

Direction

- For Crust:
- Beat butter at medium speed with an electric mixer until creamy; add 2 cups flour and 1/2 cup powdered sugar. Beat until mixture forms a smooth dough. Press mixture into a lightly greased 13- x 9-inch baking pan.
- Bake at 350° for 20 to 22 minutes or until lightly browned.
- ****
- For Topping:
- Whisk together remaining 1/4 cup flour, granulated sugar, and next 6 ingredients; pour over baked crust.
- Bake at 350° for 28 to 30 minutes or until set.
- Cool in pan on wire rack.
- Sprinkle evenly with 1 tablespoon powdered sugar, and cut into bars.
- Garnish with rind strips, if desired.

135. Cobblestone Bars Recipe

Serving: 24 | Prep: | Cook: 10mins | Ready in:

Ingredients

- 1/2 cup unsalted butter
- 1-6 ounce package chocolate chips
- 1-6 ounce package butterscotch chips
- 1 cup peanut butter
- 1 cup coconut
- 1 cup chopped nuts
- 1 package mini-marshmallows

Direction

- In pan, melt butter, chocolate chips, butterscotch chips, and peanut butter over low heat.
- Do not burn.
- Stir until creamy.
- Add remaining ingredients.
- Spread mixture in a 9 X 13" dish.
- When cool, cut into bars.
- Cut in the size bars that you prefer.

136. Coconut Angel Bars Recipe

Serving: 10 | Prep: | Cook: | Ready in:

Ingredients

- 1 prepared angel food cake, sliced into 2-3 inch cubes or "fingers"
- 2 containers of vanilla or chocolate frosting
- 1 bag of coconut flakes

Direction

- Remove the frosting from the containers and stir well.
- Roll the cake pieces into the frosting, using a flat knife to coat well.
- Roll the cake into the coconut!
- Yep, it's just that easy!
- If you're serving a large group, you can always buy more than one cake or even use pound cakes or a plain commercial sheet cake.
- You can roll the cake into sprinkles of any color or sugared shapes and sugar glitter. The kids will love this!

137. Coconut Bars Recipe

Serving: 16 | Prep: | Cook: 30mins | Ready in:

Ingredients

- 1 cup + 2 TBLS unsifted all-purpose flour
- 1/2 tsp baking soda
- 1/4 tsp salt
- 1/2 cup (1 stick) unsalted butter, softened
- 2/3 cup packed light-brown sugar
- 1 large egg
- 2 tsp vanilla extract
- 1 cup sweetened flaked coconut
- 3/4 cup semisweet mini chocolate chips
- 1/2 cup toasted almonds, chopped

Direction

- Preheat oven to 350 degrees F.
- Line 8-inch square baking pan with foil, extending foil beyond 2 sides of pan.
- Lightly coat with cooking spray.
- In small bowl mix flour baking soda and salt.
- In another small bowl with electric mixer, beat butter and brown sugar on medium speed 2 minutes.
- Beat in egg and vanilla.
- On low speed, beat in flour mixture just until blended.
- Stir in all but 3 TBS of the coconut; stir in mini chips and almonds.
- Spread in prepared pan, sprinkle with remaining coconut.
- Bake 30-32 minutes, until wooden pick inserted in center comes out with moist crumbs attached
- Let cool completely in pan or rack.
- Lift by foil ends, transfer to cutting board.
- Cut into 16 squares.

138. Coconut Blueberry Cheesecake Bars Recipe

Serving: 32 | Prep: | Cook: 30mins | Ready in:

Ingredients

- 1/2 cup butter
- 3/4 cup finely crushed graham crackers
- 1/2 cup flour
- 1/2 cup flaked coconut
- 1/2 cup ground pecans
- 1/4 cup sugar
- 1 1/2 8 oz pkg cream cheese, softened (it works with fat free or regular!)
- 2/3 cup sugar
- 4 eggs
- 1 tbsp milk
- 1 tsp vanilla
- 2 cups blueberries

Direction

- Preheat oven to 350 degrees and grease a 9 X 13 in baking pan
- In saucepan heat butter on medium heat until color of light brown sugar, remove from heat and set aside
- In bowl, stir together graham crackers, flour, coconut, pecans, and 1/4 cup sugar
- Stir in butter until combined
- Evenly press mixture along bottom of baking dish
- Bake 8-10 minutes or until lightly browned
- In large mixing bowl, beat cream cheese and 2/3 cup sugar on medium until combined
- Add eggs, milk, and vanilla and beat until combined.
- Pour mixture over hot crust and then sprinkle on blueberries
- Bake 20 minutes or until center looks set
- Cool in pan on rack, then cover and refrigerate 3 hours before cutting

139. Coconut Brownies

Serving: 0 | Prep: | Cook: | Ready in:

Ingredients

- 1 package fudge brownie mix (13x9-inch pan size)
- 1 cup sour cream
- 1 cup coconut-pecan frosting

- 2 large eggs
- 1/4 cup water
- 1 cup semisweet chocolate chips

Direction

- Preheat oven to 350°. In a large bowl, combine brownie mix, sour cream, frosting, eggs and water just until moistened.
- Pour into a 13x9-in. baking dish coated with cooking spray. Bake 30-35 minutes or until center is set (do not overbake). Sprinkle with chocolate chips; let stand 5 minutes. Spread chips over brownies.
- Nutrition Facts
- 1 each: 203 calories, 9g fat (4g saturated fat), 25mg cholesterol, 117mg sodium, 29g carbohydrate (21g sugars, 1g fiber), 3g protein.

140. Coconut Candy Bar Cake Recipe

Serving: 36 | Prep: | Cook: 115mins | Ready in:

Ingredients

- 14 squares BAKER'S Semi-Sweet baking chocolate, divided
- 1/2 cup (1 stick) butter or margarine
- 1 cup sugar
- 2 eggs
- 1-1/2 tsp. vanilla
- 1-2/3 cups flour, divided
- 3/4 tsp. baking soda
- 1/8 tsp. salt
- 1 cup water
- 1 pkg. (14 oz.) BAKER'S angel flake coconut (5-1/3 cups)
- 1 can (14 oz.) sweetened condensed milk
- 3/4 cup whipping cream
- 2 Tbsp. butter or margarine

Direction

- PREHEAT oven to 350°F. Place 4 of the chocolate squares and 1/2 cup butter in large microwaveable bowl. Microwave on HIGH 1 to 1-1/2 min. or until butter is melted. Stir until chocolate is completely melted. Blend in sugar. Add eggs, 1 at a time, beating on low speed after each addition until well blended. Add vanilla; mix well. Add 1/3 cup of the flour, the baking soda and salt; beat well. Add remaining 1-1/3 cups flour alternately with the water, mixing until well blended. Pour into greased and floured 13x9-inch baking pan.
- BAKE 30 min. or until toothpick inserted in center comes out clean. Cool completely in pan on wire rack.
- MIX coconut and sweetened condensed milk until well blended; spread over cake. Microwave whipping cream and 2 Tbsp. butter in large microwaveable bowl on HIGH 2 min.; stir. Microwave an additional 30 sec. or until mixture comes to boil. Add remaining 10 chocolate squares; stir until chocolate is completely melted. Cool until mixture is of desired spreading consistency, stirring frequently. Spread over cake. Let stand until chocolate layer is firm.

141. Coconut Dream Squares Recipe

Serving: 36 | Prep: | Cook: 25mins | Ready in:

Ingredients

- 1-1/4 cup sifted cake flour
- 1-1/4 cup firmly packed brown sugar
- 1/3 cup soft butter
- 2 eggs
- 1/2 teaspoon baking powder
- 1 teaspoon vanilla
- 1 cup chopped walnuts
- 1-1/3 cup flaked coconut

Direction

- Combine 1 cup of the flour and 1/4 cup of the sugar.
- Add butter and blend well then press firmly in ungreased square pan.
- Bake 15 minutes at 350.
- Meanwhile beat eggs until light.
- Add 1 cup sugar gradually beating constantly until fluffy.
- Sift 1/4 cup flour and baking powder then fold into egg mixture.
- Add vanilla, nuts and coconut then mix well.
- Spread over baked mixture in pan and bake 25 minutes.
- Cool and cut into squares.

142. Coconut Blueberry Cheesecake Bars Recipe

Serving: 32 | Prep: | Cook: 18mins | Ready in:

Ingredients

- Chill: 3 hours
- 1/2 cup butter
- 3/4 cup finely crushed graham crackers
- 1/2 cup all-purpose flour
- 1/2 cup flaked coconut
- 1/2 cup ground pecans
- 1/4 cup sugar
- 1-1/2 8-oz. pkg. cream cheese, softened
- 2/3 cup sugar
- 4 eggs
- 1 Tbsp. brandy or milk
- 1 tsp. vanilla
- 2 cup blueberries

Direction

- Preheat oven to 350 degrees F. Lightly grease a 13x9x2-inch baking pan; set aside.
- For crust, in a small saucepan heat butter over medium heat until the color of light brown sugar. Remove from heat; set aside.
- In medium bowl stir together graham crackers, flour, coconut, pecans, and 1/4 cup sugar. Stir in butter until combined. Evenly press on bottom of prepared pan. Bake 8 to 10 minutes or until lightly browned.
- Meanwhile, in large mixing bowl beat cream cheese and 2/3 cup sugar on medium until combined. Add eggs, brandy, and vanilla. Beat until combined. Pour over hot crust. Sprinkle with blueberries.
- Bake 18 to 20 minutes or until center appears set. Cool in pan on rack. Cover and refrigerate. Cut into bars. Store, covered, in refrigerator.

143. Coffee Crisp Bars Recipe

Serving: 12 | Prep: | Cook: 25mins | Ready in:

Ingredients

- 1/4 cup "light" margarine (I use Becel)
- 2/3 cup brown sugar
- 1/2 cup non-fat milk (I used potato milk, but soy or rice would work too)
- 1 cup flour
- 1/4 cup unsweetened cocoa powder
- 2 tsp instant espresso powder
- 1 teaspoon baking powder
- 7 "snack size" coffee Crisp bars (16g each), chopped

Direction

- Lightly coat the bottom only of a 9' pan with non-stick cooking spray.
- Melt margarine in a large bowl.
- Beat in sugar and milk.
- Sift in flour, cocoa powder, espresso powder and baking powder, mixing until just combined.
- Fold in candy pieces.
- Bake 20-25 minutes.
- Cool completely on a wire rack before cutting.

144. Coffeebreak Chocolate Coconut Cookie Bars Recipe

Serving: 24 | Prep: | Cook: 20mins | Ready in:

Ingredients

- 6 HERSHEY'S milk chocolate bars(1.55 oz. each)
- 1 cup (2 sticks) butter or margarine, softened
- 1 cup packed light brown sugar
- 1/2 cup granulated sugar
- 1 egg
- 1 tablespoon milk
- 1-1/2 teaspoons vanilla extract
- 2-1/4 cups all-purpose flour
- 1 teaspoon baking soda
- 1/4 teaspoon salt
- 1 cup MOUNDS sweetened coconut Flakes
- 1 cup walnut pieces
- vanilla DRIZZLE(recipe follows)

Direction

- 1. Heat oven to 375°F. Unwrap and coarsely chop chocolate bars; set aside.
- 2. Beat butter, brown sugar and granulated sugar in large bowl until well blended. Add egg, milk and vanilla; beat well. Stir together flour, baking soda and salt; gradually beat into butter mixture. With wooden spoon work chocolate bar pieces, coconut and walnuts into mixture. (Dough will be stiff.) Press mixture in ungreased 13x9x2-inch baking pan.
- 3. Bake 20 to 22 minutes or until edges are golden brown. (Do not overbake.) Cool completely in pan on wire rack. Drizzle VANILLA DRIZZLE over surface; allow to set. Cut into bars. About 24 bars.
- VANILLA DRIZZLE: Combine 1/2 cup powdered sugar and 2 teaspoons milk in small bowl. Add additional milk, 1/2 teaspoon at a time, until of desired consistency.

145. Congo Bars Recipe

Serving: 32 | Prep: | Cook: 25mins | Ready in:

Ingredients

- 1 stick butter, plus 2 T for greasing pan
- 2 1/4 c all purupose flour, plus extra for flouring pan
- 2 t baking powder
- 1/8 t salt
- 1 16 oz box light brown sugar
- 3 large eggs
- 12 oz best-quality semi-sweet or dark chocolate chips

Direction

- Preheat oven to 350, with a rack in center.
- Butter a 9x13 baking pan generously, ten dust with flour.
- Shake out any excess flour.
- Sift together flour, baking powder and salt, set aside.
- Melt butter in a large, heavy saucepan over medium heat.
- Remove from heat and add sugar, stirring until dissolved and mixture is smooth.
- Let mixture cool 3 to 4 minutes, the stir in eggs, 1 at a time.
- Stir in dry ingredients and finally chocolate chips.
- The chips may start to melt slightly.
- Scrape batter into prepared and smooth the top.
- Bake until a tester comes out clean, 20-30 minutes.
- Cool to room temperature.
- Cut into 32 squares.
- Store in airtight container at room temp.

146. Cran Kin Bars Recipe

Serving: 18 | Prep: | Cook: 25mins | Ready in:

Ingredients

- 2/3 cup packed light brown sugar
- 4 tbsp reduced-calorie margarine
- 1 cup canned pumpkin
- 1/2 cup buttermilk
- 1 1/4 cup spelt flour
- 1 1/2 cup uncooked rolled oats
- 1 tbsp cornstarch
- 1 tbsp pumpkin pie spice
- 1/2 tsp baking soda
- 1/2 tsp salt
- 1/3 cup dried cranberries
- 1/3 cup fresh or frozen chopped cranberries

Direction

- Heat oven to 350°F and lightly grease a 9x13-inch pan with cooking spray.
- Cream sugar and margarine. Then beat in pumpkin and buttermilk.
- In medium bowl, combine flour, oats, cornstarch, pumpkin pie spice, baking soda and salt.
- Stir into pumpkin mixture just until moistened.
- Fold in both types of cranberries.
- Bake 20-25 minutes.

147. Cranberry Cake Squares Recipe

Serving: 32 | Prep: | Cook: 35mins | Ready in:

Ingredients

- Base:
- 2 cups all-purpose flour
- 1/2 cup granulated sugar
- 1 cup butter, at room temperature
- ==============================
- Filling:
- Two 12 oz packages cranberries
- 2 cups brown sugar
- 4 eggs
- 2 tsp pure vanilla extract
- 1 tsp baking powder
- 2/3 cup all-purpose flour
- 1/4 tsp salt
- ==============================
- Garnish:
- icing sugar

Direction

- Preheat oven to 350°F
- In a large bowl, sift together flour and sugar.
- Cut in butter until crumbly.
- Pat into a 13 x 9-inch baking dish.
- Bake for 15 to 20 minutes, or until golden brown.
- Cool.
- In a pot, combine cranberries with 1/4 cup brown sugar.
- Cook over low heat until berries pop and soften.
- Let cool.
- In a bowl, beat eggs together lightly.
- Add remaining sugar gradually, beating until thickened.
- Stir in vanilla.
- In a separate bowl, sift together baking powder, flour and salt.
- Add the dry ingredients to egg mixture until blended.
- Fold in cranberries.
- Spread over base and bake for 30 to 35 minutes, or until set.
- When cool, dust with sifted icing sugar and cut into squares.
- Makes about 32 squares.

148. Cranberry Pear Bars Recipe

Serving: 32 | Prep: | Cook: 25mins | Ready in:

Ingredients

- 2 cups all-purpose flour
- 1/2 cup packed brown sugar
- 3/4 cup butter, cut into pieces
- 1 cup regular rolled oats
- 2/3 cup pear nectar or apple juice
- 2/3 cup packed brown sugar
- 2 cups fresh cranberries
- 1/8 tsp ground nutmeg

Direction

- Preheat oven to 350 F. For crust, combine flour and 1/2 cup brown sugar in a food processor. Cover and process with one or two on-off turns to mix. Add butter; pulse several times until fine crumbs form. Add oats; pulse once to mix. (Or combine flour and brown sugar in a medium bowl. Cut in butter with a pastry blender until mixture resembles fine crumbs. Stir in oats.) Reserve 1 cup crumb mixture. Press remaining crumb mixture on bottom of ungreased 13x9x2-inch baking pan. Bake in preheated oven for 15 minutes or until crust is lightly brown.
- Meanwhile, for filling, combine pear nectar and 2/3 cup brown sugar in a medium saucepan. Bring to boiling, stirring to dissolve sugar. Add cranberries, return to boiling; reduce heat. Simmer, uncovered, for 10 minutes or until filling is slightly thickened, stirring occasionally. Remove from heat; stir in nutmeg.
- Spread filling evenly over baked crust. Sprinkle with reserved crumb mixture. Bake in preheated oven for about 25 minutes or until top is lightly browned. Cool completely in pan on wire rack. Cut into bars. Makes 32.
- To store: Place bars in layers separated by pieces of waxed paper in an airtight container; cover. Store at room temperature for up to 3 days or freeze for up to 1 month.

149. Cranberry Squares Recipe

Serving: 24 | Prep: | Cook: 60mins | Ready in:

Ingredients

- 1 1/2 c. sugar
- 2 large eggs
- 3/4 c. (1 1/2 sticks) unsalted butter, melted, cooled slightly
- 1 tsp. almond extract
- 1 1/2 c. AP flour
- 2 c. fresh or frozen cranberries (about 8 oz.)
- 1/2 c. chopped pecans or almonds (about 2 1/4 oz.) (optional)
- coarse sugar to sprinkle on top before baking

Direction

- Preheat oven to 350 degrees F.
- Butter a 9-inch square baking pan.
- Using an electric mixer, beat sugar and eggs in large bowl until slightly thickened, about 2 minutes.
- Bean in melted butter and almond extract.
- Add flour and stir until well blended.
- Stir in cranberries and pecans or almonds.
- Pour batter into prepared pan.
- Bake until tester inserted into centre comes out clean, about 1 hour.
- Transfer to rack and cool completely.
- Cut into squares and serve.
- Enjoy! :)

150. Cream Cheese Pear Bars Recipe

Serving: 24 | Prep: | Cook: 60mins | Ready in:

Ingredients

- cookiE CRUST:
- 1 pkg butter or sugar cookies, finely crushed
- 10 T butter, melted
- FILLING:
- 3 fresh pears, cored and sliced
- 1/4 cup brown sugar
- 2T cornstarch
- 1 tsp ground nutmeg

- juice from 1/2 lemon
- ----------------------------
- 12oz cream cheese, softened
- 1 egg
- 3T honey
- 2tsp vanilla(or 1 each vanilla and almond)
- TOPPING:
- 1 1/2 sticks butter, softened
- 1 1/2 cups flour
- 1 cup packed brown sugar
- 1 cup shredded coconut or finely chopped nuts or oats

Direction

- Combine crust ingredients in glass 9X13 dish adding butter, slowly to get right amount to form mixture able to press into bottom to form crust.
- Bake at 350 for about 15 minutes until crumbs lose their shiny appearance and just beginning to brown on edge.
- In medium bowl, combine pears, lemon juice, cornstarch, 1/4 cup brown sugar and nutmeg and toss to combine.
- Whip cream cheese and add honey. Mix until combined.
- Add egg and combine, again.
- Add vanilla and mix until thoroughly combined.
- Combine all topping ingredients and cut together until crumbly mix is formed.
- Pour cream cheese mixture over crust, then top with sliced pears (remove from bowl with slotted spoon so as not to get too much liquid with them.
- Crumble topping completely over pears.
- Bake about 45 minutes until brown and bubbly.
- Cool some before cutting into squares. Serve with ice cream or fresh whipped cream seasoned with a bit of nutmeg, if desired.
- **Apples can be substituted in this recipe and cinnamon replacing the nutmeg, but I do prefer the pears.

151. Cream Cheese Squares Recipe

Serving: 16 | Prep: | Cook: 35mins | Ready in:

Ingredients

- Crust:
- 1/3 cup brown sugar
- 1 cup flour
- 1/2 cup chopped walnuts
- 1/2 cup softened butter
- Filling:
- 8 oz softened cream cheese
- 1/4 cup sugar
- 1 egg
- 2 tbsp milk
- 1 tbsp lemon extract
- 1 tsp vanilla
- Topping:
- Topping of your choice if any

Direction

- Grease an 8" square pan.
- Mix all ingredients for crust in bowl.
- Layer bottom of pan with 1/3 mixture of crumb mixture.
- Bake 12-15 minutes at 350.
- Mix all Filling ingredients in bowl till blended.
- In baked crust pan.
- Top with filling mixture.
- Sprinkle with remaining crumbs.
- Bake 25 minutes.
- Cool.
- Cut into squares.
- Top with topping if you choose.

152. Creamy Baked Apple Squares Recipe

Serving: 12 | Prep: | Cook: 35mins | Ready in:

Ingredients

- Filling:
- 1 cup sour cream
- 1 egg
- 2 tablespoons brown or white sugar
- Crust and crumb topping:
- 1 box super-moist yellow cake mix (the kind with pudding added to the mix)
- ½ cup butter, softened
- ¼ cup packed brown sugar
- ½ teaspoon cinnamon
- 2 apples, peeled, cored and thinly sliced

Direction

- Mix together filling ingredients and set aside.
- For crust and crumb topping, combine cake mix and butter until crumbly (I use a fork); reserve 2/3 cup for topping, adding the brown sugar and cinnamon to it.
- Press remaining crumb mixture into bottom on ungreased 9x13 baking dish.
- Arrange apple slices over crust.
- Spread sour cream mixture over apples (it's easiest to just place dollops of the mixture over the apples, then spread them together with the back of a spoon).
- Sprinkle reserved crumb mixture over top of sour cream mixture.
- Bake at 350 until top is browned nicely, about 35 minutes.
- Serve warm, with whipped cream or ice cream, if desired.
- Refrigerate leftovers (I never do, but leftovers never last more than a day - if you're keeping it longer than that, then it would probably be best to keep chilled).
- NOTE: I have not tried this, but after I made this at my daughter's recently, we were talking about how good a cream cheese filling would be in place of the sour cream layer. If anyone tries this, please let me know - I think it would be very good!

153. Creamy Dreamy Candy Bar Dessert Recipe

Serving: 18 | Prep: | Cook: 3mins | Ready in:

Ingredients

- CRUST
- 3 cups crushed vanilla wafers
- 2/3 cup butter, melted
- 1/4 cup sugar
- 1/2 tsp. cinnamon
- FILLING
- 1 milk chocolate candy bar (7 ounces), plain or with almonds, broken into pieces
- 1 package (10 ounces) large marshmallows
- 1 cup milk
- 2 cups whipping cream, whipped
- 1/2 sp. vanilla extract
- sliced almonds, toasted, optional

Direction

- In a bowl, combine wafer crumbs, butter, sugar and cinnamon.
- Mix well.
- Set aside 1/3 cup for topping.
- Press remaining crumb mixture into a greased 13 x 9 inch pan. Refrigerate until firm. In a saucepan, heat the candy bar, marshmallows and milk over medium low heat until chocolate and marshmallows are melted, stirring often.
- Remove from the heat and cool to room temperature.
- Fold in whipped cream and vanilla; pour over crust.
- Chill for 3 to 4 hours.
- Sprinkle with reserved crumb mixture and almonds if desired.

154. Creamy Lemon Oat Bars Recipe

Serving: 16 | Prep: | Cook: 30mins | Ready in:

Ingredients

- 1 can (14 oz.) sweetened condensed milk
- 3 teaspoons grated lemon zest
- 1/4 cup fresh lemon juice
- 1 1/4 cups flour
- 1 cup old fashioned oats
- 1/2 cup packed brown sugar
- 1/2 cup unsalted butter, softened
- 1/4 teaspoon baking soda
- 1/4 teaspoon salt

Direction

- Heat oven to 375F degrees.
- Coat 8x8 inch pan with non-stick cooking spray.
- Mix milk, lemon zest and lemon juice in medium bowl until thickened; set aside. Mix remaining ingredients in medium bowl until crumbly.
- Press half of the crumbly mixture in pan; bake about 10 minutes or until set.
- Spread lemon milk mixture over baked crust. Sprinkle remaining crumbly mixture over the lemon milk mixture, press down gently.
- Bake about 20 minutes or until edges are golden brown and center is set but soft. Cool completely. Cut 4 rows by 4 rows.

155. Crumb Topped Date Bars

Serving: 16 | Prep: | Cook: 17mins | Ready in:

Ingredients

- 1 package (8 ounces) chopped dates
- 1/2 cup sugar
- 1/2 cup water
- 1 tablespoon lemon juice
- 2 cups Basic Cookie Dough

Direction

- In a saucepan, bring the dates, sugar, water and lemon juice to a boil. Reduce heat; simmer, uncovered, for 5 minutes, stirring occasionally. Remove from the heat; cool.
- Press half of the cookie dough into a greased 9-in. square baking pan. Spread with date mixture. Crumble remaining dough over filling. Bake at 375° for 25-30 minutes or until top is golden brown. Cool on a wire rack. Cut into bars.
- Nutrition Facts
- 1 bar: 141 calories, 5g fat (3g saturated fat), 17mg cholesterol, 77mg sodium, 23g carbohydrate (15g sugars, 1g fiber), 2g protein.

156. Crunchy Peanut Brickle Bars Recipe

Serving: 1 | Prep: | Cook: 20mins | Ready in:

Ingredients

- 2 cups quick cooking oats
- 1 1/2 cups all purpose flour
- 1 cup chopped dry roasted peanuts
- 1 cup firmly packed brown sugar
- 1 teaspoon baking soda
- 1/2 teaspoon salt
- 1 cup butter or margarine, melted
- 1 (14 oz) can sweetened condensed milk(NOT evaporated!)
- 1/2 cup peanut butter
- 1 (6-oz) package almond brickle chips OR 6 (1 3/16 oz) milk chocolate bars

Direction

- Preheat oven to 375 degrees F.
- In a large bowl, combine oats, flour, peanuts, sugar, baking soda and salt; stir in butter until crumbly.

- Reserving 1 1/2 cups crumb mixture, press remainder on bottom of greased 13x9 inch baking pan
- Bake for 12 minutes.
- In small bowl, beat sweetened condensed milk with peanut butter until smooth; spread evenly over prepared crust to within 1/4 inch of edge.
- In medium bowl, combine reserved crumb mixture and brickle chips.
- Sprinkle evenly over peanut butter mixture; press down firmly
- Bake 20 minutes or until golden brown.
- Cool and cut into bars.
- Store loosely covered at room temperature.
- ***
- -All human wisdom is summed up in two words.... wait & hope-
- ***

157. DOUBLE DELICIOUS COOKIE BARS Recipe

Serving: 18 | Prep: | Cook: 30mins | Ready in:

Ingredients

- 1 1/2 C. graham cracker crumbs
- 1/2 C. (1 stick) butter or margarine
- 1 (14-oz.) can sweetened condensed milk
- 1 C. (6 oz) semi-sweet chocolate chips
- 1 C. (6 oz.) peanut butter-flavored chips

Direction

- Preheat oven to 350°F (325°F for glass dish).
- In small bowl, combine graham cracker crumbs and butter; mix well. Press crumb mixture firmly on bottom of 13X9-inch baking pan.
- Pour Sweetened Condensed Milk evenly over crumb mixture.
- Layer evenly with remaining ingredients; press down firmly with fork.
- Bake 25 to 30 minutes or until lightly browned.
- Cool.
- Cut into bars.
- Store leftovers covered at room temperature.

158. Dads Fave Sour Cream Raisin Bars Recipe

Serving: 20 | Prep: | Cook: 45mins | Ready in:

Ingredients

- 1 c brown sugar
- 1 c butter
- 1 3/4 c oatmeal
- 1 3/4 c flour
- 1 tsp soda
- 1 3/4 c raisins
- 1 1/2 c sugar
- 3 eggs
- 2 1/3 Tb cornstarch
- 1 1/2 c sour cream
- Dash salt
- 1/2 tsp cinnamon
- 1/2 tsp cloves
- 1 Tb butter
- 1 tsp vanilla

Direction

- Mix first 5 ingredients together.
- Pat 1/2 of mixture in a 9x13 pan.
- Boil raisins in 1 cup water.
- Add other ingredients except 1 Tb butter and vanilla and boil until thick.
- Add 1 Tb butter and vanilla.
- Pour over pan mixture.
- Top with remaining crumb mixture.
- Bake at 350 for 30 minutes.

159. Date Bars Recipe

Serving: 30 | Prep: | Cook: 25mins | Ready in:

Ingredients

- CRUST INGREDIENTS
- 1 3/4 cups   oatmeal
- 1 1/2 cups   flour
- 1/2 tsp   baking powder
- 1 tsp   baking soda
- 3/4 cup   butter, melted
- 1 cup   brown sugar
- 1/2 tsp   salt
- date FILLING
- 1 lb   chopped dates
- 3/4 cup   sugar
- 1 cup   water
- 1 Tbs   butter
- 1 tsp   vanilla
- 1 cup   chopped walnut

Direction

- Make the filling: Boil dates, sugar, and water until thick, about 5-10 minutes.
- Add 1 TBSP butter, the vanilla, and the walnuts.
- Set aside to cool a bit.
- Prepare the crust: Combine all dry ingredients with the melted butter.
- Firmly press half of the mixture into a lightly greased 13 x 9 pan.
- Cover with filling mixture and top with remaining half of crust mixture.
- Press lightly.
- Bake at 350 degrees for 25 minutes.
- NO LONGER THAN THAT!
- Cut into squares when cool.

160. Date Nut Bar Delight Recipe

Serving: 10 | Prep: | Cook: 30mins | Ready in:

Ingredients

- 1 3/4 cups old-fashioned oats
- 1 1/2 cups all-purpose flour
- 1 cup packed brown sugar
- 1 teaspoon baking soda
- 1/2 teaspoon salt
- 1 cup cold butter or margarine
- 2 1/2 cups chopped dates
- 3/4 cup sugar
- 3/4 cup water
- 1/2 cup chopped walnuts
- Optional, whipped cream

Direction

- In a large bowl, combine oats, flour, brown sugar, baking soda and salt.
- Cut in butter until mixture resembles coarse crumbs. Press half into a greased 13-in. x 9-in. x 2-in. baking pan. In a saucepan, combine dates, sugar and water. Cook for 10 mins or until thickened, stirring frequently. Stir in walnuts. Spread over crust sprinkle the rest of the oat mixer over the top. Bake at 350 degrees F for 30 mins. Cool on a wire rack. Cut into squares; optional, top with whipped topping.

161. Date Squares Recipe

Serving: 24 | Prep: | Cook: 20mins | Ready in:

Ingredients

- Base
- 1 1/2 cups cake flour
- 1 1/2 cups rolled oats
- 1 cup packed brown sugar
- 1/2 tsp baking soda
- 1/4 tsp salt
- 3/4 cups butter or margarine
- date Paste
- 1 pound dried dates
- 1/3 cup brown sugar (optional as dates are very sweet)

- 1/2 cup orange juice
- 1/2 cup water
- 1/2 tsp vanilla extract

Direction

- Pre-heat oven to 350 f.
- Place dates in a pot with sugar, orange juice and water over medium heat
- Cook and mash with a fork or potato masher until you get a paste
- Add vanilla and set aside to cool
- Mix all of the dry ingredients together and add butter or margarine
- With your hand combine everything until you get a crumbly mixture
- Split mixture in half and place in a 9x9 inch greased pan
- Press down slightly to create a crust
- Carefully place the date paste on top of the crust
- Loosely place the rest of the "crumbs" on top of the date paste but DO NOT press down on it to create a crust
- Place in the oven for 20 mins
- Let it cool before cutting
- Enjoy!

162. Delicious Raspberry Walnut Shortbread Bars Recipe

Serving: 24 | Prep: | Cook: 20mins | Ready in:

Ingredients

- 1 1/4 Cups all purpose flour
- 1/2 Cup sugar
- 1/2 Cup butter
- Topping:
- 3/4 Cup raspberry jam (Use the best you can find!)
- 1/3 Cup firmly packed brown sugar
- 2 eggs
- 1 Tsp vanilla
- 3 Tbs all purpose flour
- 1/2 tsp salt
- 1 Cup chopped walnuts

Direction

- In a medium bowl, combine 1 1/4 Cups flour and 1/2 Cup sugar. With a pastry blender, cut in 1/2 cup butter until crumbly.
- Press mixture in bottom of greased 9 inch square baking pan.
- Bake in preheated 350 degree oven for 18 to 20 minutes or until edges are lightly golden brown. (Watch the last few minutes)
- Spread Raspberry Jam over crust.
- In a small bowl combine brown sugar, eggs, and vanilla. Beat at medium speed until well mixed (about 2 minutes)
- Stir in 3 Tbsp. flour and salt until well mixed. Stir in walnuts. Pour over Jam, spread carefully to cover.
- Continue baking 20 to 24 minutes or until golden brown and filling is set. Cool completely. Cut into bars.
- These are fabulous.

163. Diabetic Chocolate Chip Pumpkin Bars Recipe

Serving: 36 | Prep: | Cook: 25mins | Ready in:

Ingredients

- 1 cup flour
- 1 cup whole wheat flour
- 3/4 cup sugar
- 1/2 cup finely chopped pecans or walnuts
- 2 teasp. baking powder
- 1 teasp. cinnamon
- 1/2 teasp. baking soda
- 1/2 teasp. salt
- 1 (15-ounce) can pumpkin
- 4 eggs slightly beaten or (1 cup frozen egg product, thawed)
- 1/2 cup canola oil

- 1/4 cup fat-free milk
- 1/2 cup miniature semi-sweet chocolate chips

Direction

- Preheat oven to 350' F.
- Lightly coat 15 x 10 x 1 inch baking pan with cooking spray.
- In large bowl combine flour, whole-wheat flour, sugar, pecans, baking powder, cinnamon, baking soda, and salt.
- In medium bowl combine pumpkin, eggs, oil and milk.
- Add pumpkin mixture and 1/3 cup of the chocolate chips to flour mixture.
- Stir until just combined.
- Spread evenly in baking pan.
- Sprinkle the remaining chocolate chips over the top.
- Bake about 25 minutes or until a toothpick comes out clean.
- Cool on a wire rack.
- Cut into bars.
- ....
- Per serving: 90 cal.
- 4 g total fat ...1 g sat. Fat.... 0 mg chol
- 77 mg sodium
- 12 g carb
- Exchanges.... 1 carb,
- 0.5 fat
- Carb choices...1

164. Disappearing Butterscotch Chocolate Bars Recipe

Serving: 12 | Prep: | Cook: 35mins | Ready in:

Ingredients

- 1 cup butterscotch chips
- 1 stick unsalted butter
- 1-1/2 cups flour
- 2/3 cup brown sugar, firmly packed
- 2 teaspoons baking powder
- 1/2 teaspoon salt
- 1 teaspoon vanilla
- 2 eggs, slightly beaten
- 2 cups miniature marshmallows
- 12 ounce package semi-sweet chocolate chips
- 1/2 cup chopped pecans

Direction

- In heavy pan on stove, melt over medium heat the butterscotch chips and butter.
- Stir constantly until melted.
- Cool to lukewarm.
- In large bowl, combine flour brown sugar, baking powder, salt.
- Add the melted butterscotch chip/butter mixture.
- Add the beaten eggs.
- Mix thoroughly.
- Fold marshmallows, chocolate chips, and nuts into all.
- Spread into a greased 9 X 13 baking dish or pan.
- Bake at 350 degrees for about 35 minutes.
- Don't overcook.
- Center will be jiggly, but firm when cool.
- Cut into bars.

165. Dotty Golden Squares Recipe

Serving: 8 | Prep: | Cook: 50mins | Ready in:

Ingredients

- 3 tbsp golden corn syrup
- 2 tbsp honey
- 1 tbsp sugar
- 1 tbsp salted butter, cold
- 3 oz millet puffs
- 2 tbsp miniature chocolate chips

Direction

- Line an 8" pan with parchment and heavily grease.
- Heat syrup, honey, and sugar in a large heavy-bottomed pan until bubbling.
- Boil for 2 minutes, then remove from heat, stir in the butter until melted and add the puffs.
- Mix well and press into the pan.
- Sprinkle chocolate chips immediately onto squares and place in a hot oven for 1 minute to melt (I heat the broiler, turn it off and then put the pan in).
- Cool 15 minutes, then remove from pan and cut into squares. Cool completely before indulging!

166. Double Chocolate Bars

Serving: 0 | Prep: | Cook: | Ready in:

Ingredients

- 1 package (15-1/2 ounces) Oreo cookies, crushed
- 3/4 cup butter, melted
- 1 can (14 ounces) sweetened condensed milk
- 1 package (10 ounces) miniature semisweet chocolate chips, divided

Direction

- Combine cookie crumbs and butter; pat onto the bottom of an ungreased 13-in. x 9-in. baking pan.
- In a microwave, heat milk and 1 cup chocolate chips; stir until smooth. Pour over crust. Sprinkle with remaining chips.
- Bake at 350° for 10-12 minutes or until chips begin to melt but do not lose their shape. Cool on a wire rack.
- Nutrition Facts
- 1 each: 132 calories, 8g fat (4g saturated fat), 10mg cholesterol, 83mg sodium, 16g carbohydrate (12g sugars, 1g fiber), 1g protein.

167. Double Chocolate Peanut Butter Bars Recipe

Serving: 35 | Prep: | Cook: 20mins | Ready in:

Ingredients

- 1 cup firmly packed brown sugar
- 1/2 cup LandO Lakes margarine, softened
- 1/2 cup chunky peanut butter
- 2 eggs
- 1 teaspoon vanilla
- 1 3/4 cups all-purpose flour
- 1/2 teaspoon baking powder
- 1/4 teaspoon baking soda
- 1 cup mini real semi-sweet chocolate chips
- 2 tablespoons sugar
- 35 milk chocolate candy kisses

Direction

- Heat oven to 350 degrees F.
- Line 13 x9-inch baking pan with aluminum foil, leaving a 1-inch overhang; set aside.
- Combine brown sugar, margarine and peanut butter in large bowl.
- Beat at medium speed, scraping bowl often, until creamy.
- Add eggs and vanilla; continue beating until well mixed.
- Reduce speed to low; add flour, baking powder and baking soda.
- Beat until well mixed.
- Stir in chocolate chips.
- Pat dough into prepared pan.
- Sprinkle with sugar.
- Bake for 20 to 22 minutes or until golden brown.
- Immediately press evenly spaced chocolate candies into warm bars.
- Cool completely.
- Remove bars from pan using edges of foil; cut into bars, cutting between candies.
- 35 bars

168. Double Chocolate Squares Recipe

Serving: 68 | Prep: | Cook: 5mins | Ready in:

Ingredients

- 3 tablespoons butter or margarine, melted
- 2 tablespoons sugar
- 1 cup graham cracker crumbs
- 1/2 cup milk
- 1 (6.0 oz.) HERSHEY'S milk chocolate Bar, broken into pieces
- 1/2 cup HERSHEY'S Mini chips Semi-sweet chocolate
- 1 cup (1/2 pt.) cold whipping cream
- sweetened whipped cream
- Sliced sweetened strawberries
- sweetened whipped cream

Direction

- Stir together butter and sugar in small bowl. Add graham cracker crumbs; mix well. Spread mixture firmly onto bottom of 8-inch square pan. Refrigerate 1 to 2 hours or until firm.
- Meanwhile, heat milk to boiling in small saucepan; remove from heat. Immediately add chocolate bar pieces and small chocolate chips; stir until chocolate melts and mixture is smooth. Pour into medium bowl; cool to room temperature.
- Beat whipping cream in small bowl on high speed of mixer until stiff; fold gently into chocolate mixture. Pour onto prepared crust; freeze several hours or until firm. Cut into squares. Just before serving, garnish with whipped cream and strawberries.

169. Double Trouble Chocolate Nut Bars Recipe

Serving: 12 | Prep: | Cook: 35mins | Ready in:

Ingredients

- 1 1/2 C. unsifted flour
- 3/4 C. confectioners sugar
- 1/3 plus 1/4 C. unsweetened cocoa
- 1/4 t. salt
- 3/4 C. margarine or butter melted
- 2 eggs
- 1 (14 oz) can Eagle Brand sweetened condensed milk
- 2 t. vanilla extract
- 1/2 t. baking powder
- 1 (6 oz) pkg. semi sweet chocolate chips
- 1 C. chopped walnuts

Direction

- Preheat oven to 350.
- In medium bowl, combine 1-1/4 C. flour, sugar, 1/3 C. cocoa and salt. Stir in margarine and 1 egg; mix well.
- Spread onto bottom of greased 9x13 baking pan.
- In mixer bowl, combine Eagle Brand, 1/4 C. flour, 1/4 C. cocoa, 1 egg, vanilla and baking powder; mix well. Spoon evenly over crust. Top with chips and walnuts.
- Bake 30-35 minutes.
- Cool. Cut into bars. Store

170. Double Chocolate And Caramel Bars Recipe

Serving: 72 | Prep: | Cook: 35mins | Ready in:

Ingredients

- Bars:
- 3 cups Gold Medal® all-purpose flour
- 3/4 cup packed brown sugar
- 2/3 cup baking cocoa
- 1 egg, beaten
- 1 1/2 cups firm butter or margarine
- 1 1/2 cups chopped walnuts

- 1 bag (12 oz) semisweet chocolate chips (2 cups)
- 48 caramels
- 2 cans (14 oz each) sweetened condensed milk
- chocolate Glaze:
- 1 bag (6 oz) semisweet chocolate chips (1 cup)
- 1 teaspoon shortening or vegetable oil

Direction

- Heat oven to 350°F. Line 15x10x1-inch pan with foil, leaving about 2 inches of foil hanging over sides of pan.
- In large bowl, stir together flour, brown sugar, cocoa and egg. Cut in 1 1/4 cups of the butter, using pastry blender (or pulling 2 table knives through ingredients in opposite directions), until crumbly. Stir in walnuts; reserve 3 cups of the crumb mixture. Press remaining mixture firmly in bottom of pan; sprinkle with 2 cups chocolate chips. Bake 15 minutes.
- Meanwhile, in heavy 2-quart saucepan, melt caramels with sweetened condensed milk and remaining 1/4 cup butter over low heat, stirring constantly. Pour over crust. Top with reserved crumb mixture. Bake about 20 minutes longer or until bubbly. Cool completely, about 2 hours.
- In small microwavable bowl, microwave 1 cup chocolate chips and the shortening uncovered on High 1 to 3 minutes, stirring halfway through heating time, until melted and thin enough to drizzle. Drizzle over bars. For bars, cut into 12 rows by 6 rows to get a yield of 72 bars. You can cut them anyway you like or any size.

171. Dreamy Coconut Squares Recipe

Serving: 0 | Prep: | Cook: 2hours | Ready in:

Ingredients

- 1/2 cup butter, at room temperature
- 2 tbsp powdered sugar
- 1 cup cake flour
- 2 eggs, at room temperature
- 1 1/4 cups brown sugar, packed
- 2 tbsp flour
- 1/4 tsp salt
- 1 1/2 tsp baking powder
- 1 cup chopped walnuts
- 1 cup shredded coconut

Direction

- Preheat the oven to 350 F.
- Butter and flour an 8 inch square baking pan.
- Cream the butter and the powdered sugar.
- Stir in the flour.
- Spread the mixture in the prepared pan.
- Bake for 30 minutes.
- Beat the eggs and the brown sugar until thick.
- Sift together the flour, salt, and baking powder.
- Stir into the egg mixture.
- Stir in the nuts and coconut.
- Spread over the crust.
- Bake for 30 minutes longer.
- Cool and cut into squares

172. Dried Fruit Oat Bars Recipe

Serving: 24 | Prep: | Cook: 25mins | Ready in:

Ingredients

- 1/2 cup chopped Medjool dates
- 1/3 cup chopped dried apricots
- 1/4 cup dried cranberries
- 1 1/2 cups water
- 1 cup maple syrup, divided
- 3/4 cup water
- 1 1/2 cups oatmeal
- 1 cup quinoa flakes (optional, swap with more oatmeal if necessary)
- 1 1/2 cups whole wheat flour

- 1/2 tsp salt
- 1/2 tsp baking soda

Direction

- Preheat oven to 350F.
- Combine dried fruits, water and 1/4 cup of maple syrup in a pot.
- Heat, stirring, until thickened - 5-7 minutes. Cool slightly.
- Combine remaining syrup and water, stir into remaining ingredients.
- Press half of the oat mixture into the bottom of a lightly greased 13x9" pan with lightly moistened hands.
- Spread the fruit filling overtop the crust.
- Crumble the remaining crust ingredients overtop the fruit.
- Bake 25 minutes. Cut while still warm.

173. Dulce De Leche Apple Bars With Browned Butter Icing Recipe

Serving: 16 | Prep: | Cook: 30mins | Ready in:

Ingredients

- BARS:
- 1½ cups all-purpose flour
- ¾ tsp baking powder
- ¾ tsp baking soda
- ¾ tsp ground cinnamon
- ½ tsp salt
- ½ cup butter (1 stick), softened
- 1 cup packed light brown sugar
- 2 large eggs
- 1 tsp vanilla extract
- 1½ cups chopped, peeled apples
- ½ cup dulce de leche
- ICING:
- 2 Tbs butter
- 1½ cups powdered sugar
- ¼ tsp vanilla extract
- 1½ to 2 Tbs half and half cream

Direction

- Preheat oven to 350°F. Grease and flour a 9x9-inch square baking pan.
- Combine flour, baking powder, baking soda, cinnamon and salt. Set aside.
- In a large mixing bowl, beat butter, sugar, eggs and vanilla until fluffy.
- Stir flour mixture into sugar mixture, just until combined. Carefully stir in apples.
- Spoon 2/3 of the batter into the prepared pan. Drop Dulce de Leche by heaping Tablespoons over batter. Drag a butter knife through Dulce de Leche to swirl through the batter. Drop remaining batter over Dulce de Leche.
- Bake 25 to 30 minutes, or until browned and firm to touch. Let cool completely.
- Prepare icing: In a small saucepan, heat butter over medium until it begins to brown. Remove from heat. Add to a bowl with powdered sugar, vanilla and half/half. Beat on high speed with electric mixer until creamy. Drizzle and spread over bars, and chill until icing is set.
- For cleanest cuts, chill completely and slice into the bars with a sharp, thin knife. Keep refrigerated until ready to serve.
- Cooking Tips
- *You can make your own Dulce de Leche or purchase it already made. We can usually find it in a can in the Latin section of our local grocery store. The stuff in the can is pretty darn good. You just might want to heat it up for 20 seconds in the microwave before scooping it onto the bars.

174. Dulce De Leche Frosted Squares Recipe

Serving: 10 | Prep: | Cook: 40mins | Ready in:

Ingredients

- FOR THE cookies
- 300 grs. butter
- 3 cups flour
- 4 egg yolks
- 1/2 cup sugar
- 1 tbsp. vanilla
- FILLING
- 400 grs. dulce de leche or fruit preserves
- FOR frosting
- 1/2 cup powder sugar

Direction

- COOKIE DOUGH
- Preheat the oven to 350 degrees.
- Lightly grease a baking sheet.
- Cream butter, add sugar, then the egg yolks and vanilla.
- Add flour.
- Process until a dough forms.
- SHAPE
- Cut dough into squares half just a square and the other half cut a little square inside, you can use whatever form you like.
- Bake for approx. 25 to 35 min.
- Let them stand for 1/2 hour.
- FILLING AND DECORATION
- With a pipe draw a square inside the cookie and fill it.
- Frost with powder sugar the cookies that have a little square and put them over the bases that have the Dulce de Leche.
- You're done! Enjoy!!!

175. EASY EASY LEMON CHEESE SQUARES Recipe

Serving: 24 | Prep: | Cook: 38mins | Ready in:

Ingredients

- 1 box (18 1/2 oz.) lemon cake mix
- 1/2 c. butter, melted
- 3 eggs
- 1 can (16 oz.) lemon cream frosting
- 1 pkg. (8 oz.) cream cheese

Direction

- Mix together cake mix, melted butter and one egg. Put in a greased 9 x 13 inch pan.
- Blend cream cheese, 2 eggs, and frosting. Pour over cake dough. Bake in 350 degree oven for 35 to 40 minutes until brown. Remove from oven cool slightly and cut into
- squares. (dust with sifted confectionary sugar, if desired).

176. Easy Blueberry Lemon Bars Recipe

Serving: 24 | Prep: | Cook: 45mins | Ready in:

Ingredients

- 2 c. fresh or frozen blueberries
- 1 T. sugar
- 2 T. fresh lemon juice
- zest of 1 lemon, divided
- 1 box yellow cake mix
- 4 eggs
- 1 stick butter, softened
- 2 3/4 c. powdered sugar
- 8 oz. cream cheese

Direction

- Preheat oven to 325.
- Combine blueberries with sugar, lemon juice and half of the lemon zest. Set aside.
- Mix cake mix with 1 egg, butter, and the rest of the lemon zest. Pat into a buttered and floured 13X9 baking pan.
- Beat powdered sugar, cream cheese, and remaining 3 eggs until smooth. Gently stir in blueberry mixture; pour over cake. Bake 45-55 minutes, or until browned. Let cool completely; chill and cut into squares. Dust with powdered sugar.

177. Easy Cherry Dream Bars Recipe

Serving: 1 | Prep: | Cook: 30mins | Ready in:

Ingredients

- 1 (18.25 ounce) box white or yellow cake mix
- 1/2 cup butter or margarine, divided
- 1 1/4 cups oatmeal, divided
- 1 egg
- 1 can cherry pie filling
- 1/2 cup nuts, chopped
- 1/4 cup brown sugar

Direction

- Mix cake mix, 6 tablespoons butter and 1 cup oatmeal. Mix until crumbly. Reserve 1 cup crumbs for topping.
- To remaining crumbs, add egg, mixing until well blended. Press into a 13 x 9-inch baking pan. Pour pie filling over crust, spreading to cover.
- To the reserved crumbs add 1/4 cup oatmeal, 2 tablespoons margarine, nuts and brown sugar. Beat until thoroughly mixed. Sprinkle over cherry mixture.
- Bake at 350 degrees F for 30 to 40 minutes.

178. Espresso Chocolate Squares Recipe

Serving: 24 | Prep: | Cook: 45mins | Ready in:

Ingredients

- Crust
- 1 1/4 cup all purpose flour
- 3/4 cup confectioner's sugar
- 1/4 cup unsweetened cocoa powder
- 3/4 cup (1 1/2 sticks) butter, chilled and cut into pieces
- 1/2 cup miniature semi-sweet chocolate chips
- Filling:
- 1/4 cup heavy cream
- 1 tbsp instant espress coffee powder
- 2 8 oz bricks of cream cheese, softened
- 1/4 cup (1/2 stick) butter, softened
- 3/4 cup sugar
- 1 tbsp all purpose flour
- 1/4 tsp ground allspice
- 2 eggs
- Glaze:
- 6 tbsp miniature chocolate chips
- 1 tbsp heavy cream
- 1/2 tbsp butter
- 1/4 tsp instant espresso coffee powder

Direction

- Crust:
- Preheat oven to 350 degrees. Line a 9X13" baking pan with foil, butter the bottom of foil.
- Whisk together 1 1/4 cup flour, confectioner's sugar and cocoa together in a medium bowl, add 1/2 cup butter. Using a pastry blender of 2 knives, cut in butter until butter is the size of small peas.
- Stir in 1/2 cup chocolate chips; press into bottom of pan.
- Bake 20 minutes or until toothpick comes out clean; cool slightly.
- Filling:
- Stir 1/4 cup cream and 1 tbsp. instant espresso together until coffee is dissolved. Using an electric mixer, beat cream cheese and 1/4 cup butter together. Add sugar, 1 tbsp. flour and allspice; beat until blended. Slowly beat in cream and coffee mixture. Add eggs, one at a time beating until smooth. Pour batter over crust.
- Bake 20 to 25 minutes or until edges are slightly puffed and center is set; set pan on a cooling rack.
- Glaze;
- Melt 6 tbsp. chocolate chips with 1/4 tsp. instant espresso in a medium saucepan over

low heat, stirring constantly. Drizzle over bars and refrigerate until set.
- Cover and store bars in the refrigerator for up to 1 week.

179. Frozen Chocolate Bar Cookie Cake Recipe

Serving: 9 | Prep: | Cook: | Ready in:

Ingredients

- 1 package of your favorite chocolate chip cookies
- 1 Litre tub of frozen whipped topping
- Some milk (for dunking the cookies…about a cup and a half)
- 3 chocolate bars like Butterfinger, Skor or Crispy Crunch (I use Crispy Crunch) — put in the blender to make chunky crumbs

Direction

- First, make sure you leave the frozen topping in the fridge for the day so that it's soft and spreadable…or leave on the counter for a few hours. You also need a 9×9 inch square dish that is okay to put in the freezer.
- Take a cookie and dunk completely in some milk, but don't make it soggy. Place on the bottom of the dish…repeat until you have a layer of cookies.
- Cover the cookies with half of the softened whipped topping and sprinkle half of the chocolate bar crumbs. Next, repeat with another layer of cookies and whipped topping and finally top with the remaining chocolate crumbs…AND YOU'RE DONE!! Just place in the freezer and wait a few hours until frozen. Enjoy!

180. Frozen Chocolate Mousse Squares Recipe

Serving: 16 | Prep: | Cook: 10mins | Ready in:

Ingredients

- 12 OREO chocolate Sandwich cookies, crushed
- 1/4 cup (1/2 stick) butter or margarine, melted
- 2 containers (8 oz. each) cream cheese spread
- 1 can (14 oz.) sweetened condensed milk
- 4 squares Semi-Sweet baking chocolate, melted
- 1 cup thawed Cool Whip whipped topping

Direction

- MIX crushed cookies and the butter in foil-lined 9-inch square pan. Press firmly onto bottom of pan to form crust.
- BEAT cream cheese in large bowl with electric mixer on low speed until creamy. Gradually add milk, mixing well after each addition. Blend in chocolate. Gently stir in whipped topping. Spoon over crust; cover.
- FREEZE at least 6 hours or overnight. Remove from freezer 15 min. before serving to soften slightly. Cut into 16 squares to serve. Store leftover dessert in freezer.

181. Fruit And Nut Bars Recipe

Serving: 16 | Prep: | Cook: 35mins | Ready in:

Ingredients

- 1/3 cup (95 grams) all purpose flour
- 1/8 teaspoon baking soda
- 1/8 teaspoon baking powder
- 1/4 teaspoon salt
- 1/3 cup (70 grams) light brown sugar
- 1 1/2 cups (145 grams) walnuts (can also use pecans, hazelnuts, or almonds), chopped

- 1/2 cup (65 grams) dried cherries or cranberries
- 1 1/2 cup dates, pits removed and cut into quarters
- 1 cup (165 grams) dried apricots, cut into bite size pieces
- 1 large egg
- 1/2 teaspoon pure vanilla extract

Direction

- Preheat oven to 325 degrees F (160 degrees C) and place the rack in the center of the oven. Have ready an 8 x 8 inch (20 x 20 cm) square baking pan that has been lined across the bottom and up the two opposite sides with aluminum foil. Set aside.
- In a large bowl, whisk together the flour, baking soda, baking powder and salt. Stir in the brown sugar, walnuts, and dried fruit. Use your fingers to make sure that all the fruit and nuts have been coated with the flour mixture.
- In a separate bowl, beat (with a wire whisk or hand mixer) the egg and vanilla until light colored and thick (this will take several minutes). Add the egg mixture to the fruit and nut mixture and mix until all the fruit and nut pieces are coated with the batter. Spread into the prepared pan, pressing to even it out.
- Bake for about 35 to 40 minutes, or until the batter is golden brown and has pulled away from the sides of the pan. Remove from oven and place on a wire rack to cool. When cooled, lift the bars from the pan by the edges of the aluminum foil. Use a sharp knife to cut into 16 squares.
- Can be stored for about 10 days at room temperature or longer if refrigerated.
- Makes 16 - 2 inch (5 cm) squares.

182. Fudge Fantasy Bars Recipe

Serving: 36 | Prep: | Cook: 15mins | Ready in:

Ingredients

- 1 package(s) (17.5 ounces) sugar cookie mix
- 1/2 cup cocoa (not drink mix
- 1/2 cup butter or margarine, melted
- 1 large egg
- 2/3 cup toasted chopped pecans
- 1/2 cup sweetened flaked coconut
- 1 package (12 ounces) semisweet chocolate chips
- 2/3 cup whipping (heavy) cream
- 1 block (8-ounce) cream cheese, softened
- 1/2 cup chocolate syrup
- 2 cup frozen whipped topping, thawed

Direction

- Heat oven to 350°F. Line a 13x9x2-inch baking pan with foil. Let some foil hang over the edges. Set aside.
- Stir cookie mix and cocoa powder in large mixing bowl until well mixed. Add butter and egg, stirring until soft dough forms. Add pecans and coconut; knead to combine.
- With wet fingers, press dough evenly over prepared baking pan. Bake for 12-15 minutes or just until set. Cool completely.
- Place chocolate chips and whipping cream in medium saucepan over low heat, stirring until melted and the mixture is smooth. Spread 1 cup evenly over cooled cookie base.
- Meanwhile, beat cream cheese and chocolate syrup at medium speed with an electric mixer until smooth. Add whipped topping and beat until light and fluffy. Spread cheese mixture evenly over ganache layer. Carefully spread remaining ganache evenly over cheese filling.
- Refrigerate for 6 to 8 hours or overnight. Lift bars with foil handles. Run wet knife around edges of cookie to peel off foil. Cut into bars. Store covered in refrigerator.

183. Fudgy Almond Bars Recipe

Serving: 12 | Prep: | Cook: 19mins | Ready in:

Ingredients

- 1 3/4 cups all-purpose flour
- 3/4 cup confectioners' sugar
- 1/4 cup baking cocoa
- 3/4 cup cold butter
- 1 can (14 ounces) sweetened condensed milk
- 1 teaspoon vanilla extract
- 2 cups (12 ounces) semisweet chocolate chips, divided
- 1 cup coarsely chopped honey roasted almonds
- 1/2 cup flaked coconut
- l

Direction

- In a bowl, combine flour, sugar and cocoa. Cut in butter until mixture resembles coarse crumbs. Press firmly into a greased 13 by 9 by 2 inch baking pan. Bake at 350 degrees for 10 minutes. Meanwhile, in a saucepan, heat milk, vanilla and 1 cup chocolate chips, stirring until smooth. Pour over the crust. Sprinkle with nuts, coconut and remaining chocolate chips; press down firmly. Bake for 18 - 20 min.

184. GERMAN LEBKUCHEN HONEY BARS Recipe

Serving: 48 | Prep: | Cook: 6mins | Ready in:

Ingredients

- 3 cups sifted flour
- 1 tsp ground cinnamon
- 1/2 tsp baking soda
- 1/2 tsp ground allspice
- 1/2 tsp ground cloves
- 1/2 tsp ground nutmeg
- 1 cup dark corn syrup
- 1/3 cup sugar
- 1 egg
- 2 tablespoons lemon juice
- 2 tsp grated lemon rind
- 1/2 cup confectioners' sugar
- 1 tablespoon water
- candied cherry halves

Direction

- Stir together first 6 ingredients. In 1-quart saucepan, bring corn syrup and sugar to a boil. Cool.
- In a large bowl stir together corn syrup mixture, egg, lemon juice and rind. Gradually stir in flour mixture until well blended. Divide dough into fourths. Cover; chill at least 1 hour or until easy to handle.
- On a well-floured surface, roll out dough 1/4 at a time to 1/4" thickness. Cut with 2" cookie cutters. Place on greased cookie sheet. Bake in 400°F oven 6 minutes or until lightly browned. Remove from cookie sheet immediately; place on rack.
- Mix confectioners' sugar and water. While still warm, brush with glaze. Top with candied cherry half. Cool.
- May be stored in tightly covered container up to 4 weeks.
- Makes about 4 dozen.

185. GOOEY COCONUT BARS Recipe

Serving: 12 | Prep: | Cook: 45mins | Ready in:

Ingredients

- 1 (18.25 ounce) box French vanilla cake mix
- 2 eggs
- 1/2 cup (1 stick) butter or margarine, melted
- 8 ounces cream cheese, softened
- 2 eggs

- 1 teaspoon vanilla extract
- 1/2 teaspoon almond extract
- 1 (16 ounce) box confectioners' sugar
- 1 1/2 cups shredded coconut

Direction

- Preheat oven to 350 degrees. Spray a 13x9 inch baking pan with Pam. Combine the first 3 ingredients. Press into bottom about 1 inch up the sides of prepared baking pan.
- Mix together the next 6 ingredients and pour over crust.
- Bake for 45 minutes, or until golden brown on top. Let cool completely to set and cut into small squares.

186. German Chocolate Bars Recipe

Serving: 48 | Prep: | Cook: 35mins | Ready in:

Ingredients

- 2/3 cup butter or margarine, softened
- 1 box Betty Crocker® SuperMoist® German chocolate cake mix
- 1 cup semisweet chocolate chips
- 1 container Betty Crocker® Rich & Creamy coconut pecan frosting
- 1/4 cup milk

Direction

- Heat oven to 350°F (325°F for dark or non-stick pan). Lightly grease or spray bottom and sides of 13x9-inch pan.
- In medium bowl, cut butter into cake mix, using pastry blender or fork, until mixture looks like fine crumbs. Press half of the mixture (2 1/2 cups) in bottom of pan.
- Bake 10 minutes. Sprinkle chocolate chips over baked layer. Drop frosting by tablespoonfuls over chocolate chips. Stir milk into remaining cake mixture. Drop by teaspoonfuls onto frosting layer.
- Bake 24 to 28 minutes or until cake portion is slightly dry to touch; cool completely. Refrigerate until firm. For 48 bars, cut into 8 rows by 6 rows. Store loosely covered.

187. Ginger Pumpkin Praline Squares Recipe

Serving: 15 | Prep: | Cook: 40mins | Ready in:

Ingredients

- Filling Ingredients:
- 1 cup firmly packed brown sugar
- 1/4 cup sugar
- 1 (29-ounce) can pumpkin
- 1 (12-ounce) can evaporated milk
- 5 eggs
- 2 teaspoons ground cinnamon
- 1/2 teaspoon ground ginger
- 1/2 teaspoon ground cloves
- Topping Ingredients:
- 3/4 cup all-purpose flour
- 1/2 cup firmly packed brown sugar
- 1/4 cup cold LAND O LAKES® butter
- 1/2 cup chopped pecans

Direction

- Garnish Ingredients:
- LAND O LAKES™ Heavy Whipping Cream, whipped, sweetened, if desired
- Ground cinnamon, if desired
- Preparation:
- Heat oven to 350°F. Combine all filling ingredients in large bowl. Beat at medium speed, scraping bowl often, until smooth.
- Pour into greased 13x9-inch baking pan. Bake for 25 to 30 minutes or until partially set.
- Meanwhile, combine 3/4 cup flour and 1/2 cup brown sugar in small bowl; cut in butter with pastry blender or fork until mixture resembles coarse crumbs. Stir in pecans.

Sprinkle topping over hot, partially baked pumpkin filling. Continue baking for 15 to 20 minutes or until knife inserted in centre comes out clean. Cool 30 minutes. Refrigerate until cooled completely (1 1/2 hours).
- To serve, dollop each serving with whipped cream; sprinkle with cinnamon, if desired. Store refrigerated.

188. Gingerbread Squares Recipe

Serving: 10 | Prep: | Cook: 55mins | Ready in:

Ingredients

- 1/2 cup plus 2 tbs butter or margarine, divided
- 1/2 cup corn syrup
- 1/2 cup walnut halves or pieces
- 1 large pear or apple, cored and chopped
- 1/2 cup sugar
- 3/4 cup molasses
- 2 eggs
- 2 cups all-purpose flour
- 1/2 tsp each, baking powder and baking soda
- 1/2 tsp each, ground ginger and cinnamon
- 1/4 tsp each, salt and ground cloves
- 1/2 cup buttermilk

Direction

- Combine 2 tbsp. butter and corn syrup in small saucepan. Cook over medium heat until butter is melted and syrup is hot, stirring frequently. Pour into 9" square baking dish. Sprinkle walnuts and chopped pear evenly over syrup.
- Beat together 1/2 cup butter and sugar until light and fluffy. Gradually beat in molasses. Add eggs, one at a time, beating well. Combine flour, baking powder, soda, ginger, cinnamon, salt and cloves in a medium bowl; mix well. Add flour mixture alternately with buttermilk to molasses mixture, beating well.

Pour over pear mixture in dish. Bake in a 350° oven for 50 to 55 mins or till a wooden pick inserted in centre comes out clean.
- Transfer to cooling rack; let stand 10 mins. Loosen edges and turn out onto a serving plate; cool at least 15 mins. Serve warm or at room temperature. Makes 8 to 10 servings.

189. Glendas Best Zucchini Bars Recipe

Serving: 24 | Prep: | Cook: 20mins | Ready in:

Ingredients

- 2 c. sugar
- 1 c oil
- 3 eggs
- 2 c flour
- 1 tsp cinnamon
- 1 tsp salt
- 2 tsp soda
- 1/4 tsp baking powder
- 1 tsp vanilla
- 2 c shredded zuchinni
- 1 carrot shredded
- 3/4 c rolled oats
- 1 c chopped nuts, (hickory, walnut or which ever you choose)
- ~@~
- Frosting:
- 1/2 c soft sweet butter
- 1/4 tsp almond extract
- 2 tsp vanilla
- 2 1/2 c confectioners sugar
- 1 - 3oz pkg cream cheese, softened

Direction

- Beat sugar and eggs and oil.
- Combine flour, cinnamon, salt, soda baking powder and beat in.
- Add vanilla.
- Beat for 1 to 2 minutes until well mixed.

- Fold in zucchini, carrot, oats and nuts.
- Pour into prepared 15x10x1 jellyroll pan.
- Bake at 350 degrees for 15 - 20 minutes.
- Combine frosting ingredients and frost when cooled.

190. Gooey Coconut Bars Recipe

Serving: 1 | Prep: | Cook: 45mins | Ready in:

Ingredients

- 1 (18.25 ounce) box French vanilla cake mix
- 2 eggs
- 1/2 cup (1 stick) butter or margarine, melted
- 8 ounces cream cheese, softened
- 2 eggs
- 1 teaspoon vanilla extract
- 1/2 teaspoon almond extract
- 1 (16 ounce) box confectioners' sugar
- 1 1/2 cups shredded coconut

Direction

- Heat oven to 350 degrees F. Spray a 13 x 9-inch baking pan with Pam.
- Combine first 3 ingredients. Press into bottom about 1 inch up the sides of prepared baking pan.
- Mix together next 6 ingredients and pour over crust. Bake for 45 minutes, or until golden brown on top. Let cool completely to set, and cut into small squares.

191. Granola Bars Recipe

Serving: 32 | Prep: | Cook: 2mins | Ready in:

Ingredients

- 1 tsp butter
- 1 1/4 cups rolled wheat
- 1 1/2 cups toasted pecans, cashews, and almonds rough chopped
- 1/2 cup ground flax seed
- 1 1/2 cups granola oats from the bottom third of TJ's granola
- 1 cup dried mixed berries
- 1 cup mesquite honey
- 1/3 cup turbinado sugar
- 1 tsp vanilla extract
- 1/2 tsp fine grain sea salt

Direction

- Use the butter to grease an 11" x 16" sheet pan.
- In a small pan heat the honey, sugar, vanilla, and salt over medium-low heat until the sugar dissolves.
- Put all the dry ingredients into a bowl and mix well.
- Pour the sugar mixture over the dry ingredients and mix well until thoroughly combined.
- Pour into the sheet pan and using wax paper press the mixture into the pan so it is firmly and evenly dispersed.
- Let it cool and then cut into bars and serve.
- I wrapped mine in wax paper squares and stored them in the refrigerator in a Ziploc bag.

192. Granola Nut Protein Bar Recipe Recipe

Serving: 12 | Prep: | Cook: 3mins | Ready in:

Ingredients

- 2-1/2 cups natural peanut butter
- 2 cups honey
- 2-1/4 cups protein powder
- 3 cups uncooked oatmeal
- 1/2 cup chopped walnuts
- 1/2 cup raisins
- 1/4 cup wheat bran
- 1/2 teaspoon cinnamon

Direction

- Preparation: In a double boiler, warm the peanut butter and honey to a smooth consistency. This step can be done in the microwave as well--just heat both ingredients for 70 to 90 seconds. In a mixing bowl, stir together all remaining dry ingredients. Pour in the peanut-butter mixture and stir until completely combined. Spread uniformly into a brownie pan. Slice into 12 to 16 pieces, and then wrap each piece in plastic wrap.
- Each Granola Nut Protein Bar costs 25 to 35 cents to make, as opposed to 99 cents and up for store-bought energy bars. On top of that, if you do use organic ingredients, you won't believe the difference!
- Nutritional information:
- 200 calories per bar 9 grams fat 3 to 4 grams fiber 15 grams protein 26 grams carbohydrates
- These bars are definitely not low-fat (they have four times as much fat as a Power Bar), so you may want to reserve them for when you're working out hard.

193. Grasshopper Bars Recipe

Serving: 36 | Prep: | Cook: 60mins | Ready in:

Ingredients

- Bars:
- 1 pouch(1lb 1.5oz.)Betty Crocker doble chocolate chunk cookie mix
- 1/3c vegetable oil
- 2Tbs. water
- 1egg
- Frosting:
- 3c powdered sugar
- 1 pkg.(3oz) cream cheese,softened
- 1/4c butter,softened
- 2Tbs. milk
- 1/4tsp mint extract
- 3-4 drops green food color
- Glaze:
- 1 oz. unsweetened baking chocolate
- 1Tbs butter

Direction

- Heat oven to 350 Spray bottom of 13x9" pan with cooking spray.
- In a large bowl, stir all Bar ingredients until soft dough forms. Press into pan; bake 15 mins. Cool about 10 mins.
- In a large bowl, stir all frosting ingredients until smooth. Spread over bars.
- In small microwaveable bowl, microwave all glaze ingredients on high 30 seconds; stir till smooth. Drizzle over frosting Refrigerate 30 mins or till set. For bars, cut into 9 rows by 4 rows. Store covered in frig.
- Line baking pan with foil for easier cutting!

194. Gutte Kuchen Recipe

Serving: 12 | Prep: | Cook: 20mins | Ready in:

Ingredients

- 2 cups AP flour
- 1 teaspoon baking powder
- 3/4 cup of sugar
- 3/4 cup butter flavored shortening
- 1 egg
- 1 teaspoon vanilla extract
- 1/2 teaspoon cinnamon
- 2 Tablespoons milk
- Jar of favorite jam,jelly,preserves or fruit spread

Direction

- Preheat oven to 400.
- Butter a small cookie sheet and set aside.
- Combine flour through milk and knead gently.
- Divide dough in half.
- Press one half of the dough into prepared baking sheet.
- Spread Jam over the dough.

- Cover with the rest of the dough ((I roll it out and cut shapes with a cookie cutter for the top) its artistic license. I've also made a lattice for the top, which was trickier but beautiful)).
- Bake for 20 minutes or so until it starts to brown.
- Cool in pan and cut into squares.
- Layer on waxed paper.

195. HEATH BAR CAKE Recipe

Serving: 8 | Prep: | Cook: 32mins | Ready in:

Ingredients

- 1 BOX chocolate cake mix
- 1 CAN EAGLE BRAND milk
- 1/2 CAN chocolate syrup
- 1/2 JAR caramel topping
- 1/2 JAR BUTTERSCOTH TOPPING
- 1- 12OZ COOLWHIP
- 2 HEATH BARS CRUSHED

Direction

- BAKE CAKE AND LET COOL USING A WOODEN SPOON POKE HOLES IN THE CAKE
- POUR EAGLE BRAND MILK OVER THE CAKE ALONG WITH TOPPINGS
- SPREAD ON CAKE
- WAIT TIL TOPPINGS SOAK INTO CAKE
- TOP WITH CRUSHED BARS AND COOL WHIP

196. Halloween Magic Bars Recipe

Serving: 24 | Prep: | Cook: 25mins | Ready in:

Ingredients

- 2 cups (500ml) chocolate cookie crumbs
- 3/4 cup (175 ml) butter, melted
- 1 can (300 ml) Eagle Brand Condensed Milk
- 1 pkg (300g) peanut butter chips
- 1 pkg (250g) milk chocolate chips
- 1 cup (250 ml) sweetened flaked coconut
- orange-covered chocolate or peanut candy pieces (smarties I think are the best)

Direction

- Combine cookie crumbs with butter; press evenly onto parchment paper-lined 13 x 9 inch (3 L) baking pan.
- Pour Eagle Brand evenly over crumbs.
- Sprinkle with chips and coconut; press down firmly.
- Bake in preheated 350°F (180°C) oven for 20-25 minutes or until edges become lightly browned.
- Remove from oven and press orange candy pieces on top. Cool thoroughly and chill before cutting into bars.

197. Heath Bar Apple Dip Recipe

Serving: 15 | Prep: | Cook: | Ready in:

Ingredients

- 1 8oz block cream cheese, softened
- 1/2 c sugar
- 3/4 c brown sugar
- 1 t vanilla
- 1/2 bag Heathbar Bits (or Skor)
- apple wedges (granny smith, or roma)

Direction

- Cream together cream cheese, sugars, and vanilla
- Stir heath bar bits in with spoon
- Serve with granny smith or roma apple wedges

- (Cut apples into pineapple juice to keep from turning brown)

198. Heath Bar Brownies Dated 1964 Recipe

Serving: 12 | Prep: | Cook: 55mins | Ready in:

Ingredients

- 1 cup pecans chopped
- 6 large heath toffee bars broken into small pieces
- 1-1/4 cup granulated sugar
- 5 ounces unsweetened chocolate chopped
- 1/2 cup soft unsalted butter
- 4 eggs at room temperature
- 1 tablespoon pure vanilla extract
- 1/4 teaspoon salt
- 2/3 cups cake flour

Direction

- Position rack in center of oven and preheat to 325.
- Grease and flour square baking pan.
- Place heath bars and pecans in food processor and chop with steel knife until coarse.
- Remove and set aside.
- Combine sugar and chocolate in food processor and mix until chocolate is fine as sugar.
- Transfer to large mixing bowl then add butter and blend 1 minute.
- Add eggs, vanilla and salt then blend until fluffy scraping down sides.
- Add flour and toffee mixture then blend until flour is incorporated.
- Turn batter into prepared pan and spread evenly.
- Bake 50 minutes for wetter brownies and 55 minutes for cake like brownies.
- Let cool in pan on rack then cut into squares and store in airtight container.

199. Heath Bar Coffee Cake Recipe

Serving: 32 | Prep: | Cook: 30mins | Ready in:

Ingredients

- 1 stick butter
- 1 cups brown sugar
- 1/2 cup white sugar
- 2 cups flour
- Place these in a bowl and mix well in an electric mixer. Take out 1/2 cup of this mixture to use for the topping. In the bowl with the remaining mixture in it, add the following and mix until all dry ingredients are moistened:
- 1 cup buttermilk
- 1 egg
- 1 tsp. vanilla
- 1 tsp. baking soda
- For the topping, add the following to the 1/2 cup of reserved mix:
- 5 oz. crushed Heath bars (roughly 1/4 inch square pieces)
- 1/4 chopped pecans
- Pour the batter into prepared baking dish and spread until even. Sprinkle the topping over the batter evenly. Bake at 350 degrees for about 30 minutes or until a toothpick inserted in the center comes out clean. Slice into bars and serve

Direction

- Preheat oven to 350 degrees. Grease a 9x13 inch Pyrex® baking dish.
- Makes about 32 bars.

200. Heath Bar Poundcake Recipe

Serving: 6 | Prep: | Cook: 80mins | Ready in:

Ingredients

- 1 stick butter
- 4 oz. cream cheese
- 1 cup sugar
- 2 eggs
- 1 tbl vanilla extract
- 1 cup flour
- 1 heath bar-ground in food processor or blender
- ¼ cup light brown sugar

Direction

- In a medium bowl, mix butter, cream cheese and sugar together until smooth. Add eggs and vanilla; stir together. Add flour; mix well.
- Combine ground heath bar with brown sugar. Grease glass loaf dish with butter; coat bottom and sides with sugar mixture. Pour batter into loaf dish; sprinkle with remaining sugar mixture. Bake in preheated 300 degree oven one hour to one hour and ten minutes until knife "just" comes out clean.

201. Heavenly Brownie On Shortbread Bars Recipe

Serving: 1 | Prep: | Cook: 60mins | Ready in:

Ingredients

- Shortbread
- 1-1/3 cups all-purpose flour
- 1/3 cup granulated sugar
- ¼ teaspoon salt
- 4 ounces (1 stick) cold, unsalted butter cut into ½-inch slices
- 1 teaspoon pure vanilla extract
- Heavenly Brownie
- 2/3 cup all-purpose flour
- 1/8 teaspoon salt
- 1 stick unsalted butter cut into 1/-inch slices
- 5 ounces bittersweet chocolate coarsely chopped
- 1 cup firmly packed light brown sugar
- 3 large eggs
- 1 teaspoon pure vanilla extract
- 1 cup packed hazelnuts, finely chopped to yield 1 cup

Direction

- Before baking: Center a rack in the oven and preheat the oven to 350 degrees F. Press a sheet of aluminum foil to cover the outside bottom and sides of a 9 by 2-inch square pan. Lift off the foil, invert the pan, and gently press the foil into the pan to fit the contours.
- To make the shortbread: In a food processor, combine the flour, sugar, and salt and process briefly to blend. Scatter the butter pieces over the top and process with 1-second bursts. Add the vanilla and continue with 1-second bursts until the ingredients form small clumps. Stop before the mixture forms a ball.
- Scatter the clumps over the bottom of the prepared pan, and press with fingertips to line the bottom evenly.
- Bake the shortbread until it is pale gold and firm to the touch, 27 to 32 minutes. Let cool in the pan, about 20 minutes.
- To make the Heavenly Brownie: Briefly whisk together the flour and salt in a medium bowl to blend; set aside. In a small, heavy saucepan, melt the butter and chocolate over very low heat, stirring with a silicone spatula until smooth. Remove from the heat and stir the sugar into the chocolate mixture, combining thoroughly. Set aside for 5 to 7 minutes.
- In a medium bowl, whisk the eggs until lightly beaten. Add the slightly cooled chocolate mixture to the eggs, stirring to blend. Stir in the vanilla, then the flour mixture. Pour the batter over the shortbread, and spread evenly with a rubber spatula. Sprinkle the nuts evenly over the batter. Gently pat them in place.
- Bake the brownie until the top looks slightly cracked about 1 inch from the edge around the pan and feels soft to the touch, 27 – 30 minutes. Don't overbake; the brownie will firm as it cools. Transfer to a wire rack and let cool

completely in the pan, at least 3 hours or up to overnight.
- To serve, using the edges of the foil as handles, lift the brownie slab onto a cutting board.
- Using a sharp knife, cut the brownies straight down through the shortbread into 1-1/2-inch squares.
- To store, return the bars to the pan, cover with aluminum foil, sealing the foil around the edges of the pan, and keep at room temperature for up to 3 days.

202. Heavenly Candy Bar Cake Recipe

Serving: 12 | Prep: | Cook: 25mins | Ready in:

Ingredients

- 9 fun-size or 21 mini chocolate-coated caramel and creamy nougat bars
- 1/2 cup butter or margarine
- 2 cups sugar
- 1 cup shortening
- 3 large eggs
- 2 1/2 cups all-purpose flour
- 1 teaspoon salt
- 1 1/2 cups buttermilk
- 1/2 teaspoon baking soda
- 1 teaspoon vanilla extract
- Chocolate-Marshmallow frosting
- Garnishes: chopped frozen fun-size chocolate-coated caramel and creamy nougat bars, candy corn

Direction

- Melt candy bars and butter in a heavy saucepan over low heat about 5 minutes, stirring until smooth. Set aside.
- Beat sugar and shortening at medium speed with an electric mixer about 3 minutes or until well blended.
- Add eggs, 1 at a time, beating just until blended after each addition.
- Combine flour and salt. Stir together buttermilk and baking soda. Gradually add flour mixture to sugar mixture, alternately with buttermilk mixture, beginning and ending with flour mixture.
- Beat at low speed just until blended after each addition.
- Stir in melted candy bar mixture and vanilla.
- Spoon batter into 3 greased and floured 9-inch cake pans.
- Bake at 350° for 30 minutes or until a wooden pick comes out clean. Cool in pans on a wire rack 10 minutes; remove cakes from pans, and let cool completely on wire rack. Spread half of Chocolate-Marshmallow Frosting evenly between cake layers. Spread remaining frosting evenly over top and sides of cake.
- Garnish, if desired. Prep: 15 min., Cook: 5 min., Bake: 30 min.
- Note: For testing purposes only, we used Milky Way Bars

203. Hershey Bar Cake Recipe

Serving: 14 | Prep: | Cook: 80mins | Ready in:

Ingredients

- 2 sticks butter softened
- 4 large eggs
- 1 cup buttermilk
- 2 teaspoons pure vanilla extract.
- 2 cups sugar
- 2 1/2 cups all-purpose flour
- 1/2 ts. baking soda,mix into buttermilk.
- 1 cup pecans (optional)
- 8 Hershey Bars 1 can hershey chocolate syrup.(Melt together on low heat)

Direction

- In a bowl mix, mix together first 7 ingredients listed.
- Melt Hershey bars add syrup into it.

- Fold the chocolate mixture gently into flour mixture.
- Pour into well-greased and floured Bundt pan or square pans.
- Bake in preheated 350 degree oven about 1 1/4 hours till toothpick comes out clean.
- Remove from oven.
- Cover with foil till cool.
- FROSTING:
- 1 bar Bakers Sweet chocolate
- 1 tablespoon unsalted butter
- 1/4 cup water
- Melt together on low heat.
- Mix in 1 cup sifted confectioners' sugar.
- Blend together. Add 1 teaspoon pure vanilla extract.
- Pour over cake allowing it to drip down sides of the cake.
- Let set.
- Yum!

204. Hershys Cookie Layered Bars Recipe

Serving: 12 | Prep: | Cook: 25mins | Ready in:

Ingredients

- * 3/4 cup (1-1/2 sticks) butter or margarine
- * 1-3/4 cups vanilla wafer crumbs
- * 6 tablespoons HERSHEY'S cocoa
- * 1/4 cup sugar
- * 1 can (14 oz.) sweetened condensed milk (not evaporated milk)
- * 1 cup HERSHEY'S SPECIAL dark chocolate chips or HERSHEY'S semi-sweet chocolate chips
- * 3/4 cup HEATH BITS 'O BRICKLE Toffee Bits
- * 1 cup chopped walnuts

Direction

- Directions:
- 1. Heat oven to 350 F. Melt butter in 13x9x2-inch baking pan in oven. Combine crumbs, cocoa and sugar; sprinkle over butter.
- 2. Pour sweetened condensed milk evenly on top of crumb mixture. Top with chocolate chips and toffee bits, then nuts; press down firmly.
- 3. Bake 25 to 30 minutes or until lightly browned. Cool completely in pan on wire rack. Chill, if desired. Cut into bars. Store covered at room tem

205. Ho Ho Bars Recipe

Serving: 24 | Prep: | Cook: 37mins | Ready in:

Ingredients

- 1 choc cake mix (Betty Crocker Super Moist) make according to directions, put in a 1/2 sheet cake pan. Bake 18 - 20 min. Cool completely.
- 1 can chocolate frosting
- Filling:
- 3/4 cup sugar
- 1 stick butter - softened (not melted)
- 2/3 cup shortening
- 1/2 cup evapoarted milk
- 1 tsp. vanilla

Direction

- Beat first 3 ingredients until creamy. Slowly add evaporated milk. Beat 8 - 10 minutes on high. Add vanilla and mix well. Spread on cool cake.
- Melt frosting in microwave 30 - 45 seconds, stir. Pour over filling and smooth out.
- It's best to let the frosting dry overnight, otherwise the bars are messy to eat.
- Enjoy!!!

206. Holiday Magic Bars Recipe

Serving: 16 | Prep: | Cook: 30mins | Ready in:

Ingredients

- 2 cups ginger cookie crumbs (I use Anna's ginger Thins, but any crisp gingersnap-type cookie will do)
- 3 tbsp. butter, melted
- 1 1/2 cups chocolate chips
- 1 cup white chocolate chips (I use Ghirardelli - they seem to melt better and don't scorch as easily)
- 3/4 cup dried cranberries
- 1/2 cup dried apricots, chopped
- 2 tsp. minced candied ginger
- 3/4 cup chopped pecans
- 3/4 cup shredded coconut
- 1 14-oz. can sweetened condensed milk

Direction

- Preheat oven to 350 degrees F. Butter an 8" x 8" or 9" x 9" inch baking dish.
- Combine crumbs and butter, and press into bottom of baking dish.
- Sprinkle with chocolate/white chocolate morsels, cranberries, apricots, ginger, nuts and coconut.
- Drizzle with sweetened condensed milk
- Bake for 30 minutes or until golden brown.
- Let cool completely, then cut into squares with a sharp knife.
- Measurements are estimates - a little more or less of anything is fine.

207. Homemade Snickers Bars Recipe

Serving: 15 | Prep: | Cook: 7mins | Ready in:

Ingredients

- Step one:
- 1 cup milk chocolate chips
- 1/4 cup creamy peanut butter
- 1/4 cup butterscotch chips
- Step two:
- 1/4 cup butter
- 1/4 cup evaporated milk
- 1/4 cup creamy peanut butter
- 1 1/2 cup chopped salted peanuts
- 1 cup white sugar
- 1 1/2 cup marshmallow cream
- 1 tsp vanilla
- Step three: caramel Layer
- 14 oz. caramels(usually around 30 pre-wrapped caramels)
- 1/4 cup whipping cream

Direction

- Layer 13x9 dish with foil. Butter foil.
- Step One: Combine first three ingredients in step one in saucepan.
- Stir over low heat until melted and smooth.
- Pour into dish.
- Chill until set
- Step two:
- Melt butter in saucepan over medium heat.
- Add sugar and evaporated milk.
- Bring to a gentle boil
- Reduce heat to medium-low boiling and stirring for 5 minutes
- Remove from heat and stir in marshmallow cream, peanut butter and vanilla.
- Add peanuts.
- Spread over chocolate layer and chill until set
- Step Three:
- Combine caramels and whipping cream in saucepan and stir over low heat until melted and smooth.
- Cook and stir for 4 minutes more
- Spread over filling and chill until set
- Step Four: Repeat step one.
- Chill at least 4 hours and remove from fridge 20 minutes before cutting

208. Homemade Twix Bars Recipe

Serving: 15 | Prep: | Cook: 5mins | Ready in:

Ingredients

- Club crackers
- 1 cup of club cracker crumbs
- 1 stick butter
- 3/4 cup brown sugar
- 1/2 cup of granulated sugar
- 1/3 cup milk
- 1 cup chocolate chips
- 3/4 cup peanut butter

Direction

- Line a 9x13 inch pan with whole crackers.
- Boil butter, cracker crumbs, sugars, and milk.
- Cook for 5 minutes.
- Pour over crackers.
- Add another layer of crackers.
- Melt chocolate and peanut butter together.
- Spread over crackers.
- Allow to cool, and then serve.

209. Honey Almond Bars Recipe

Serving: 9 | Prep: | Cook: 40mins | Ready in:

Ingredients

- 3/4 cup of unsalted butter
- 1 cup of all purpose flour
- 1/3 cup of honey
- 1 cup of sliced almonds
- 1/2 cup of sifted confectioner's sugar
- 1/4 tsp of salt
- 2 tsp of lemon juice
- 1/2 tsp of almond extract

Direction

- In a large bowl, cream together 1/2 cup of the butter and the confectioner's sugar.
- Stir in flour and salt.
- Pat evenly into an ungreased 9 inch square cake pan.
- Bake in 350 degree oven for 12 to 15 minutes or until lightly golden.
- Meanwhile, in a small saucepan, melt remaining butter.
- Stir in honey and lemon juice.
- Bring to a boil over medium high heat, stirring constantly.
- Remove from heat.
- Stir in almonds and almond extract.
- Spread evenly over hot baked layer and return to oven for about 15 minutes until evenly golden brown.
- While hot, cut in squares, allow to cool in pan.

210. I Want That Recipe Bars Recipe

Serving: 24 | Prep: | Cook: 30mins | Ready in:

Ingredients

- Crust
- 3/4 cup butter
- 1/4 cup plus 1 Tbsp. sugar
- 1½ cups flour
- Filling
- 1 cup graham cracker crumbs
- 1/2 cup chocolate chips
- 1/2 cup walnuts
- 1/4 tsp salt
- 1 tsp. baking powder
- 14 oz. can sweetened condensed milk
- Frosting
- 1 1/2 cups powdered sugar
- 1 tsp vanilla
- 1/3 cup butter
- 3 oz. cr. cheese

Direction

- Crust
- Mix crust ingredients & pat into a 9 x 13 pan.
- Bake at 350 for 10 minutes.
- Filling
- Mix filling ingredients and spread over baked crust. No need to cool the crust first.
- Bake for 15-20 minutes.
- Cool.
- Frosting
- Blend together butter and cream cheese.
- Add vanilla and beat in powder sugar until creamy.
- Frost bars.
- Note: These should be stored in the fridge because of the cream cheese but taken out a little before serving. For easier cutting, cut before refrigerating.
- Note: I think these could also be very good made with white chocolate chips and macadamia nuts instead of chocolate chips and walnuts.

211. Ice Cream Crunch Bars Recipe

Serving: 16 | Prep: | Cook: | Ready in:

Ingredients

- 50 vanilla wafers, finely crushed
- 1 cup finely chopped toasted pecans
- 1 cup coconut toasted
- 1/4 cup butter melted
- 1 pint vanilla ice cream softened
- 1 pint chocolate ice cream softened

Direction

- Mix wafers, pecans, coconut and butter until well blended. Press 1 cup of the wafer mixture firmly onto bottom of 9-inch square pan.
- Spoon vanilla ice cream over crust; carefully spread to form even layer. Freeze 25 minutes or until firm. Sprinkle with 1/4 cup of the remaining wafer mixture then cover with the chocolate ice cream. Sprinkle with the remaining wafer mixture. Freeze 4 hours or until firm. Let stand 10 minutes at room temperature to soften slightly. Cut into 16 bars to serve. Store leftover bars in airtight container in freezer.

212. Ice Cream Marshmallow Bars Recipe

Serving: 12 | Prep: | Cook: | Ready in:

Ingredients

- 1 13 oz. jar of marshmallow cream
- 1 1/2 cups of chocolate syrup
- 1 cup of peanut butter
- 1 15 oz. box of grahm crackers (you will have extras)
- 2 1/2 cups of ice cream
- 2 tablespoons sugar
- 1/3 cup butter
- Grahm cracker Crust
- 5 sheets of graham crackers - f needed use more
- 2 tablespoons sugar
- 1/3 cup butter

Direction

- Prep does not include chill time
- Directions for graham cracker crust:
- Crush graham crackers in a bag into crumbs.
- Mix the sugar in with the graham crackers.
- Put the butter in the microwave for 15 seconds, or until melted completely.
- Pour the cracker sugar mixture into a bowl and gradually stir in the melted butter.
- When mixed pour into a 7x11 in. pan and press against sides and bottom.
- Put into the refrigerator for 15 minutes.
- Directions for marshmallow mix:
- Pour 1 cup of chocolate syrup on top of the graham cracker crust.

- Pour 1 cup of peanut butter on top of the chocolate syrup.
- Lay a sheet of un-crumbled graham crackers on top of the peanut butter.
- Put the ice cream in the microwave for about 15 seconds, or until soft.
- Spread onto graham cracker sheet until flat.
- Lay another sheet of graham crackers on top of the ice cream.
- Scoop the marshmallow cream into a bowl.
- Now mix 1/2 cup of chocolate syrup with the marshmallow cream until light brown. (Add chocolate more if needed)
- Put the mixture into the microwave for about 15 seconds.
- Pour on top of the sheet of graham crackers.
- Put in freezer for 2 hours, cut into 12 squares and enjoy!!

213. Jane Parker A P Spanish Bar Cake Recipe

Serving: 12 | Prep: | Cook: 35mins | Ready in:

Ingredients

- 4 cups water
- 2 cups raisins
- 1 cup shortening
- 4 cups all purpose flour
- 2 cups white sugar
- 2 teaspoons baking soda
- 1 teaspoon ground cloves
- 1 teaspoon ground nutmeg
- 1 teaspoon ground cinnamon
- 1 teaspoon ground allspice
- 1/2 teaspoon salt
- 2 eggs
- 1 cup chopped walnuts

Direction

- Preheat oven to 350 degrees F (175 degrees C).
- Lightly grease one 9 x 13 pan

- Cook raisins and water for 10 minutes over medium heat.
- Stir in the shortening.
- Remove from heat and let mixture cool.
- Combine flour, sugar, baking soda, ground cloves, ground nutmeg, ground cinnamon, ground allspice and salt.
- Add flour mixture to the cooled raisin mixture and blend well.
- Stir in the beaten eggs.
- Add the chopped nuts (if desired).
- Pour batter into prepared pan.
- Bake at 350 degrees F (175 degrees C) for 35 minutes, OR, until center springs back when lightly touched.
- When cake is cool, spread your favorite vanilla frosting on top.

214. Kahlua Praline Bars Recipe

Serving: 30 | Prep: | Cook: 25mins | Ready in:

Ingredients

- Crust:
- 1/3 cup packed brown sugar
- 2/3 cup all-purpose flour
- 1/3 cup butter or margarine
- 1/2 cup finely chopped pecans
- Filling:
- 2 ounces unsweetened chocolate
- 1/4 cup butter-flavored shortening
- 1/4 cup butter or margarine
- 1/2 cup packed brown sugar
- 1/4 cup granulated sugar
- 1 teaspoon vanilla
- 2 eggs
- 1/4 cup Kahlua liqueur
- 1/2 cup all-purpose flour
- 1/4 teaspoon salt
- 1/2 cup chopped pecans
- Frosting:
- 2 tablespoons butter or margarine, softened

- 1 tablespoon Kahlua liqueur
- 2 cups confectioners' sugar
- 1 tablespoon milk or cream

Direction

- Preheat oven to 350 degrees.
- Line an 8- or 9-inch-square pan with parchment, letting two opposite ends hang slightly over sides of pan.
- Crust:
- In large bowl, combine brown sugar, flour, margarine and pecans; mix well. Pat into bottom of prepared pan.
- Filling:
- In saucepan, melt chocolate, shortening and butter.
- Remove from heat; stir until smooth and slightly cooled.
- Beat in sugars and vanilla.
- Beat in eggs, one at a time.
- Stir in Kahlua, flour and salt.
- Add pecans.
- Pour over crust.
- Bake for 25 minutes or until fudgy.
- Do not overbake.
- Cool.
- Frosting:
- Beat together butter, Kahlua, confectioners' sugar and milk.
- Add more Kahlua if necessary to achieve spreading consistency. Frost cooled cake (either in the pan, or lifted out by the parchment paper handles).
- Let frosting set; slice into bars.
- Refrigerate.

215. Key Lime Bars Recipe

Serving: 36 | Prep: | Cook: 45mins | Ready in:

Ingredients

- 1 cup butter
- 1/2 cup powdered sugar
- 2 cups flour
- 4 eggs, beaten
- 2 cups sugar
- pinch salt
- 6 Tbls. bottled key lime juice
- 1 Tsp. baking powder
- additional confectioner's sugar for dusting

Direction

- Preheat oven to 350.
- For crust: Mix butter, 1/2 cup powdered sugar and 2 cups flour. Pat into a 9X13 inch greased pan.
- Bake for 20 minutes, or until pale golden in color.
- Beat together eggs, sugar, lime juice, add flour, salt and baking powder. Mix well and pour on top of crust. Bake for 25 minutes.
- Remove. When cool dust with powdered sugar. Cut into squares.
- Keep any remaining bars chilled.
- Note: Original recipe doesn't call for it, but I like to add fresh lime zest for extra lime flavor*

216. Killer Hazelnut Brownie Bars Recipe

Serving: 25 | Prep: | Cook: 25mins | Ready in:

Ingredients

- 1 stick butter, softened, plus extra for greasing the pan
- 1c turbinado sugar
- 1/2 vanilla bean, split and seeds scraped
- 1/4 tsp vanilla extract
- 2 eggs
- 1/4 c flour
- 1/4 c cake flour
- 1/4 c unsweetened cocoa powder
- 1/4 tsp baking powder
- 1/4 tsp salt
- 1/3 c chopped hazelnuts

- grenadine Frosting:
- 1 stick butter, softened
- 2 c powdered sugar
- 2 Tbs grenadine

Direction

- Preheat oven to 350.
- Line 8x8" baking pan with parchment. Lightly grease and flour.
- In standing mixer with paddle attachment, cream together butter, sugar, vanilla seeds and vanilla extract. Add eggs and mix till well incorporated.
- Mix together dry ingredients and add slowly to egg mixture. Mix till well incorporated.
- Pour the batter into prepared pan. Spread evenly, add hazelnuts to the top.
- Bake 22 to 25 mins until brownies are set and begin to pull away from the side.
- Remove from oven and let cool on wire rack. Once cooled, remove brownies from pan and cut into 1 1/2" squares for individual bites.
- Frosting: In large bowl use mixer to cream butter and slowly add powdered sugar. Add grenadine and mix until frosting consistency is reached.
- Prepare frosting in piping bag and pipe onto individual brownie bites.

217. Kit Kat Bars Recipe

Serving: 1 | Prep: | Cook: | Ready in:

Ingredients

- Ritz crackers
- 1-1/2 c. graham crackers, crushed
- 3/4 c. brown sugar
- 1 c. granulated sugar
- 3/4 c. butter or margarine
- 1/3 c. milk
- 1 tsp. vanilla
- 1 c. butterscotch chips
- 1 c. semisweet chocolate chips
- 3/4 c. smooth peanut butter

Direction

- Put graham crackers, brown sugar, white sugar, butter, milk in a saucepan; bring it to a boil. Boil for 5 minutes. Remove from heat and add vanilla.
- Place a layer of Ritz Crackers in a 13x9" pan and pour 1/2 of the mixture over it. Make another layer of Ritz Crackers and pour the remaining mixture. Add one last row of Ritz Crackers.
- Over low heat, melt both chips and peanut butter. When melted, spread evenly over the top layer of crackers. When cool, cut into desired bars or squares.

218. Lamington Bar Cake Recipe

Serving: 16 | Prep: | Cook: 45mins | Ready in:

Ingredients

- ¾ cup butter, softened
- ¾ cup caster sugar
- 3 eggs, lightly beaten
- 1 ¼ cups self raising flour
- 2 tbsp cocoa powder
- Icing:
- 1 ¾ oz dark chocolate, broken into pieces
- 5 tbsp milk
- 1 tsp butter
- ¾ cup icing sugar
- About 8 tbsp shredded coconut
- 150ml heavy cream

Direction

- Lightly grease a 1lb loaf tin about 3x10inches.
- Cream together butter and sugar until fluffy. Gradually add eggs, beating well after each addition. Sieve flour and cocoa powder. Fold into the mixture. Pour the mixture in the

prepared tin and level the top. Bake in a preheated oven, 350F, for 40 minutes or until springy to the touch. Leave to cool for 5 minutes in the tin, and then turn out to a wire rack to cool.
- Place chocolate, milk and butter in a heatproof bowl set over a pan of hot water. Stir until the chocolate has melted. Add the icing sugar beat until smooth. Leave to cool until thick enough to spread, and then spread it all over the cake. Sprinkle with the shredded coconut and allow the icing to set.
- Cut a V – shape wedge from the top of the cake. Put the cream in a piping bag fitted with a star nozzle. Pipe the cream down the center of the wedge and replace the wedge of the cake on top of the cream. Pipe another line of cream down either side of the wedge of cake. Serve.

219. Layered Chocolate Bars Recipe

Serving: 4 | Prep: | Cook: 1mins | Ready in:

Ingredients

- 1-1/2 c. finely crushed thin pretzels
- 3/4 c. (1-1/2 sticks) butter or margarine, melted
- 1 can (14 oz) sweetened condensed milk (not evaporated milk)
- 4 bars (4 oz) unsweetened baking chocolate, broken into pieces
- 2 c. Campfire miniature marshmallows
- 1 c. Mounds sweetened coconut Flakes
- 1 c. coarsely chopped pecans
- 4 bars (4 oz) Semi-Sweet baking chocolate, broken into pieces
- 1 Tbsp. shortening

Direction

- Heat oven to 350 degrees. Combine pretzels and melted butter in small bowl; press evenly into bottom of 13x9-inch baking pan.
- Place sweetened condensed milk and unsweetened chocolate in small microwave-safe bowl. Microwave at HIGH 1 to 1-1/2 minutes or until mixture is melted and smooth when stirred. Pour over pretzel layer in pan. Top with marshmallows, coconut and pecans; press firmly down onto chocolate layer. Bake 25 to 30 minutes or until lightly browned; cool completely in pan on wire rack.
- Melt semi-sweet chocolate and shortening in small microwave-safe bowl at HIGH for 1 minute or until melted when stirred; drizzle over entire top. Refrigerate 15 minutes or until set. Cut into bars.

220. Layered Chocolate Cheesecake Bars Recipe

Serving: 16 | Prep: | Cook: 45mins | Ready in:

Ingredients

- Crust:
- 20 chocolate wafer cookies
- 3 tablespoons unsalted butter, melted
- 1 tablespoon sugar
- 1/2 teaspoon ground coffee beans
- 1/4 teaspoon fine salt
- Filling:
- 8 ounces semisweet chocolate, finely chopped
- 8 ounces cream cheese, room temperature
- 2/3 cup sugar
- 1/2 cup sour cream
- 2 large eggs, room temperature
- Glaze:
- 4 ounces bittersweet chocolate, chopped
- 2 tablespoons unsalted butter
- 1 teaspoon light or dark corn syrup
- 2 tablespoons sour cream, room temperature
- 1/2 cup crushed candy canes (or walnuts)

Direction

- Preheat oven to 350 degrees F. Line an 8-inch square baking dish with foil.
- For the crust: Process the chocolate wafers in a food processor with the butter, sugar, coffee, and salt until fine. Evenly press the crust into the prepared dish covering the bottom completely. Bake until the crust sets, about 15 minutes.
- Meanwhile, make the filling: Put the chocolate in a medium microwave-safe bowl; heat at 75 percent power until softened, about 2 minutes. Stir, and continue to microwave until completely melted, up to 2 minutes more. (Alternatively put the chocolate in a heatproof bowl. Bring a saucepan filled with an inch or so of water to a very slow simmer; set the bowl over, but not touching, the water, and stir occasionally until melted and smooth.)
- Blend the cream cheese, sugar, and sour cream together in the food processor until smooth. Scrape down the sides, as needed. Add the eggs and pulse until just incorporated. With the food processor running, pour the chocolate into the wet ingredients and mix until smooth.
- Pour the filling evenly over the crust. Bake until filling puffs slightly around the edges, but is still a bit wobbly in the centre, about 25 to 30 minutes. Cool on a rack.
- For the Glaze: Put the chocolate, butter and corn syrup in microwave safe bowl. Heat glaze in the microwave at 75 percent power until melted, about 2 minutes. Stir the ingredients together until smooth; add the sour cream. Spread glaze evenly over the warm cake and scatter the crushed candy canes over top. Cool completely, then refrigerate overnight.
- Cut into small bars or squares. Serve chilled or room temperature.
- Store cookies covered in the refrigerator for up to 5 days.
- Cook's Note: To crush the candy canes, remove wrappers and place in a resealable plastic bag. Use a rolling pin to roll and break the candy up into small pieces, about 1/4 inch or so.

221. Layered Chunks Of Chocolate Squares Recipe

Serving: 16 | Prep: | Cook: 40mins | Ready in:

Ingredients

- vanilla cookie layer ....
- 8- tablespoons (1 stick) unsalted butter, melted and cooled to tepid...
- 1 2/3 cups vanilla wafer cookie crumbs (such as crumbs from Nabisco Nilla wafers)..
- Batter........
- 1 1/4 - cups bleached all-purpose flour
- 1/4- cup unsweetened cocoa powder
- 1/4- teaspoon baking powder
- 1/4- teaspoon salt
- 1/2- pound (2 sticks) unsalted butter, melted and cooled to tepid
- 6- ounces unsweetened chocolate, melted and cooled to tepid
- 5- large eggs.....
- 2- cups superfine sugar
- 2 1/2 - teaspoons vanilla extract
- 6- ounces bittersweet chocolate, coarsely chopped , for sprinkling on dark chocolate batter.......
- Powdered sugar for sifting over the top of the squares...

Direction

- Preheat oven to 325 degrees F.
- Film the inside of a 10 x 10 x 2inch baking pan with non-stick cooking spray.
- Pour the melted butter into the prepared pan.
- Spoon the cookie crumbs evenly over the bottom of the pan and press down lightly with the underside of a small metal spatula, so that the crumbs absorb the butter.
- Bake the cookie layer in the preheated oven for 4 minutes.
- Place the baking pan on a rack to cool for 10 minutes.

- Sift the flour, cocoa powder, baking powder, and salt onto a sheet of waxed paper.
- Whisk the melted butter and melted chocolate in a medium size mixing bowl until smooth.
- Ina large mixing bowl, whisk the eggs for 1 minute to blend, add sugar and whisk for another 45 seconds to 1 minute or until incorporated.
- Blend in the melted butter and chocolate mixture, mixing thoroughly.
- Blend in vanilla extract.
- Sift the flour mixture over and slowly stir (or whisk) it in, mixing until the particles of flour are absorbed.
- Stir in the 6 ounces of chopped chocolate.
- Spoon the batter in large dollops on the cookie crumb layer.
- Carefully spread the batter over the cookie layer, using a flexible knife or spatula.
- Scatter the 4 ounces of chopped chocolate on top of the batter.
- Bake the bars in a preheated oven for 35 to 40 minutes, or until set.
- Let the bars stand in the pan on a cooling rack for 2 hours. then refrigerate for 1 hour, or until firm enough to cut.
- Cut bars into quarters then cut each square into 4 quarters.
- Remove squares from baking pan, store in airtight container if you don't get them all eaten.
- Sift powdered sugar on squares before serving.
- Makes 16 squares.

222. Lemon Bars Recipe

Serving: 88 | Prep: | Cook: 35mins | Ready in:

Ingredients

- 1¼ cups flour
- ½ cup Confectioners sugar
- ½ teasp salt
- 12 tbsp butter, cut into 12 pieces and softened
- 7 egg yolks, Large
- 2 eggs, Large and whole
- 1 cup and 2 tbsp Granulated sugar
- ⅔ cup lemon juice (fresh)
- ¼ cup lemon zest (grated) (I sometimes use more for more flavor)
- 3 tbsp heavy cream

Direction

- Adjust oven rack to middle position and preheat to 350. Line a 9" square baking pan with two pieces of aluminum foil at right angles (to form a sort of sling). Lightly coat foil with vegetable oil.
- Mix together flour, confectioners' sugar and salt. Using a pastry cutter (or food processor) incorporate 8 tbsp. of the butter until the mixture is pale yellow and resembles coarse cornmeal.
- Sprinkle the mixture into the prepared pan and press firmly into an even layer. Bake until the crust starts to brown slightly, about 20 minutes.
- While crust is baking, whisk together egg yolks and whole eggs in a medium non-reactive saucepan.
- Whisk in granulated sugar until combined, then whisk in lemon juice, lemon zest, and a pinch of salt.
- Add remaining 4 tbsp. of butter and cook over medium-low heat, stirring constantly until the mixture thickens slightly and registers 170 degrees (F) on an instant-read thermometer, about 5 minutes.
- Strain the mixture immediately into a non-reactive bowl and stir in cream. Pour the warm curd over the hot crust. Bake until the filing is shiny and opaque and the center jiggles slightly when shaken, 10 to 15 minutes.
- Let cool completely on a wire rack, about 2 hours, before removing from the pan using foil and cutting into squares.
- Dust with confectioners' sugar just before serving.

- Note: it is important to pour the warm curd over the hot crust when making these intensely flavored bars. This ensures that the filling cooks through evenly. You will need about four lemons for zest and juice.

223. Lemon Cheesecake Bars Recipe

Serving: 16 | Prep: | Cook: 30mins | Ready in:

Ingredients

- 2 cups graham cracker crumbs
- 1/2 cup finely chopped pecans
- 1/2 cup sugar
- 1/2 cup butter, melted
- 2 (8 ounce) packages cream cheese, softened
- 1 (14 ounce) can sweetened condensed milk
- 2 eggs
- 1/2 cup+ lemon juice

Direction

- In a bowl, combine the cracker crumbs, pecans and sugar. Add butter; mix well. Set aside 1/2 cup. Press the remaining crumb mixture into a greased 13-in. x 9-in. x 2-in. baking dish. Bake at 325 degrees F for 8 minutes.
- Meanwhile, in a small mixing bowl, beat the cream cheese until smooth. Add the milk, eggs and lemon juice; beat until smooth. Spoon over crust. Sprinkle with the reserved crumb mixture. Bake for 30 minutes or until center is almost set. Cool on a wire rack. Store in the refrigerator.

224. Lemon Cream Cheese Bars Special Recipe

Serving: 10 | Prep: | Cook: 26mins | Ready in:

Ingredients

- Crust:
- 1 box of cake mix (Lemon, butter, Yellow or White)
- 1 1/2 sticks of melted butter (3/4 cup)
- 1/2 cup chopped walnuts (optional)
- Topping:
- 1 8oz. of cream cheese (you can use fat free)
- 2 cups powder sugar (extra for sprinkling after cooked)
- 2 Lg. eggs
- 1 large fresh lemon (1/3 cup juice)
- zest of 1 lemon (optional)

Direction

- Spray 9x13 baking pan, set oven at 350*
- Mix crust ingredients together until crumbly. Press into pan.
- Beat Topping ingredients until smooth. Pour over crust and bake.
- Check after 25 min. when lightly browned and not too jiggly, it will be done.
- Sprinkle with Powdered sugar when cool.

225. Lemon Custard Bars Recipe

Serving: 12 | Prep: | Cook: 25mins | Ready in:

Ingredients

- 1/3 cup butter
- 1 cup granulated sugar
- 1 cup all purpose flour
- 2 eggs
- 2 tablespoons all purpose flour
- 2 teaspoons finely shredded lemon peel
- 3 tablespoons lemon juice
- 1/4 teaspoon baking powder
- 1/8 teaspoon salt
- powdered sugar

Direction

- For crust in a medium mixing bowl beat butter with an electric mixer on medium to high speed until softened.
- Add 1/4 cup of the sugar and beat until thoroughly combined.
- Beat in 1 cup flour until mixture resembles fine crumbs.
- Press mixture into an ungreased square baking pan and bake at 350 for 15 minutes.
- Meanwhile for lemon mixture in the same mixing bowl beat eggs with an electric mixer on medium speed just until foamy then add remaining sugar, flour, lemon juice, baking powder and salt.
- Beat on medium speed for 3 minutes then stir in lemon peel.
- Pour lemon mixture over baked crust and bake at 350 for 25 minutes.
- Cool in pan on a rack.
- Sift powdered sugar over top.

226. Lemon Raspberry Cheesecake Bars Recipe

Serving: 30 | Prep: | Cook: 45mins | Ready in:

Ingredients

- Crust:
- Non-stick cooking spray
- 3/4 cup Crisco® butter flavor shortening (or 3/4 stick)
- 1/2 cup firmly packed brown sugar
- 1-1/4 cups all-purpose flour
- 1 cup uncooked oats
- 1/4 teaspoons salt
- Filling:
- 3/4 cup Smucker's® Seedless Red raspberry jam
- 16 ounces cream cheese, softened
- 3/4 cup sugar
- 2 tablespoons all-purpose flour
- 2 large eggs
- 3 tablespoons fresh lemon juice, no seeds please
- 2 teaspoons freshly grated lemon peel

Direction

- Preheat oven to 350°.
- Spray a 13x9x2-inch baking pan with non-stick cooking spray. Set aside.
- Crust:
- In a bowl, combine shortening and brown sugar, beat with an electric mixer at medium speed until well blended.
- Gradually add 1-1/4 cups flour, oats and salt.
- Beat at low speed until well blended.
- Press crust mixture into bottom of prepared pan.
- Bake for 20 minutes or until lightly browned.
- Filling:
- Let crust stand after removing from oven for 2 minutes.
- Spoon raspberry jam onto hot crust.
- Spread carefully to cover.
- In a bowl, combine cream cheese, sugar and 2 tablespoons flour.
- Beat with an electric mixer at low speed until well blended.
- Add eggs and beat again until well blended.
- Add lemon juice and lemon peel. Beat until smooth.
- Pour over the raspberry layer.
- Bake 25 minutes or until set.
- Remove pan and put on wire rack to cool.
- Let cool to room temperature.
- Cut into 30 bars.
- Cover and refrigerate any un-eaten portions.

227. Lemon Squares Recipe

Serving: 20 | Prep: | Cook: 45mins | Ready in:

Ingredients

- 1 C all purpose flour
- 1/2 C butter or margarine, softened

- 1/4 C Imperial sugar Confectioners powdered sugar or Dixie Crystals Confectioners powdered sugar
- 1 C Imperial sugar Extra Fine Granulated sugar or Dixie Crystals Extra Fine Granulated sugar
- 2 tsp grated lemon peel
- 2 T lemon juice
- 1/2 tsp baking powder
- 1/4 tsp salt
- 2 eggs

Direction

- Preheat oven to 350 degrees.
- Mix thoroughly flour, butter and powdered sugar in a small bowl. Press evenly with hands in bottom and about 5/8 inch up sides of an ungreased 8-inch square pan.
- If dough is sticky, flour fingers.
- Bake 20 minutes. Beat remaining ingredients in a medium bowl on medium speed until light and fluffy.
- Pour over hot crust. Bake just until no indentation remains when touched lightly in center, about 25 minutes. Let stand until cool, then cut into about 1 1/2 inch squares.

228. Lemonberry Jazz Bars Recipe

Serving: 36 | Prep: | Cook: 30mins | Ready in:

Ingredients

- Shortbread Crust Layer:
- 2 cups flour
- 1/2 cup confectioners sugar
- 1/2 stick butter, melted
- pinch of salt
- Lemon Curd* Layer:
- 4 medium sized lemons(or 5 small)
- 1 cup sugar
- 6 egg yolks
- 1 stick cold butter, cut into 16 pieces
- *about 2 cups of lemon curd will be needed so this layer can be made using 2 jars(8-10oz, each) of commercial lemon curd at room temperature
- Blueberry Layer:
- 2pts fresh blueberries, washed
- lemon Mousse Layer:
- 1 large package Cook and Serve vanilla pudding(NOT instant)
- 2 lemons
- milk as per directions, minus about 1/4 cup
- 2 cups heavy whipping cream, chilled
- 1/4 cup sugar
- white chocolate Layer:
- 6oz premium white chocolate(can use baking chocolate, but NOT confectioners coating)

Direction

- To Prepare Crust:
- Combine flour, confectioners' sugar and salt in medium bowl.
- Add melted butter and combine with fork (or hands) until mixed and mixture will stick when small amount is pressed together
- Press into bottom of a sprayed, glass 9X13 pan
- Bake at 350 for about 25 minutes until edges are just starting to lightly brown.
- Lemon Curd Layer:
- Set up double broiler, or medium stainless steel bowl over a slightly smaller bowl of boiling water, being careful that the bottom of the top pan does not touch the water.
- While water is heating, beat egg yolks and sugar in the stainless steel bowl. Whisk together until smooth, then add juice and zest from all 4 lemons, and continue to whisk until combined.
- Place pan over the simmering water and heat while folding and stirring mixture constantly, until it thickens, well. This will take about 10 minutes.
- Add butter pieces one at a time, whisking thoroughly after each, until all are added and mixed in.
- Remove from heat and set in fridge to cool

- Once cooled, carefully spread over cooled crust, covering to edges
- Top this layer with the fresh blueberries
- Lemon Mousse Layer:
- Prepare pudding per package directions, using 1/4 cup less, milk.
- When thickened and done, add the zest and juice of 2 lemons and stir to combine.
- Let cool completely in fridge.
- Once pudding has cooled, whip the whipping cream and sugar in mixer at medium high speed until stiff peaks form.
- Fold small amount of whipped cream into bowl of cooled pudding, and gently stir until somewhat incorporated.
- Then add this mixture back into mixing bowl with remaining whipped cream, and fold gently until mixture is a uniform color, and well combined.
- Carefully spread this layer over blueberries, covering to edge.
- Cool in fridge for about 10 minutes
- White Chocolate Layer:
- Melt 6oz white chocolate in microwave for 2-3 minutes, stirring well every minute, until melted and smooth.
- Drizzle chocolate over mousse layer using a plastic bag or cake decorator method. Continue to drizzle in layers until all chocolate is gone. This will give you a drizzled appearance, but a near solid layer of chocolate.
- Chill bars in fridge a few hours for layers to set up. Cut.
- ~~Please note that the lovely drizzling of the chocolate did not hold up well to cutting into bars. A possible solution to this would be to chill well and cut into bars BEFORE adding the chocolate, then just chill the individual bars, slightly after drizzling individual bars.

229. Linzer Torte Bars Recipe

Serving: 24 | Prep: | Cook: 25mins | Ready in:

Ingredients

- 1 C all-purpose flour
- 1 C powdered sugar
- 1 C ground walnuts
- 1/2 C margarine or butter, softened
- 1/2 tsp. ground cinnamon
- 2/3 Red raspberry preserves
- (To make apricot Linzer Bars: Substitute ground almonds for the ground walnuts and apricot preserves for the raspberry preserves.)
- Be sure and use the pan size called for in this recipe. cookie dough needs to be spread to the sides and into the corners of the pan.

Direction

- Heat oven to 375 degrees.
- Mix all ingredients except preserves until crumbly.
- Press two-thirds of mixture in ungreased square pan, 9X9X2-inches.
- Spread with preserves.
- Sprinkle with remaining crumbs.
- Press gently into preserves.
- Bake 20 to 25 minutes or until light golden brown. (Cookies are done when a toothpick is inserted into the centre of the pan. If it comes out wet, they need more time.)
- Cool completely in the pan. Cut into 48 bars or 18 for a larger bar.

230. Luscious Layer Bars Recipe

Serving: 1 | Prep: | Cook: 45mins | Ready in:

Ingredients

- 1 pouch (1 lb 1.5 oz) Betty Crocker® chocolate chip cookie mix
- 1/2 cup butter or margarine, softened
- 1 egg
- 1 cup butterscotch chips

- 1 cup milk chocolate chips or semisweet chocolate chips
- 1 cup flaked coconut
- 1 cup chopped walnuts
- 1 can (14 oz) sweetened condensed milk (not evaporated)

Direction

1. Heat oven to 350°F. Spray bottom of 13x9-inch pan with cooking spray.
2. In large bowl, stir cookie mix, butter and egg until soft dough forms. Press dough in bottom of pan using floured fingers.
3. Bake 15 minutes. Sprinkle with butterscotch chips, chocolate chips, coconut and walnuts. Drizzle evenly with condensed milk.
4. Bake 30 to 35 minutes or until light golden brown. Cool completely, about 2 hours. For bars, cut into 9 rows by 4 rows.

231. Macadamia Fudge Squares Recipe

Serving: 12 | Prep: | Cook: 15mins | Ready in:

Ingredients

- 1 cup all-purpose flour, spooned in and leveled
- 1/4 teaspoon ground cinnamon
- 1/4 teaspoon salt
- 1 cup (2 sticks) unsalted butter
- 4 ounces unsweetened chocolate, coarsely chopped
- 1 cup (lightly packed) very fresh dark brown sugar
- 1 cup granulated sugar
- 4 large eggs, well beaten
- 1 teaspoon pure vanilla extract
- 1 1/2 to 1 3/4 cups coarsely chopped, salted macadamia nuts
- 1 small recipe Midnight chocolate glaze (recipe follows)
- Midnight chocolate glaze Ingredients:
- 1/2 cup water
- 1/4 cup granulated sugar
- 2 tablespoons light corn syrup
- 4 ounces fine-quality bittersweet chocolate, such as Lindt, finely chopped
- 1/4 cup strained powdered sugar
- 1 tablespoon Dutch-process cocoa powder
- 1 teaspoon pure vanilla extract
- 1/4 teaspoon lemon juice
- Pinch of salt
- 1 tablespoon unsalted butter, soft

Direction

- Position the rack in the middle of the oven. Heat the oven to 375°F. Line a 10 1/2 x 15 1/2 x 1-inch jelly roll pan with aluminum foil and butter the foil.
- In a medium bowl, thoroughly whisk together the flour, cinnamon, and salt. Set aside.
- In a large bowl set over a pot of barely simmering water, slowly melt the butter and the chocolate. Stir occasionally. Remove from the heat and, using a whisk, blend the brown sugar into the mixture, stirring until melted. Gradually mix in the granulated sugar. Stir in the eggs and the vanilla. Add the dry ingredients, stirring just until combined. Do not over mix.
- Spread the batter evenly in the prepared pan, smoothing it with the back of a tablespoon. Sprinkle the surface with the macadamia nuts and press them gently into the batter.
- Bake for 13 to 15 minutes, or until the top is set and the bar begins to pull away from the sides of the pan. Do not over bake. The squares should remain slightly moist on the inside. (Note: If the batter rises in the pan during baking, prick the bubbles gently with a fork to release the air.) Remove from the oven and let stand until almost cool.
- While the bar is cooling, make the glaze. To web the bar, dip a small whisk into the glaze and squiggle it across the pan. If the glaze becomes too thick, thin it with a little very hot water. Let stand until the glaze is set.

- Carefully lift the bar from the pan by grasping the foil on both sides and place it on a large cutting board. Pull down the sides of the foil and cut into 2-inch squares using a thin-bladed, sharp knife.
- Storage: Store in an airtight container, layered between strips of wax paper, for up to 5 days. These cookies may be frozen.
- Directions for the Midnight Chocolate Glaze:
- Place the water in a 3-quart heavy-bottomed saucepan. Add the granulated sugar and corn syrup, but do not stir. Cover and bring to a slow boil on medium-low heat. After 1 minute, check to see if any sugar crystals remain. If so, gently stir the mixture. Continue to cook the syrup uncovered for 3 to 4 minutes. (Large bubbles will form on the surface.)
- Remove the pan from the heat and sprinkle the chopped chocolate over the syrup. Push the chocolate gently into the syrup, but do not stir. Let stand for 2 to 3 minutes, until the chocolate is melted, then stir gently with a small whisk.
- When smooth, stir in the powdered sugar and cocoa powder, then blend in the vanilla, lemon juice, and salt. Stir gently with the whisk until smooth, then blend in the butter. If the glaze is not pourable, add 3 or 4 teaspoons of very hot water until the desired consistency is reached.
- Note: This glaze is best used immediately. Storage: Leftover glaze can be refrigerated for several weeks.

232. Macadamia Layer Bars Recipe

Serving: 36 | Prep: | Cook: 30mins | Ready in:

Ingredients

- 2 1/2 cups chocolate cookie crumbs*
- 1/2 cup butter, melted
- 1/4 cup sugar
- 1 (14-oz.) can sweetened condensed milk
- 2 (12-oz.) pkg. white baking chips
- 1 1/2 cups sweetened flaked coconut
- 1 1/2 cups unsalted macadamia nuts, chopped

Direction

- Heat oven to 325°F. Line 13x9-inch pan with foil; spray with cooking spray. Line bottom with parchment paper; spray with cooking spray.
- Combine cookie crumbs, melted butter and sugar in medium bowl; press firmly into bottom of pan. Pour condensed milk over crust, covering evenly. Sprinkle with white baking chips, coconut and nuts; press down evenly.
- Bake 30 to 35 minutes or until lightly browned. Cool completely. Remove bars with foil; slide off foil and parchment paper. Cut into 36 bars.
- TIP *Crush chocolate wafer cookies or chocolate sandwich cookies in food processor or in plastic bag with rolling pin (about 50 wafer cookies or 23 sandwich cookies).

233. Magic Cookie Bar Mix For Gifts Recipe

Serving: 12 | Prep: | Cook: 25mins | Ready in:

Ingredients

- 1-6oz. package chocolate chips
- 1-3 1/2oz. bag flaked coconut or 1 1/3 C.
- 1 C. chopped pecans
- 1 1/2 C. graham cracker crumbs

Direction

- Use a 1 quart, wide-mouth canning jar.
- Pack each layer.
- To the jar add the chocolate chips, the coconut, and the pecans.
- Place the graham cracker crumbs into a plastic sandwich bag or sealing bag and place the bag in the jar on top of the packed ingredients.

- Seal and decorate the jar, and attach the following instructions on a recipe tag.
- MAGIC COOKIE BARS
- You will need:
- 1/2 c. butter, melted
- 1-14oz. can condensed milk
- Use a 9x13x2" baking pan and pour in the melted butter.
- Spread the graham cracker crumbs.
- In a large bowl, add the condensed milk and the jar contents and mix.
- Pour onto the crumbs and pack firmly in the pan.
- Bake at 350 degrees for 25-30 minutes or until lightly golden.
- Cool.

234. Magic Cookie Bars Recipe

Serving: 36 | Prep: | Cook: 30mins | Ready in:

Ingredients

- 1/2 cup margarine or butter
- 1 1/2 cups graham cracker crumbs or digestive biscuit crumbs
- 14 ounce can of sweetened condensed milk
- 6 ounces of semi-sweet chocolate chips
- 3 1/2 ounce can of flaked coconut (1 1/3 cups)
- 1 cup chopped nuts

Direction

- Preheat oven to 350 degrees.
- If using a glass dish preheat to 325 degrees.
- In 13 x 9 inch baking dish, melt margarine in oven.
- Sprinkle crumbs over margarine.
- Pour sweetened condensed milk evenly over the crumbs.
- Top with remaining ingredients: the chocolate chips, coconut and nuts.
- Press down on the mixture with a spatula.
- Bake 25 to 30 minutes or until lightly browned.
- Cool.
- Chill if desired.
- Cut into bars.
- Store loosely covered at room temperature.

235. Mals Magic Bars Recipe

Serving: 12 | Prep: | Cook: 50mins | Ready in:

Ingredients

- For the coconut mixture:
- 1 small bag coconut flakes, chopped fine in blender
- 1 Tbspn room temp, unsalted butter
- 3-4 eggs
- 1 capful vanilla extract
- 1/3 cup granulated sugar
- 1/4 cup dark brown sugar
- 1/4 cup unsweetened cocoa powder
- 2 Tbspns milk
- _
- For fudge mixture:
- 1/2 box worth of Duncan Hines or Betty Crocker chocolate cake mix
- Substitute oil for room temp butter, but use half of what the box calls for.
- Use half the eggs it asks for, rounding up. (i.e. if it says three, use two)
- 1/3 cup granulated sugar
- 1 cup marshmellow fluff
- 1 capful vanilla extract
- 1 capful almond extract
- tspn salt
- 1/2 small bag of semi-sweet chocolate chips
- chocolate syrup
- Extra coconut for garnish

Direction

- First you have to screw up... I mean concoct the coconut mixture. Add the chopped coconut, the sugars, cocoa powder, butter, extract and all but one of the eggs into a large

mixing bowl and beat until blended, then add milk.
- Not sure if this had anything to do with the consistency, but you can bake it for a little while first, then mix it up and add the last egg, but you don't have to. If you're lazy you can just use it raw, but it helps if it's been refrigerated for at least 2 hours before using it in the bars.
- When you're ready, preheat the oven to 350F.
- Combine cake mix, butter, eggs, sugar, extracts and a teaspoon of salt to a mixing bowl and blend well. DO NOT add milk. It will look like brownie mix, that's good.
- In a greased and floured rectangle baking dish, spread the mixture evenly so it coats the entire bottom. It will be thin, that's okay.
- Bake at 350 F until done, 20-25 minutes, until cake tester or toothpick comes out clean. Remove from oven but don't turn it off or attempt to take the cake out of the pan.
- This is the tricky part... flatten coconut mixture in a thin layer over the cake without ripping the cake. This will involve getting your hands dirty. If you do it while the cake is still hot, the mixture will melt a bit, that's okay. Try to get a uniform layer over the fudge base, and not to leave any holes.
- (Then clean your hands, they'll be gooey) Stick the pan back into the oven for 10 minutes until your coconut layer has browned slightly at the edges.
- After that, use a spoon or spatula to spread a layer of marshmallow fluff over the whole mess. Then add a whole bunch of chocolate chips.
- Squeeze some chocolate syrup over the marshmallow. Get creative with the designs!
- Add whatever leftover coconut you may have over it and viola, you're done!
- For best results, stick the whole mess in the fridge to let it set. Cut into squares, serve and enjoy!

236. Maraschino Cherry Bars Recipe

Serving: 36 | Prep: | Cook: 15mins | Ready in:

Ingredients

- MARASCHINO CHERRY BARS
- Crust:
- 2 cups flour
- 1/3 cup sugar
- 3/4 cup butter (or marg.), softened
- Filling:
- 2 eggs, slightly beaten
- 1 cup firmly packed brown sugar
- 1/3 cup flour
- 1 1/2 tsp. baking powder
- 1/2 tsp. salt
- 1/2 tsp. vanilla
- 10-oz. jar maraschino cherries, drained/chopped (reserve juice)
- 1/2 cup chopped walnuts
- Frosting:
- 2 Tbsp. butter (or marg.), softened
- 2 1/2 cups powdered sugar
- 3 to 4 Tbsp. reserved cherry juice
- 3 to 4 Tbsp. flaked coconut

Direction

- Heat oven to 350 degrees. In large bowl, combine first 3 ingredients; blend until crumbly. Press mixture into ungreased 13x9-inch pan.
- Bake at 350 for 12 to 15 minutes or until lightly browned.
- In small bowl, combine all filling ingredients; mix well. Pour over crust. Bake at 350 for 20 to 25 minutes or until toothpick inserted in center comes out clean. Cool.
- In small bowl, combine all frosting ingredients except coconut; beat until light and fluffy. Spread frosting over cooled bars; sprinkle with coconut. Cut into 36 bars.

237. Marbled Chocolate Nut Bars Recipe

Serving: 1 | Prep: | Cook: 30mins | Ready in:

Ingredients

- 1 box German chocolate cake mix
- 1-8 oz. cream cheese, softened
- 1/2 c. sugar
- 1 c. milk chocolate chips, divided
- 1/2 to 3/4 c. chopped nuts

Direction

- Prepare cake mix according to directions. Pour into a 10×15 inch baking pan.
- In a small bowl, mix cream cheese and sugar. Stir in 1/4 to 1/2 cup chocolate chips. Drop by teaspoonfuls over batter. Cut through batter with a knife to swirl the cream cheese mixture. Sprinkle remaining chocolate chips and nuts over top. Bake @ 350° for 30 minutes or until a toothpick inserted comes out clean. Cool and cut into bars.

238. Mars Bar Chocolate Muffins Recipe

Serving: 12 | Prep: | Cook: 20mins | Ready in:

Ingredients

- 2 cups all-purpose flour
- 1/2 cup sugar
- 4 Tbsp cocoa powder
- 2 Tsp baking powder
- 1/2 tsp baking soda
- 1/2 tsp salt
- dash of cinnamon
- 1 cup milk
- 1/2 cup veg oil
- 1 egg slightly beaten
- 1 or 2 Mars Bars, cut into small, bite-sized chunks

Direction

- Preheat oven to 350F / 170C / Gas Mark 4.
- Line muffin tin with cupcake papers, or oil and flour.
- Combine dry ingredients in mixing bowl (mix together with a whisk).
- Add milk, oil and egg. Mix with spoon until dry ingredients are moist.
- Stir in Mars Bar chunks.
- Fill cups to top.
- Bake for 20 minutes. (Do not open oven door for the first 10 minutes.)
- Let cool in pan for a few minutes, then transfer to cooling rack.

239. Mars Bar Squares Recipe

Serving: 8 | Prep: | Cook: 5mins | Ready in:

Ingredients

- 5-6 regular sized Mars Bars candy bars
- 1 tbsp margarine or butter
- 1 cup rice Krispies or chocolate flavor rice Krispies
- 1 tbsp honey
- 1/2 cup chopped almonds
- 1/2 of a baking chocolate bar (semisweet is fine)

Direction

- Soften the Mars Bars in a bowl in the microwave until just soft and easy to stir, do not completely melt- only soften please!
- Mix the margarine or butter and stir into the softened Mars Bars.
- Add the honey and combine well.
- Add in the Rice cereal (chocolate flavor the best) folding carefully so not to crush cereal the mixture.
- Stir in the almonds.

- Pour the mixture into a square cake pan, so that the thickness of the bars will be approx. 1 inch.
- Melt the cooking chocolate over slow heat or microwave.
- Coat the Mars Bars with chocolate in a buttered cake pan.
- The amount would depend on how much chocolate you like.
- Spread melted chocolate out to edges and sprinkle more chopped almonds on, pressing some into melted chocolate.
- Chill till firm and cut into bars.

240. Marshmallow Creme Banana Bars Recipe

Serving: 24 | Prep: | Cook: 20mins | Ready in:

Ingredients

- ½ cup solid shortening
- 1 cup white sugar
- ¼ cup brown sugar
- 1 egg
- ¼ cup sour cream
- 1 teaspoon baking soda, dissolved in 1 tablespoon water
- 1 teaspoon vanilla extract
- ½ teaspoon banana flavoring (I rarely have this on hand, and it can be omitted)
- 1½ cups mashed ripe bananas
- 1½ cups flour
- 1 teaspoon baking powder
- ¼ teaspoon salt
- 7 ounce jar marshmallow crème
- Browned butter caramel Frosting (recipe posted separately)

Direction

- Cream together shortening and both sugars.
- Stir in egg thoroughly, then stir in sour cream, baking soda/water mixture, extract, and flavoring (if using); blend well.
- Add mashed bananas to creamed mixture alternately with dry ingredients; mix together until all ingredients are incorporated into batter.
- Pour batter into lightly sprayed or greased 10x15 baking sheet.
- Bake at 350 degrees for about 18 to 22 minutes, or until top springs back when poked with your finger.
- Remove pan from oven and immediately drop spoonfuls of marshmallow crème over top of bars.
- Allow crème to set on bars for a couple minutes, allowing the heat from the bars to melt the crème enough to allow you to use the back of a spoon to spread the crème over the top of the bar (use a soft touch or you will pull up the top of the bars as you spread).
- NOTE: Do not spread the crème to the very edge of the pan – it will melt down between the pan and the bars, making a mess when trying to cut the bars. I leave just an inch or so between the crème and the edge of the baking pan.
- When bars have cooled completely, frost very gently with the browned butter caramel frosting – you don't want to pull up the crème as you frost, so I use a pretty thin frosting, almost like a glaze, and gently spread over the crème.

241. Marshmallow Whipped Hershey Bar Pie Recipe

Serving: 8 | Prep: | Cook: 10mins | Ready in:

Ingredients

- 1 prepared graham cracker crust, homemade or store-bought
- 1/3 cup milk
- 18 - 20 large marshmallows, Jet Puffed
- 6 Hershey milk chocolate Bars (approximately 9 oz)

- 1 cup heavy whipping cream
- 1/2 teaspoon vanilla

Direction

- In a double boiler or a bowl set over a pot of water, combine milk and marshmallows.
- Heat, stirring occasionally to melt marshmallows, until marshmallows are partially melted.
- Add Hershey Bars and stir often until everything is melted.
- Remove from heat and let cool completely (approximately 1 hour)
- In a bowl, preferably metal, whip the heavy cream until fluffy.
- Stir in the vanilla.
- Fold the whipped cream into the cooled chocolate mixture.
- Scoop it all into the graham cracker pie shell.
- Chill for 4 hours or better yet, overnight.
- Note: If you are using a small store-bought graham cracker crust, it may overflow.
- This pie should serve 8-10 and pushing it at 12 people
- Homemade Graham Cracker Crust:
- Mix together 1-1/4 cups graham cracker crumbs, 3 Tablespoons sugar and 6 Tablespoons melted butter.
- Press into a greased 9 inch glass pie plate and bake at 350 for 8-10 minutes.
- Allow to cool completely before placing ingredients in.

242. Marzipan Bars Recipe

Serving: 36 | Prep: | Cook: 60mins | Ready in:

Ingredients

- Crust:
- 21/2c flour
- 3/4c sugar
- 1/2tsp salt
- 1c9icks) cold unsalted butter,cut up
- 1 large egg,beaten
- Filling:
- 11/4c sugar
- 3/4c blanched or natural almonds
- 1/4c flour
- 1/2c(1 stick) unsalted butter,softened
- 3 lg. eggs
- 1 tsp almond extract
- 1tsp vanilla
- 2 to 3 drops green food coloring,if desired
- 1/2c seedless raspberry jam
- 6 oz. bittersweet chocolate,chopped
- 2tsp vegetable shortening.
- 3/4c hazelnuts,toasted,skins removed

Direction

- Crust: Preheat oven to350. Line a jelly roll pan with foil, letting foil extend 2" at ends. In food processor, pulse flour, sugar and salt to combine. Add butter and pulse till mixture is texture of coarse meal.
- Add egg and pulse until dough begins to hold together. Press dough evenly over bottom and sides of pan. Refrigerate 15 mins. Bake 20 to 22 mins, or till crust is browned at edges and golden in the center. Cool on rack while making filling.
- Filling: In food processor, process sugar, almonds, hazelnuts and flour till nuts are finely ground. Add butter and 1 egg. Process till smooth. Add remaining eggs, almond extract, vanilla extract, and green food coloring if using. Process till blended.
- Spread jam filling over bottom of crust. Spoon filling over jam and spread to cover. Bake 30 to 35 mins, until filling is golden brown and firm in center. Let cool completely on wire rack.
- Melt chocolate with shortening. Spread over filling. Refrigerate till chocolate sets. Cut into squares, decorate if desired.

243. Melting Moments Lemon Bars Recipe

Serving: 36 | Prep: | Cook: 45mins | Ready in:

Ingredients

- Base:
- 2 cups flour
- 2/3 cup powdered sugar
- 1 cup butter, softened but not melted
- Filling:
- 4 eggs, beaten until frothy
- 6 tablespoons fresh squeezed lemon juice
- ¼ cup flour
- 1 teaspoon baking powder
- 2 cups white sugar
- 2 tablespoons fresh grated lemon rind
- Glaze:
- 1 cup powdered sugar
- 1 teaspoon vanilla extract
- 1 tablespoons butter, melted
- enough fresh squeezed lemon juice to make it into a glaze

Direction

- Mix together the base ingredients with a pastry blender or food processor (the mixture should resemble crumbs).
- Firmly pat it into a lightly sprayed 9x13 baking dish.
- Bake at 350 degrees for 20 minutes.
- While the base is baking, prepare the filling by beating the eggs together in a medium sized bowl.
- In a separate small bowl, mix together the lemon juice, flour and baking powder to make a smooth paste. Add some of the beaten eggs if necessary, to make it smooth and runny.
- Add the sugar and grated lemon rind to the beaten eggs, then stir in the flour mixture. Mix ingredients together until smooth and well blended.
- Pour filling over the hot base and return pan to oven.
- Bake an additional 25 minutes, until filling is set.
- Prepare the glaze by mixing all ingredients together until smooth and runny enough to drizzle over the filling.
- When the bars are removed from the oven, immediately use a fork to poke several holes in the filling with the fork tines, then quickly pour the glaze over the top of the bars and let it soak into the top and into the tiny holes made by the fork tines.
- Cool bars completely before cutting into squares.

244. Mexican Bars Recipe

Serving: 32 | Prep: | Cook: 35mins | Ready in:

Ingredients

- 1/2 cup shortening (butter or combo)
- 2 cup sugar white
- 3 eggs
- 1 1/2 cups flour
- 1 tsp. baking powder
- 1/4 tsp salt
- Topping:
- 1 cup nuts (I like almonds or walnuts)chopped
- 1 cup chocolate chips
- 1 cup miniature marshmallows

Direction

- Cream together shortening and 1 cup sugar till smooth. Add one whole 1 and 2 egg yolks (set egg whites aside).
- Gradually add flour, baking powder and salt.
- Spread in a 9 x 13 pan.
- On top sprinkle nuts, chocolate chips and marshmallows.
- Beat the 2 egg whites with 1 cup sugar and spread on top of the nut, chip and marshmallow mixture.
- Bake at 350 degrees for 30-40 minutes.

- Cut while still hot - if you wait you might just have to eat the "whole" thing LOL

245. Meyer Lemon Bars Recipe

Serving: 12 | Prep: | Cook: 18mins | Ready in:

Ingredients

- 'm ashamed to admit it but I am a lemon bar snob. I'm not proud of it. Well, maybe the word snob is a bit harsh. Let's just say that I have very strong preferences when it comes to lemon bars.
- I prefer a delicate, buttery crust with a slight "snap" to it. And the crust should never be more than half the overall height of the lemon bar. I don't want to chew endlessly on an overly thick and, inevitably, tough crust. Or even worse, mash my way through the gummy mess of an underdone crust.
- I prefer a dominant lemon flavor untainted by the milkiness of cream, evaporated or condensed milk. It should be just tart enough to make my mouth pucker a teeny bit. Don't get me wrong. A creamy lemon confection has its place in my dessert kingdom, but not in the form of lemon bars. Sorry, milk, but tart is king.
- I prefer my lemon filling to be smooth and soft, but not runny. When the filling hits my tongue it should be luscious. Overcooking the filling will turn the lemon bar into a sponge. No one wants to eat a lemon flavored sponge, least of all me.
- I prefer my lemon bars dusted with confectioners' sugar. But not so heavily dusted that exhaling will shower the table (or your neighbor) with sugar.
- And finally, I prefer to eat my lemon bars with a fork. That's not snobbish, is it?

Direction

- Meyer Lemon Bars
- (Makes one 8-inch square pan)
- Crust:
- 1 cup all-purpose flour
- 1/2 cup confectioners' sugar
- 1/8 tsp. salt
- 4 ounces (1 stick) unsalted butter, cold and cut into 1/2 inch pieces
- Filling:
- 2 large eggs
- 1 cup superfine or bakers' sugar
- 2 tbsp. all-purpose flour
- 1/8 tsp. salt
- 2 tsp. finely grated Meyer lemon zest*
- 1/4 cup freshly squeezed Meyer lemon juice*
- Preheat oven to 350F. Butter and line an 8-inch square pan with parchment paper.
- To make crust:
- Combine flour, confectioners' sugar and salt in the bowl of a food processor. Add butter and pulse until the mixture is pebbly. Press evenly into the bottom of your prepared pan. Bake until lightly golden, about 18-20 minutes. Set aside crust.
- To make filling:
- In a medium bowl, whisk together eggs, sugar, flour and salt. Whisk in lemon zest and juice until well combined. Pour over crust (it's okay if crust is still hot). Bake until filling is just set, about 15 to 18 minutes. Cool completely before serving. Dust with confectioners' sugar if desired.

246. Michelles Vegan Granola Bars Recipe

Serving: 16 | Prep: | Cook: 15mins | Ready in:

Ingredients

- 1 cup quick-cooking oats
- 1 cup large-flake oats
- ¼ cup apple cider
- ¼ cup vegetable oil

- ¼ cup whole flax seeds
- ¼ cup sesame seeds
- ¼ cup chopped almonds
- ½ cup chopped, dried fruit
- ½ cup rice syrup, maple syrup or agave nectar

Direction

- Preheat oven to 350F.
- Combine all ingredients in a large bowl.
- Turn out and press into a baking pan.
- Bake 15 minutes and leave to cool completely on sheet before cutting and wrapping.

247. Milk Chocolate Bar Cake Recipe

Serving: 12 | Prep: | Cook: 25mins | Ready in:

Ingredients

- 1 package Swiss chocolate cake mix
- 1 package cream cheese, softened (I used low-fat and it was fine)
- 1 cup icing sugar
- 1/2 cup sugar
- 10 milk chocolate bars with almonds (50g each)
- 1 container frozen whipped topping, thawed

Direction

- Prepare cake mix according to package directions. Pour into 3 greased and floured 8" round cake pans.
- Bake at 325F for 20-30 mins or until wooden toothpick inserted in centre comes out clean. Cool in pans on wire racks for 10 mins. Remove from pans, and cool completely on racks.
- Beat cream cheese and both sugars at medium speed of electric mixer until creamy.
- Finely chop 8 of the chocolate bars. Fold, along with cream cheese mixture, into whipped topping.
- Spread icing between layers and on top and sides of cake.
- Chop remaining 2 chocolate bars and sprinkle half over top of cake. Press remaining along bottom edge of cake.

248. Milk Chocolate Candy Bar Cake Recipe

Serving: 18 | Prep: | Cook: 25mins | Ready in:

Ingredients

- 1 Swiss chocolate cake mix (18.25 oz)
- 1 cream cheese, softened (8 oz)
- 1 cup powdered sugar
- 1/2 cup granulated sugar
- 10 milk chocolate candy bars with almonds (I used Hersheys)(1.5 oz each)
- 1 frozen whipped topping, thawed (12 oz)

Direction

- Prepare cake batter according to the package directions.
- Pour into 3 greased and floured 8 in round cake pans.
- Bake at 350 degrees for 20 to 25 minutes.
- Cool in pans on wire racks for about 10 minutes; remove from pans and cool completely on wire racks.
- Beat cream cheese, powdered sugar and granulated sugar at medium speed until mixture is creamy.
- Chop 8 of the candy bars finely.
- Fold cream cheese mixture and chopped candy into whipped topping.
- Spread icing between layers and on top and sides of cakes.
- Chop remaining 2 candy bars.
- Sprinkle half of chopped candy bars over cake.
- Press remaining chopped candy along bottom edge of cake.

249. Millionaire Shortbread Bars Recipe

Serving: 16 | Prep: | Cook: 20mins | Ready in:

Ingredients

- For shortbread:
- 3/4 cup unsalted butter,room temperature
- 1/4 cup white sugar
- 1/2 Tsp. pure vanilla extract
- 1 1/2 cups all purpose flour
- 1/8 Tsp. salt
- For caramel filling:
- 1-14 Oz can/jar Dulce De leche
- chocolate topping:
- 6 ounces semi-sweet or bittersweet chocolate,cut into pieces.Use a good quality chocolate*
- 1/2 Tsp.unsalted butter

Direction

- Preheat oven to 350 (177 degrees C).Place rack in center of oven. Grease a 9X9 (23 X23 cm) with butter or cooking spray.
- For shortbread: With a mixer, cream the butter and sugar until fluffy. Beat in vanilla. Add flour and salt and beat until dough just comes together. Press onto the bottom of greased pan and bake for 20 minutes, or until pale golden in color. Remove from oven, place on wire rack to cool while filling is prepared.
- For caramel filling. Place caramel filling in a bowl set over a saucepan of simmering water, until warmed through. (If you cannot find Dulce De Leche -you can make your own>1 14 oz. can sweetened condensed milk, in a heat proof bowl over pan of simmering water. Cook and cover, over low heat, stirring occasionally for 45-60 minutes, until milk has thickened and has turned a light caramel color.)
- Remove from heat blend until smooth. Pour caramel over the baked shortbread and leave to set.
- For topping: Melt the chocolate and butter either in microwave oven in a heatproof bowl or over a saucepan of simmering water. Always remember to keep water away from chocolate, make sure your bowl is completely dry*
- Pour the chocolate evenly over the caramel, spreading with a rubber spatula if necessary, and leave to set. Cut the shortbread into pieces using a sharp knife.
- Store in refrigerator to keep chocolate nice and firm.

250. Millionaire Squares Recipe

Serving: 14 | Prep: | Cook: 5mins | Ready in:

Ingredients

- 1 medium package of Dad's coconut cookies, crushed finely.
- 1/2 cup melted butter
- 2 cups icing sugar
- 1/2 cup butter
- 1/2 cup chocolate chips
- 1/2 tsp. vanilla extract
- 1/2 cup chopped nuts
- 1 egg, beaten

Direction

- Crust:
- Mix cookie crumbs (reserving 1 cup) with the melted butter and press into an 8x8 baking pan.
- Bake at 400F for 5 minutes.
- Remove from oven and cool.
- Topping:
- In a saucepan over medium-low heat, melt together the 1/2 cup of butter with the chocolate chips, vanilla and nuts.
- Add in the icing sugar and beaten egg and stir until very smooth, about one minute.
- Spread this mixture atop the cooled crust.

- Sprinkle the reserved crumbs on top.
- Let sit or refrigerate before cutting into squares.
- You can leave the nuts out of this recipe very successfully. In fact, it's much creamier if you do. Freezes very well.

251. Mint Nanaimo Bars Recipe

Serving: 12 | Prep: | Cook: 20mins | Ready in:

Ingredients

- Base:
- 1/2 c butter
- 1/4 c white sugar
- 5 tbsp cocoa powder
- 1 egg, beaten
- 1 tsp vanilla
- 1 1/2 c graham cracker crumbs
- 1 c unsweetened shredded coconut
- 1/2 c chopped walnuts, toasted
- Filling:
- 1/3 c butter
- 1/4 c milk
- 3 tbsp custard powder
- 3 c icing sugar
- 1 tsp peppermint flavouring
- 2 drops of green food colouring
- Topping:
- 8 oz pkg of semi sweet chocolate morsels
- 2 tbsp butter

Direction

- Base:
- Melt butter in saucepan.
- Add sugar and cocoa. Mix well. Allow mixture to cool.
- Whisk egg with vanilla. Whisk into cooled butter mixture.
- Add graham crackers, coconut and walnuts.
- Press evenly into greased 9 x 9 square pan.
- Chill for at least 20 minutes
- Filling:
- Whip butter. Add in custard powder and milk.
- Gradually add in sugar, flavouring and food colour.
- Spread over base with spatula and return to the fridge.
- Topping:
- Melt chocolate and butter over water bath. Remove and cool down.
- Add on top of the filling layer. Spread with spatula to get even layer.
- Return to fridge for another 15 minutes.
- Cut into squares and serve.

252. Moms Apple Pie Bars Recipe

Serving: 36 | Prep: | Cook: 60mins | Ready in:

Ingredients

- Crust:
- 2 1/2 c. all-purpose flour
- 1 tsp. salt
- 1 c. shortening
- 1 egg, separated, yolk beaten with enough milk to equal 2/3c. (Reserve the egg white.)
- Filling:
- 1 c. crushed corn flake cereal
- 8 c. peeled, cored, sliced tart cooking apples - Granny Smith
- 1 c. sugar
- 1 1/2 tsp. cinnamon
- 1/2 tsp. nutmeg
- 1 reserved egg white
- 2 Tbsp. sugar
- 1/2 tsp. cinnamon
- Glaze:
- 1 c. powdered sugar
- 1 to 2 Tbsp. milk
- 1/2 tsp. vanilla

Direction

- Pre-heat oven to 350 degrees.
- Crust:
- In medium bowl combine flour and salt.
- Cut in the shortening until crumbly.
- With a fork, stir in egg yolk and milk until the mixture leaves the sides of bowl and forms a ball.
- Divide in half.
- On lightly floured surface roll half of dough into 15" x 10" rectangle; place on bottom of ungreased 15" x 10" x 1" jelly roll pan.
- Filling:
- Sprinkle crust with cereal.
- Layer apples over cereal.
- In a small bowl, combine 1c. sugar, 1 1/2 tsp. cinnamon and nutmeg.
- Sprinkle over the apples.
- Roll remaining half of dough into 16" x 11" rectangle.
- Place over apples.
- In a small bowl, beat egg white with fork until foamy.
- Brush over the top crust.
- In a small bowl, stir together 2 Tbsp. sugar and 1/2 tsp. cinnamon. Sprinkle over the crust.
- Bake for 45 to 60 min. or until lightly browned.
- Glaze:
- In a small bowl, stir together all glaze ingredients.
- Drizzle over the warm dessert.
- Cut into bars.

253. No Bake Butterfinger Bars Recipe

Serving: 32 | Prep: | Cook: | Ready in:

Ingredients

- 6 cups cornflakes, crushed
- 2 cup crunchy peanut butter
- 1 cup sugar
- 1 cup corn syrup
- 12 oz. chocolate chips

Direction

- Grease 9x13 pan with butter
- Heat peanut butter, sugar and corn syrup over low heat to melt.
- Stir in cereal.
- Pat into 9x13 greased pan.
- Melt chips and spread on top.

254. No Bake Cashew Brittle Bars Recipe

Serving: 4 | Prep: | Cook: 30mins | Ready in:

Ingredients

- 11/4c old fashioned oats
- 1c(about 5oz) salted cashews
- 11/2oz(3Tbs)unsalted butter
- 1/2c packed dark brown sugar
- 3/4tsp ground cinnamon
- 3Tbs light corn syrup
- 1Tbs molasses
- 1/2tsp coarse salt

Direction

- Line a 41/2x9" loaf pan with plastic wrap, leaving a 1" overhang on each long side. Toast oats and cashews in a large skillet over med-high heat, stirring often, until aromatic and just starting to turn golden brown, 5-6 mins. Transfer to med. bowl.
- Add butter, sugar, cinnamon, corn syrup, molasses and salt in skillet, and cook over med. heat, stirring, until butter melts and mixture bubbles, 2-3 mins. Pour hot mixture over oats and cashews, and stir to combine.
- Transfer mixture to loaf pan. Using a spatula, press mixture into an even layer. Refrigerate till set, about 30 mins Remove chilled mixture from pan using plastic, discard plastic wrap and cut into 1" thick bars.

255. No Bake Chocolate Peanut Butter Bars Recipe

Serving: 5 | Prep: | Cook: | Ready in:

Ingredients

- 2 cups peanut butter, divided
- 3/4 cup(1 1/2 sticks of butter), sofened
- 2 cups powdered sugar, divided
- 3 cups graham cracker crumbs
- 2 cups (12-ounce package) semi sweet chocolate chips, divided

Direction

- Grease 13x9 inch baking pan.
- Beat 1 1/4 cup peanut butter and butter in large bowl until creamy.
- Gradually beat in 1 cup powdered sugar.
- With hands or wooden spoon, work remaining powdered sugar, graham cracker crumbs and 1/2 cups chocolate chips.
- Press evenly into prepared pan.
- Smooth top with spatula.
- Melt remaining peanut butter and remaining chocolate chips in saucepan over low heat stirring constantly, until smooth.
- Spread over graham cracker crust in pan.
- Refrigerate for at least 1 hour or until chocolate is firm; cut into bars. Store in refrigerator.
- Enjoy!

256. No Bake Chocolate Peanut Butter Oatmeal Bars Recipe

Serving: 24 | Prep: | Cook: 30mins | Ready in:

Ingredients

- vegetable cooking spray
- 9 oz finely ground chocolate wafers (2 cups) I used 8 of the oreo hundred calorie packs
- 1 1/2 cups old fashioned oats
- 1 1/4 cups powdered sugar
- 1/4 tsp course salt
- 5 oz unsalted butter (1 stick plus 2 tbsp)
- 1 cup chunky peanut butter
- 3/4 cup plus 3 tbsp smooth peanut butter
- 10 oz semi sweet chocolate, melted
- 1 1/2 oz milk chocolate, melted (i used 1 regular hershey bar)

Direction

- Spray a 9X13 pan with cooking spray, then line with parchment paper for easy bar removal/clean-up leaving over hang around the edges of the pan (I just used aluminum foil).
- Combine wafers, oats, sugar, and salt in large bowl.
- Melt butter in sauce pan over medium heat, then add crunchy peanut butter and 3/4 cup smooth peanut butter. Stir until creamy and combined.
- Add peanut butter mixture to wafer mixture and stir until well mixed.
- Transfer mixture to baking dish and press down so it is fairly even.
- Refrigerate for 30 minutes.
- Pour semi-sweet chocolate over chilled mixture and spread so that it creates a thin even layer.
- Refrigerate until hardened, about 30 minutes.
- Heat 3 tbsp. smooth peanut butter in sauce pan until runny, drizzle over chilled chocolate.
- Melt 1 1/2 oz. milk chocolate and drizzle over top of peanut butter.
- Refrigerate about 30 minutes.
- Lift block of bars out of pan using parchment paper or foil.
- Cut into bars of desired size.

257. No Bake Cereal Bars

Serving: 12 | Prep: | Cook: 25mins | Ready in:

Ingredients

- 2 cups sugar
- 2 cups corn syrup
- 1 jar (40 ounces) chunky peanut butter
- 6 cups Cheerios oat cereal
- 6 cups Chex crisp rice cereal

Direction

- In a large saucepan, cook and stir sugar and corn syrup until the sugar is dissolved. Remove from the heat. Add peanut butter; mix well. Stir in cereals. Spread quickly into two lightly greased 15x10x1-in. pans. Cut into bars while warm.
- Nutrition Facts
- 1 each: 95 calories, 5g fat (1g saturated fat), 0 cholesterol, 79mg sodium, 12g carbohydrate (7g sugars, 1g fiber), 3g protein.

258. No Bake Chocolate Cookie Squares Recipe

Serving: 16 | Prep: | Cook: | Ready in:

Ingredients

- 1/2 cup (1 stick) butter
- options:
- ======
- 1)=1 pkg. (8 squares) Semi-Sweet baking chocolate ,OREO Chocolate Sandwich cookies ,chopped pecans
- 2)=2 pkg. (4 oz. each) GERMAN'S sweet chocolate , chips AHOY! Real chocolate chip cookies , toasted slivered almonds
- 3)=1 pkg. (8 squares) Semi-Sweet baking chocolate, NUTTER butter peanut butter Sandwich cookies , chopped COCKTAIL peanuts
- 4)=1-1/3 pkg. (8 squares) Premium White baking chocolate ,OREO Chocolate Sandwich cookies ,chopped Macadamias

Direction

- MICROWAVE BAKER'S Chocolate and butter in large microwaveable bowl on HIGH 2 min. or until butter is melted. Stir until chocolate is completely melted.
- Add 1 cup each broken cookies and PLANTERS Nuts; mix well.
- Spread into greased foil-lined 8-inch square pan.
- Refrigerate 3 hours or until firm.
- Cut into 16 squares to serve.
- Store leftover.

259. No Bake Butterscotch Coconut Squares Recipe

Serving: 25 | Prep: | Cook: 40mins | Ready in:

Ingredients

- squares
- 1/8 c margarine
- 1/2 c butterscotch chips
- 1 t vanilla
- 1 egg
- 1/4 t salt
- 1 c coconut
- 1/2 c chopped nuts
- 2 c graham cracker crumbs
- icing
- 2 T soft margarine
- 1 c icing sugar
- 1/2 t vanilla
- 1 T custard powder
- 1 1/2 T milk (more if necessary)

Direction

- Squares
- Melt margarine over low heat.

- Add rest of ingredients, mix.
- Put into 9x9 pan.
- Icing
- Blend ingredients and spread on squares.
- Chill.

260. No Bake Chocolate Peanut Butter Bars Recipe

Serving: 8 | Prep: | Cook: | Ready in:

Ingredients

- 1 cup butter or margarine, melted
- 2 cups graham cracker crumbs
- 2 cups powdered sugar
- 1 cup peanut butter
- 1 1/2 cups semisweet chocolate chips
- 4 tablespoons peanut butter

Direction

- In a medium bowl, mix together the butter or margarine, graham cracker crumbs, confectioners' sugar, and 1 cup peanut butter until well blended.
- Press evenly into the bottom of an ungreased 9x13 inch pan.
- In a metal bowl over simmering water, or in the microwave, melt the chocolate chips with the 4 tablespoons peanut butter, stirring occasionally until smooth. Spread over the prepared crust. Refrigerate for at least one hour before cutting into squares.
- Store in the refrigerator.

261. Norwegian Apple Squares Recipe

Serving: 15 | Prep: | Cook: 35mins | Ready in:

Ingredients

- 1 cup butter
- 1 1/2 cups sugar
- 2 1/2 cups sifted flour
- 2 tsp baking powder
- 2 eggs
- 1/2 tsp almond extract*
- 3 apples. peeled, cored and sliced very thin
- 1/2 tsp. allspice (or cinnamon)
- 1 cup confectioner's sugar
- About 3 tbsp, hot water
- 1/2 tsp vanilla or lemon extract

Direction

- Preheat oven to 400 degrees.
- Cream butter and sugar together; blend in flour and baking powder.
- In separate bowl, beat eggs and almond extract; add to flour mixture and beat until well-blended.
- Press half the dough into bottom of a greased 13" x 9" pan - dough will be a bit sticky, but you can do it - I have faith in you.
- Spread apples over dough and sprinkle with allspice or cinnamon.
- Drop teaspoonfuls of remaining dough over top and press down slightly to cover apples (does not have to cover the apples completely).
- Bake for 35 minutes or until lightly browned. Cool and spread (or drizzle) with icing, then cut into squares.
- ICING:
- Mix together confectioner's sugar, hot water and extract to make a thin icing.
- *NOTE: Almond, Vanilla and Lemon Extracts all work well in this recipe and/or icing, except I would not use Almond in the icing.

262. Nut Goodie Bars Recipe

Serving: 36 | Prep: | Cook: 30mins | Ready in:

Ingredients

- 12 oz chocolate chips

- 12 oz butterscotch chips
- 18 oz peanut butter
- 16 oz dry roasted peanuts - or a little less depending on preference
- 1 c butter
- 1/4 c regular vanilla pudding mix - dry
- 1/2 c milk
- 2 lbs (1 bag usually) powdered sugar
- 2 tsp maple flavoring

Direction

- Melt together the chocolate and butterscotch chips with peanut butter on top of stove.
- Put 1/2 of mixture into a jelly-roll pan - wider cookie sheet with edge.
- Refrigerate.
- To the other half, add the peanuts and set aside.
- Combine butter, dry pudding mix and milk and boil 1 minute.
- Remove from heat and add powder sugar and maple flavoring.
- Beat and spread on top of first layer.
- Cool in refrigerator.
- Spread remainder of chocolate peanut mixture on top.
- Keep in refrigerator, can be frozen.
- I have doubled the chocolate/butterscotch and peanut butter parts for extra thick chocolate sections.

263. Nutella Butterscotch Bars Recipe

Serving: 24 | Prep: | Cook: 15mins | Ready in:

Ingredients

- 1 sheet puff pastry
- 1 cup butterscotch chips
- 1 cup nutella
- 2 large eggs
- 1/4 cup all-purpose flour
- 1 cup miniature chocolate chips

Direction

- Preheat oven to 400 degrees F.
- Using a rolling pin on a floured surface, roll the puff pastry to 1/8- inch thickness. Prick the dough several times with a fork, covering the surface of the pastry. Place the dough on a foil-lined cookie sheet and freeze for 15 minutes. Then, bake for 10 minutes, until dough is golden brown in color. Set aside to cool.
- In a medium bowl, stir together butterscotch chips, Nutella, eggs, flour and miniature chocolate chips. Spread the mixture onto the puff pastry, leaving a 1-inch border. Turn the oven down to 350* and bake the bars for 15-20 minutes. When the bars are done, the top will be cracked slightly and the center will have a creamy texture.
- Allow the bars to cool completely and cut with a pizza wheel or sharp knife.

264. Nutella Rocky Road Bars Recipe

Serving: 12 | Prep: | Cook: 20mins | Ready in:

Ingredients

- Crust:
- 1 ½ cup chocolate cookie crumbs (I used some flourless chocolate cookies, but I think chocolate graham crackers or Oreos would be good as well)
- 6 tablespoons unsalted butter, melted
- Filling:
- ¾ cup nutella
- 4 ounces semisweet chocolate chips
- 2/3 cup heavy whipping cream
- 1 cup marshmallows (more if you want)
- ½ cup peanuts (or more if you want)

Direction

- For the Crust:
- Spray a 14-x-4-inch rectangular tart pan with baking spray, or butter. Set aside.
- Preheat oven to 350F.
- In a small bowl, mix together cookie crumbs and melted butter. I just used a food processor since I had to make the crumbs. Mix until fully combined and you can press the crust with your hand and it stays in place.
- Dump the crust into the tart pan. Using your hands, press the tart crust evenly up the sides and in the middle of the tart pan.
- Using center rack, bake tart for 8-10 minutes. Remove from oven and let cool on wire rack.
- For the filling:
- Place chocolate chips into a medium sized bowl. Set aside.
- In a small saucepan, bring cream to a boil. Once it begins to boil, pour over chocolate chips. Let sit for 2 minutes. Then whisk until smooth.
- Whisk in the Nutella until fully incorporated. It should look glossy and smooth.
- To assemble the tart:
- Take ½ the marshmallows and ½ peanuts and scatter them onto the bottom of the tart.
- Pour Nutella filling into the tart, over top the marshmallows and nuts. Smooth out tart if needed. Top with remaining marshmallows and nuts.
- Place in refrigerator for 20 minutes. Cut and serve.

265. O Henry Bars Recipe

Serving: 8 | Prep: | Cook: 10mins | Ready in:

Ingredients

- 1c Karo syrup
- 1c sugar
- 4c Rice Krispies
- 1 1/2 c crunchy peanut butter
- 1/2c buttercotch chips
- 1/2c chocolate chips
- 9x13 pan buttered or sprayed with pam

Direction

- Measure and have all ingredients ready before beginning preparation.
- Heat syrup and sugar to boiling.
- Pour over and mix into Rice Krispies.
- In large bowl add peanut butter to above mixture and mix well.
- Put into shallow pan with smooth surface.
- Press down into pan.
- Topping
- In separate pan over low heat, melt butterscotch and chocolate chips until smooth.
- Pour over rice krispies mixture.
- Allow to cool and cut into squares.
- Enjoy!

266. OHenrie Bars Recipe

Serving: 8 | Prep: | Cook: 10mins | Ready in:

Ingredients

- 1 cup broken walnuts
- 1 cup crushed graham wafers
- 1 cup coconut
- In a saucepan, cook
- 1 cup brown sugar
- 1/2 cup margarine
- 1/2 cup milk
- 1 tsp vanilla
- Icing:
- 1/4 cup butter
- 2 cups icing sugar
- 2 tbsp cream
- 1/2 tsp salt
- 1 tsp vanilla
- Whole graham wafers

Direction

- Mix walnuts, coconut and crushed wafers together.
- In a pot, mix sugar, butter and milk. Boil 1 minute. Add vanilla and then the first mixture of walnuts and coconut.
- Butter a cookie sheet, place whole graham wafers over the bottom of the cookie sheet. Spread with above mixture. Cover everything with another layer of whole graham wafers and spread on the icing.

267. Oh Henry Bars Recipe

Serving: 18 | Prep: | Cook: 20mins | Ready in:

Ingredients

- 2/3 cup butter
- 1 cup brown sugar firmly packed
- 1 tablespoon vanilla
- 1/2 cup light corn syrup
- 4 cups quick oats
- 1 cup chocolate chips
- 2/3 cup chunky peanut butter

Direction

- Cream butter and sugar.
- Add vanilla, corn syrup and oats.
- Pat dough into lightly greased rectangular baking pan.
- Bake at 350 for 15 minutes.
- While dough is baking melt chocolate chips and peanut butter together over low heat.
- Cool dough slightly then spread chocolate mixture on top.
- Cool further then cut into bars.

268. Oreo Cream Cheese Brownie Bars Recipe

Serving: 24 | Prep: | Cook: 90mins | Ready in:

Ingredients

- Crust: (1) 1 lb 2 oz package Oreos--you will need 14 oz of this, so two full "rows", plus 4-5 cookies leftover, kept aside
- 4 tbsp melted butter
- dash salt
- Top Layer: 2.5 oz cake flour (1/2 cup plus 2 tbsp)
- 1/4 tsp salt
- 1/2 tsp baking powder
- 3 oz 70% dark chocolate chips (1 cup)
- 6 tbsp butter
- 1 cup minus 2 tbsp sugar
- 2 eggs
- 2 tsp vanilla
- Filling: 16 oz cream cheese, room temperature
- 4 tbsp sugar
- 4 tbsp cream or milk
- 1/4 tsp vanilla
- 1 egg yolk

Direction

- Preheat oven to 350.
- Line 8X8" square pan with heavy-duty foil and spray with non-stick spray.
- Crush 12 0z of the cookies in gallon zip lock or food processor until crumbly but not powdered.
- Add butter and salt, mix to combine.
- Press firmly into even layer into pan, bake for 10 minutes, then set aside to cool.
- Meanwhile, make top layer--melt chocolate chips and butter in double boiler or microwave until smooth and no lumps remain.
- Set aside to cool slightly.
- Lower oven to 325.
- Make filling: With hand-held mixer, blend filling ingredients till smooth and creamy.
- Back to brownie layer--when chocolate has cooled a bit, blend sugar and egg with hand-held mixer or whisk till creamy and pale.
- Slowly add melted chocolate mixture until well blended, then gently fold in flour mixture.

- Assemble: When crust is done, spread cream cheese mixture carefully over top, making an even layer.
- Pour brownie batter over top, trying not to disturb the cream cheese layer--you DO NOT wants swirls. (A small offset spatula works well for this.)
- Crush or chop remaining cookies coarsely, sprinkle them over the top, and press in gently.
- Bake for 60-75 minutes*, until toothpick comes out with just a few brownie crumbs and no visible cream cheese. Do not overbake.
- Cool an hour at room temperature, then refrigerate for at least 2 hours before slicing. Store in fridge.

269. PEANUT BUTTER MARSHMALLOW BARS Recipe

Serving: 12 | Prep: | Cook: 20mins | Ready in:

Ingredients

- 1/2 CUP butter flavorED CRISCO STICK/ OR 1/2 CUP Butter Flavor Crisco shortening.
- 1/4 CUP FIRMLY PACKED LIGHT BROWN SUAGR
- 1/2 CUP EXTRA crunchy peanut butter
- 1/4 CUP sugar
- 1 egg
- 1-1/4 CUPS all-purpose flour
- 1 TEASPOON baking powder
- 1/4 TEASPOON salt
- 1/2 CUP creamy peanut butter
- 4 CUPS miniature marshmallows
- 1/2 CUP chocolate FLAVORED syrup

Direction

- PREHEAT OVEN TO 350 DEGREES F. GREASE A 13 X 9 X 2 INCH GLASS BAKING DISH WITH SHORTENING
- FOR COOKIE BASE, COMBINE BROWN SUGAR, SHORTENING, EXTRA CRUNCHY PEANUT BUTTER, WHITE SUGAR AND EGG IN A LARGE BOWL. BEAT AT MEDIUM SPEED WITH A MIXER UNTIL WELL BLENDED
- COMBINE FLOUR, BAKING POWDER, AND SALT, GRADUALLY ADD TO CREAMED MIXTURE AT LOW SPEED, BEAT UNTIL WELL BLENDED.
- COVER, REFRIGERATE 15 MINUTES.
- PRESS CHILLED COOKIE BASE INTO PREPARED DISH.
- BAKE 20 MINUTES OR UNTIL LIGHT BROWN. *****DO NOT OVERBAKE******* COOL 2 TO 3 MINUTES.
- FOR TOPPING***************
- PLACE CREAMY PEANUT BUTTER IN A MICROWAVE - SAFE MEASURING CUP, MICROWAVE ON HIGH FOR 1 MINUTE.
- POUR OVER BAKED SURFACE, SPREAD TO COVER ALL.THEN COVER WITH MARSHMALLOWS, DRIZZLE CHOCOLATE SYRUP OVER MARSHMALLOWS.
- RETURN TO OVEN BAKE 5 MINUTES OR UNITL MARSHMALLOWS ARE SLIGHTLY BROWN. DO NOT OVERBAKE.
- LOOSEN FROM SIDES OF DISH WITH A KNIFE
- REMOVE DISH TO COOLING RACK COOL COMPLETLEY
- CUT WITH SHARP GREASED KNIFE INTO BARS ABOUT 2X2 INCHES.
- YIELDS 2 DOZEN BARS

270. PEANUTTY BROWNIE BARS Recipe

Serving: 36 | Prep: | Cook: 12mins | Ready in:

Ingredients

- 3/4 - cup melted butter
- 1/2- cup baking cocoa

- 1 1/2- cups sugar
- 1 1/2 teaspoons vanilla extract
- 3- eggs
- 1 1/4 - cups flour
- 1/2- cup sugar
- 1/2- cup water
- 2- cups peanut butter chips (morsels)
- 1/2- cup semisweet chocolate chips (morsels)
- 1- tablespoon shortening
- 1/4- teaspoon vanilla extract

Direction

- Combine butter and cocoa in bowl; mix well
- Add 1 1/2 cups sugar and 1 1/2 teaspoons vanilla....
- Mix well
- Beat in eggs 1 at a time
- Stir in flour
- Spread in 10x15 inch baking pan lined with greased foil.
- Bake at 350 degrees f. for 12 minutes.
- Cool in pan for 2 minutes
- Invert onto wire rack; peel off foil cool completely.
- Bring 1/2 cup sugar and water to a boil in saucepan; remove from heat.
- Stir in peanut butter chips until melted.
- Cool slightly.
- Cut baked layer into two 7 1/2 x 10 inch layers.
- Spread peanut butter mixture between and on top of layers, stacking on serving plate.
- Combine chocolate chips and shortening in a double broiler
- Heat over hot water until melted.
- Stir in 1/4 -teaspoon vanilla
- Drizzle over layers.
- Let stand until set
- Cut into bars
- Yield 3 dozen bars

271. PECAN BARS Recipe

Serving: 8 | Prep: | Cook: 35mins | Ready in:

Ingredients

- 1 pkg. yellow cake mix
- 1/2 C. butter, melted
- 1 egg
- 1 C. chopped pecans
- 1/2 C. corn syrup
- 1 tsp.. vanilla
- 3 eggs
- 1/2 C. packed brown sugar

Direction

- Reserve 3/4 cup of the cake mix.
- Combine remaining cake mix with butter and 1 egg.
- Mix till crumbly.
- Press in bottom 13x9 baking dish.
- Bake at 350 for 15 min. or until golden brown.
- Combine the reserved cake mix with brown sugar, corn syrup, and 3 eggs.
- Mix until well blended.
- Pour over baked crust; sprinkle with pecans.
- Return to oven and bake for 35 min.
- Cool and cut into squares

272. PECAN PIE BARS Recipe

Serving: 8 | Prep: | Cook: 40mins | Ready in:

Ingredients

- 2 C. all purpose. flour
- 1/4 C. firmly packed brown sugar
- 1/2 C. (1 stick) butter
- 1 1/2 C. chopped pecans
- 1 (14-oz.) can sweetened condensed milk
- 3 eggs, beaten
- 2 Tbs. lemon juice

Direction

- Preheat oven to 350°F.
- In medium bowl, combine flour and brown sugar; cut in butter until crumbly.
- Press mixture on bottom of 13x9-inch baking pan.
- Bake 10 to 15 minutes.
- In small bowl, combine pecans, sweetened condensed milk, eggs and lemon juice; pour over crust.
- Bake 25 minutes or until filling is set.
- Cool.
- Cut into bars.
- Store covered at room temperature.

273. Pay Day Bars Recipe

Serving: 10 | Prep: | Cook: 10mins | Ready in:

Ingredients

- 1 cup sugar
- 1 cup Karo syrup
- 1 tsp vanilla
- 1 cup peanut butter
- 6 cups Crispix cereal
- 2 cups peanuts

Direction

- Bring sugar and karo syrup to boil.
- Remove from heat and add remaining ingredients.
- Pour into 9x13 pan.

274. Peanut Butter Bars With Chocolate Ganache Recipe

Serving: 12 | Prep: | Cook: 40mins | Ready in:

Ingredients

- 1 cup flour
- 2 cups sugar
- 1 tsp. salt
- 1 tsp. baking soda
- 3/4 cup peanut butter
- 1 cup butter
- 1 cup water
- 2 eggs
- 1/2 cup buttermilk
- 1/2 cup semi sweet chocolate morsels
- 1/3 cup whipping cream

Direction

- Combine flour, sugar, salt and baking soda.
- In a saucepan on medium heat bring peanut butter, butter and water to a boil, stirring frequently.
- Pour into flour mixture.
- Add eggs and buttermilk, mix well.
- Pour into a greased and sugared 13x9" baking dish.
- Bake in a preheated oven of 350*F.
- Cool 30 minutes.
- In a microwaveable bowl microwave chocolate morsels and whipping cream for 1 minute, stirring half way through and spread on cake and refrigerate.
- Cut into bars when ready to serve.

275. Peanut Butter Buckeye Bars Recipe

Serving: 1 | Prep: | Cook: 30mins | Ready in:

Ingredients

- 1 (18.25 or 18.5 oz) package chocolate cake mix
- 1/4 cup vegetable oil
- 1 egg
- 1 cup chopped peanuts
- 1 (14oz) can sweetened condensed milk (NOT evaporated)

- 1/2 cup peanut butter (Favorite!!)

Direction

- Preheat oven to 350 degrees F (325 degrees for a glass dish)
- In large bowl, combine cake mix, oil and egg; beat on medium speed until crumbly. Stir in peanuts.
- Reserving 1 1/2 cups crumb mixture, press remainder on bottom of greased 13x9 inch baking pan.
- In medium bowl, beat sweetened condensed milk and peanut butter until smooth; spread over prepared crust.
- Sprinkle with reserved crumb mixture.
- Bake 25 - 30 minutes or until set.
- Cool and cut into bars.
- Store loosely covered at room temperature.
- ***
- -It try to avoid looking forward or backward; and try to keep looking upward- Charlotte Bronte
- ***

276. Peanut Butter Candy Caramel Bars Recipe

Serving: 24 | Prep: | Cook: 38mins | Ready in:

Ingredients

- peanut butter candy bar batter
- 1 1/4 - cups unsifted bleached cake flour
- 2- tablespoons plus 1 1/2teaspoon unsweetened cocoa powder
- 1/4 teaspoon baking powder
- 1/4 - teaspoon salt
- 1/4 - pound (16 tablespoons) unsalted butter, melted and cooled to tepid
- 4- ounces unsweetened chocolate, melted and cooled to tepid
- 4- large eggs
- 1 3/4- cups plus 2 tablespoons superfine sugar
- 3 - tablespoons smooth creamy peanut butter(do not use all natural here)
- 2 1/4- teaspoon vanilla
- 4- bars of chocolate covered peanut butter candy such as (butterfingers) bars cut into 3/4 inch chunks..................
- ***
- Topping ..my turtle topping previously posted............

Direction

- Preheat oven to 325 degrees f.
- Film the inside of a 9x9 x 2 inch baking pan with non-stick cooking spray.
- Mix the batter.
- Sift the flour, cocoa powder, baking powder, salt onto a sheet of waxed paper.
- In a medium-sized mixing bowl, whisk the melted chocolate until smooth.
- In a large mixing bowl, whisk eggs until blended, about 15 seconds.
- Add the sugar, vanilla extract, and peanut butter and whisk until the peanut butter is mostly integrated, about 45 seconds.
- Whisk in the melted butter- chocolate mixture.
- Sift the flour mixture over and stir to form a batter, mixing thoroughly until the particles of the flour are absorbed, using a wooden spoon or flat wooden paddle.
- Blend in the chunks of candy.
- Scrape the batter into the prepared pan, spreading it evenly into the corners.
- Smooth the top with a rubber spatula.
- Bake in the preheated oven for 35 to 38 minutes, or until set.
- Let the bars stand in the pan on a cooling rack for 1 hour.
- Spoon or drizzle the warm topping over the coolie base.
- Let it stand until the topping is firm and completely cool about 2 hours.
- With a small sharp knife cut into quarters then cut each quarter into 6 bars.
- Remove bars store air tight container or serve.
- Use within 2 days.

- Makes 2 dozen bars.

277. Peanut Butter Caramel Bars Recipe

Serving: 36 | Prep: | Cook: 30mins | Ready in:

Ingredients

- 1 pkg. (18-1/4 oz.) yellow cake mix
- 1/2 cup butter or margarine, softened
- 1 egg
- 20 minature peanut butter cups, chopped
- 2 Tbsp. cornstarch
- 1 jar (12-1/4 oz.) caramel ice cream topping
- 1/4 cup peanut butter
- 1/2 cup salted peanuts
- TOPPING:
- 1 can (16-oz.) milk chocolate frosting
- 1/2 cup chopped salted peanuts

Direction

- In a mixing bowl, combine the dry cake mix, butter and egg; beat until no longer crumbly, about 3 minutes.
- Stir in the peanut butter cups.
- Press into a greased 13x9x2-in. baking pan.
- Bake at 350 degrees for 18-22 minutes or until lightly browned.
- Meanwhile, in a saucepan, combine cornstarch, caramel topping and peanut butter until smooth.
- Cook over low heat, stirring occasionally, until mixture comes to a boil, about 25 minutes.
- Cook and stir 1-2 minutes longer.
- Remove from the heat; stir in peanuts.
- Spread evenly over warm crust.
- Bake 6-7 minutes longer or until almost set.
- Cool completely on a wire rack.
- Spread with frosting; sprinkle with peanuts.
- Refrigerate for at least 1 hour before cutting.
- Store in the refrigerator.

278. Peanut Butter Chocolate Bars Recipe

Serving: 24 | Prep: | Cook: 25mins | Ready in:

Ingredients

- 1 C. smooth or chunky peanut butter
- 6 T. butter or margarine, softened
- 3/4 C. packed brown sugar
- 1/4 C. granulated sugar
- 1 t. vanilla extract
- 3 eggs
- 1 C. flour
- 2 C. (11 1/2 oz. pkg) Nestle Toll House milk chocolate Morsels, divided
- 1 C. colored sugar or small colored candies (optional)

Direction

- Beat peanut butter, butter, brown sugar, granulated sugar and vanilla in large mixer bowl until creamy.
- Beat in eggs; beat in flour.
- Stir in 3/4 C. morsels.
- Spread into greased 9x13 baking dish.
- Bake in preheated 350 oven 20-25 minutes or until edges are lightly browned. Remove from oven, immediately sprinkle with remaining morsels. Let stand for 5 minutes; spread. Sprinkle colored sugar over melted chocolate.
- Cool in pan on wire rack.

279. Peanut Butter Cookie Candy Bars Recipe

Serving: 36 | Prep: | Cook: 12mins | Ready in:

Ingredients

- cookie Base

- 1 pouch (1 lb 1.5 oz) Betty Crocker® peanut butter cookie mix
- 3 tablespoons vegetable oil
- 1 tablespoon water
- 1 egg
- Filling
- 1/3 cup light corn syrup
- 3 tablespoons butter or margarine, softened
- 3 tablespoons peanut butter
- 1 tablespoon plus 1 1/2 teaspoons water
- 1 1/4 teaspoons vanilla
- Dash salt
- 3 1/2 cups powdered sugar
- caramel Layer
- 1 bag (14 oz) caramels, unwrapped
- 2 tablespoons water
- 1 1/2 cups unsalted dry-roasted peanuts
- Topping
- 1 bag (11.5 oz) milk chocolate chips (2 cups)

Direction

- Heat oven to 350°F. Spray bottom only of 13x9-inch pan with cooking spray. In large bowl, stir cookie base ingredients until soft dough forms. Press dough in bottom of pan. Bake 12 to 15 minutes or until light golden brown. Cool completely, about 30 minutes.
- In large bowl, beat all filling ingredients except powdered sugar with electric mixer on medium speed until creamy and smooth. Gradually beat in powdered sugar until well blended (filling will be thick). Press filling over cookie base. Refrigerate while preparing caramel layer.
- In 2-quart saucepan, heat caramels and 2 tablespoons water over low heat, stirring constantly, until caramels are melted. Stir in peanuts. Spread evenly over filling. Refrigerate about 15 minutes or until caramel layer is firm.
- In small microwavable bowl, microwave chocolate chips uncovered on High 1 to 2 minutes, stirring once, until melted. Spread evenly over caramel layer. Refrigerate about 1 hour or until chocolate is set. For bars, cut into 9 rows by 4 rows. Store covered at room temperature.

280. Peanut Butter Crunch Candy Bars Recipe

Serving: 1 | Prep: | Cook: |Ready in:

Ingredients

- 4 cups (10.5 ounce bag) miniature marshmallows
- 2 Tablespoons butter
- 1 cup crunchy peanut butter
- 1 cup smooth peanut butter
- 54 round butter-flavored cookies, crushed (1-1/2 stacks, about 2 cups)
- 1 cup semi-sweet chocolate chips, frozen
- Topping:
- 3 ounces semi-sweet chocolate bar, broken into chunks

Direction

- Line a 9 x 13-inch baking pan with non-stick foil.
- In a double-boiler, melt butter and both peanut butters, stirring to avoid scorching, until combined.
- Mix in marshmallows, half at a time, until melted and smooth. Pour into a large bowl. Let cool for 5 minutes.
- Stir in crushed crackers, then quickly add chocolate chips. (They may melt a bit, which is why they should be frozen to begin with.) Mixture will be stiff. Press into prepared pan and smooth top with a spatula. Let stand at room temperature for an hour to set.
- Clean double-boiler and dry thoroughly. (One drop of water will make the chocolate seize.) Gently melt chocolate bar stirring until smooth. You may melt chocolate in the microwave, if you wish, but be careful not to scorch it. Chocolate should be melted, but not hot.

- Pour melted chocolate into a zip-top bag, squeeze out all the air, and seal. Cut a small corner from the bag and use it as a pastry bag to drizzle chocolate in a zigzag pattern over the top of the candy bars. Chill for 30 minutes, then cut into small squares.
- Store leftovers at room temperature in an airtight container.
- Yield: 48 candy bars

281. Peanut Butter Cup Bars Recipe

Serving: 16 | Prep: | Cook: 5mins | Ready in:

Ingredients

- 1 cup butter
- 1 cup creamy peanut butter
- 1 pound powdered sugar
- 1-1/2 packages graham cracker crumbs
- 12 ounces chocolate chips

Direction

- Melt butter in saucepan over low heat.
- In large bowl mix all ingredients except chocolate chips and knead to make a soft dough.
- Spread mixture onto a cookie sheet then top with melted chocolate chips.
- Chill until firm then cut into squares.

282. Peanut Butter Granola Bars Recipe

Serving: 24 | Prep: | Cook: 15mins | Ready in:

Ingredients

- vegetable cooking spray
- 1 egg white
- 1/2 cup chunky peanut butter
- 1/3 cup brown sugar
- 1/4 cup honey
- 1/2 cup(1 stick)unsalted butter melted
- 2 cups old fashioned oats
- 1/4 cup slivered almonds,toasted (arrange nuts in single layer on baking sheet,Bake in preheated oven 350 degrees 8-10 minutes until lightly browned)
- 1/3 cup miniature chocolate chips

Direction

- Position oven rack in middle of oven.
- PREHEAT: 350 degrees.
- Spray a 7 X10 3/4 inch non-stick baking pan with vegetable cooking spray.
- Lay a 6 x 18 piece of parchment paper in the pan, allow excess to hang over sides.
- Spray the parchment paper lightly with cooking spray.
- In a medium bowl, use a hand beater, beat egg white until frothy.
- Stir in the peanut butter, brown sugar and honey.
- Add the melted butter, oats, and almonds.
- Stir to combine and add chocolate chips.
- Using a rubber spatula, spread the mixture into prepared pan, pressing lightly to form an even layer.
- Bake until the edge of the mixture begins to brown, about 15 minutes.
- Remove from oven cool at least one hour.
- Cut into 1 1/2 inch squares and serve, or wrap in plastic wrap for traveling.
- YUM!

283. Peanut Butter And Jelly Oat Bars Recipe

Serving: 24 | Prep: | Cook: 25mins | Ready in:

Ingredients

- Ingredients:

- 1 cup firmly packed dark brown sugar
- ¾ Cup butter flavor All-Vegetable shortening, plus additional for greasing
- ½ cup creamy peanut butter
- 2 cups (plus 2 tablespoons) all-purpose flour
- 1 teaspoon salt
- ½ teaspoon baking soda
- 1½ cups oats (quick, uncooked)
- 1/3 cup water
- 1 cup strawberry preserves
- .

Direction

- Directions:
- Preheat oven to 400°F. Grease 13 x 9 x 2-inch pan with shortening.
- Combine brown sugar, shortening and Peanut Butter in large bowl. Beat on medium speed of electric mixer until well blended.
- Combine flour, salt and baking soda. Add gradually to creamed mixture at low speed. Beat until well blended. Stir in oats with spoon. Mix until well blended. Stir in water 1 tablespoon at a time.
- Press half the dough into bottom of greased pan and spread Smucker's preserves over it. Flatten small amounts of remaining dough between hands. Place on preserves and arrange so dough sections touch. Fill in any spaces with dough so preserves are completely covered.
- Bake for 25-30 minutes or until golden brown and edges are slightly brown. Do not over-bake. Cut while warm into bars about 2½ x 2 inches.

284. Peanut Cake Bars Recipe

Serving: 72 | Prep: | Cook: 13mins |Ready in:

Ingredients

- 1 (18 1/4 ounce) box chocolate cake mix
- 1/2 cup water
- 1/3 cup butter or margarine, softened
- 1 egg
- Topping
- 3 cups miniature marshmallows
- 1 (10 ounce) package peanut butter chips
- 2/3 cup light corn syrup
- 1/4 cup butter or margarine
- 2 teaspoons vanilla extract
- 2 cups crisp rice cereal
- 2 cups salted peanuts

Direction

- In a bowl, combine dry cake mix, water, butter and egg until blended.
- Press into a greased 15 x 10-inch baking pan. Bake at 350 degrees F for 13 to 16 minutes or until a wooden pick inserted near the center comes out clean. Sprinkle with marshmallows. Bake 2 minutes longer.
- Cool.
- TOPPING
- In a saucepan, combine peanut butter chips, corn syrup, butter and vanilla extract. Cook over low heat until melted; stir until smooth.
- Remove from the heat; stir in cereal and peanuts. Spoon over marshmallows.
- Cool before cutting.

285. Peanutty Buttery Squares Recipe

Serving: 24 | Prep: | Cook: 30mins |Ready in:

Ingredients

- 1 cup Karo® Light or with Real brown sugar corn syrup
- 1/2 cup (1 stick) butter
- 1 cup sugar
- 2-1/2 cups creamy peanut butter or 1 (18 ounce) jar peanut butter
- Mazola Pure™ canola oil cooking spray
- 7 ounces (about 7 cups) Kellogg's® Rice Krispies or your favorite ready-to-eat cereal

- Note: fruit Loops work well too but my favorite is Kellogg's® Rice Krispies.
- 1 cup chocolate chips
- 1 cup butterscotch chips

Direction

- In a large saucepan, combine Karo® syrup, sugar and butter over medium heat and bring to a boil.
- Reduce heat to simmer and stir in peanut butter until smooth.
- Remove pan from heat.
- Mix cereal thoroughly into peanut butter and pour into 13 x 9" pan sprayed with cooking spray.
- Refrigerate pan for 20 minutes.
- Melt chocolate chips and butterscotch chips over low heat and spread over the hardened peanut butter and cereal mixture.
- Place pan back in refrigerator for until hard.
- Chill Time: 30 minutes
- Makes 24 squares

286. Pecan Squares Recipe

Serving: 8 | Prep: | Cook: 45mins | Ready in:

Ingredients

- 2 Pilsbury chocolate chip cookie dough rolls.
- 1 beaten egg
- 3/4 cup honey
- 2/3 cup milk
- 1 4-oz. Serving size instant chocolate pudding
- 1 tsp. vanilla
- 1 ½ cups pecan halves, toasted

Direction

- Spread cookie dough in the bottom of a 9 x 13" pan. Mix remaining ingredients together and spread on top of cookie dough. Bake at 350 F for 45 minutes.

287. Pecan Squares Courtesy Of The Barefoot Contessa Recipe

Serving: 24 | Prep: | Cook: 45mins | Ready in:

Ingredients

- 1 1/4 pounds unsalted butter, room temperature
- 3/4 cup granulated sugar
- 3 extra-large eggs
- 3/4 teaspoon pure vanilla extract
- 4 1/2 cups all-purpose flour
- 1/2 teaspoon baking powder
- 1/4 teaspoon salt
- Topping:
- 1 pound unsalted butter
- 1 cup good honey
- 3 cups light brown sugar, packed
- 1 teaspoon grated lemon zest
- 1 teaspoon grated orange zest
- 1/4 cup heavy cream
- 2 pounds pecans, coarsely chopped

Direction

- Preheat the oven to 350 degrees F.
- For the crust, beat the butter and granulated sugar in the bowl of an electric mixer fitted with a paddle attachment, until light approximately 3 minutes.
- Add the eggs and the vanilla and mix well.
- Sift together the flour, baking powder, and salt.
- Mix the dry ingredients into the batter with the mixer on low speed until just combined.
- Press the dough evenly into an ungreased 18 by 12 by 1-inch baking sheet, making an edge around the outside. It will be very sticky; sprinkle the dough and your hands lightly with flour.
- Bake for 15 minutes, until the crust is set but not browned.
- Allow to cool.

- For the topping, combine the butter, honey, brown sugar, and zests in a large, heavy-bottomed saucepan. Cook over low heat until the butter is melted, using a wooden spoon to stir. Raise the heat and boil for 3 minutes. Remove from the heat.
- Stir in the heavy cream and pecans. Pour over the crust, trying not to get the filling between the crust and the pan. Bake for 25 to 30 minutes, until the filling is set.
- Remove from the oven and allow to cool. Wrap in plastic wrap and refrigerate until cold.
- Cut into bars, dip one end in melted chocolate about one inch only and serve.

288. Perfectly Peanutty Banana Bars Recipe

Serving: 16 | Prep: | Cook: 30mins | Ready in:

Ingredients

- 1/4 cup low-fat peanut butter
- 1 cup ripe mashed bananas (about 3)
- 1/4 cup low-fat plain soy milk
- 1 tsp vanilla
- 3 tbsp hot water
- 1 tbsp cornstarch
- 1/2 cup flour
- 1/2 cup whole wheat flour
- 1 teaspoon baking soda
- 1 teaspoon baking powder
- 1/4 cup dry roasted peanuts, chopped

Direction

- Preheat oven to 350°F and grease an 8-inch square baking pan.
- Beat together the peanut butter and banana until smooth with electric beaters.
- Beat in the soy milk, vanilla, water, cornstarch, flour, baking soda and baking powder.
- Fold in the peanuts.
- Bake for 30 minutes until browned. Chill before slicing.

289. Pina Colada Bars Recipe

Serving: 24 | Prep: | Cook: 480mins | Ready in:

Ingredients

- 2 cup vanilla wafer crumbs
- ⅓ cup margarine, melted
- 1 8 3/4 oz. can Goya cream of coconut
- 2 8 oz. pkgs. cream cheese, Softened
- 1 8oz. container whipped topping
- 1 8oz. can crushed pineapple Drained
- ¼ cup maraschino cherries, drained and halved
- ½ cup Chopped nuts
- ½ cup flaked coconut

Direction

- Combine vanilla wafer crumbs and margarine, press into 13x9-inch pan.
- Gradually mix cream of coconut into cream cheese.
- Beat until well blended.
- Fold in whipped topping, pineapple, cherries and nuts, sprinkle with coconut.
- Chill several hours or overnight.

290. Pineapple Coconut Squares Recipe

Serving: 16 | Prep: | Cook: 35mins | Ready in:

Ingredients

- 2 T butter, melted
- 3 T sugar
- 1 egg
- 1 c flour
- 1 t baking powder

- 2 cans (8 oz each) unsweetened crushed pineapple, drained
- TOPPING
- 1 T butter, melted
- 1 c sugar
- 2 eggs
- 2 c flaked coconut

Direction

- In a bowl, beat butter and sugar. Beat in egg. Combine flour and baking powder; stir into egg mixture. Press into a 9" square baking pan coated with cooking spray. Spread the pineapple over crust; set aside.
- For topping, in a bowl, beat butter and sugar. Beat in eggs. Stir in coconut. Spread over pineapple. Bake at 325 for 35 - 40 minutes or till golden brown. Cool in pan on wire rack. Cut into bars.

291. Pineapple Oatmeal Bars Recipe

Serving: 1 | Prep: | Cook: 30mins | Ready in:

Ingredients

- 1 1/2 cups sugar
- 2 tablespoons cornstarch
- 2 1/4 cups pineapple, crushed and drained
- 1 1/2 teaspoons lemon juice
- 2 1/4 cups oats, quick-cooking
- 2 1/4 cups flour
- 1 1/2 cups brown sugar, packed
- 3/4 teaspoon baking soda
- 1 cup & 2 teaspoon butter

Direction

- Filling-Simmer first 4 ingredients over medium heat, until thick.
- Remove from stove and cool.
- Crust- Combine dry ingredients and cut in butter. Blend until crumbly.
- Press 2/3 of the mixture firmly in a 9 x 13 pan. Add filling and sprinkle remaining crust over the filling.
- Bake 350° for 30 minutes.

292. Praline Cheesecake Cookie Bars Recipe

Serving: 32 | Prep: | Cook: 50mins | Ready in:

Ingredients

- 3/4c. butter; softened
- 1c. sugar; divided
- 2t. vanilla; dvided
- 1-1/2c. flour
- 2 eggs
- 16oz. cream cheese; softened
- 1/2c. almond brickle chips
- 1/4c. caramel ice cream topping

Direction

- Mix butter, 1/2c. sugar & 1t. of vanilla until light & fluffy.
- Gradually add flour & mix until well blended.
- Press mixture onto bottom of 9x13" pan.
- Bake 20-25 min. until lightly browned.
- Meanwhile, mix cream cheese and the remaining sugar & vanilla.
- Add eggs & mix well. Stir in brickle chips.
- Pour mixture over hot crust.
- Drop teaspoonfuls of caramel topping over cream cheese mixture.
- Run a knife through the batter to swirl the topping
- Bake an additional 30 min.
- Cool then refrigerate.

293. Pumpkin Bars Can Be Made Gluten Free Recipe

Serving: 24 | Prep: | Cook: 20mins | Ready in:

Ingredients

- 1 cup flour
- 2/3 cup sugar
- 1 1/4 teaspoons baking powder (gluten free - check - Most are ok)
- 1 teaspoon cinnamon
- 1/8 teaspoon salt
- 1/2 teaspoon baking soda
- 1/8 teaspoon ground cloves
- 1 tablespoon mayonaise (gluten free - use Hellman's)
- 1 cup pumpkin
- 3 egg whites slightly beaten
- 1/4 cup plus 1 tablespoon corn oil
- 1/4 cup water
- Cream cheese frosting:
- 2 cups confection sugar
- 1/4 cup soft butter
- 3 oz. softened cream cheese
- 3/4 teaspoon vanilla

Direction

- Preheat oven 350 F and spray an 8 x12" pan with non - stick spray (gluten free check spray). Sift together the flour mixture, sugar, baking powder, cinnamon, salt, baking soda and cloves.
- Stir in the mayonnaise, pumpkin, egg whites, corn oil, and water till thoroughly combined.
- Spread in the oiled pan. Bake 20 minutes or till a toothpick inserted in the center comes out clean. Cool in the pan on a wire rack.
- Cream cheese frosting: combine 1/4 cup butter, cream cheese and vanilla in mixer/blend - slowly and confectioner sugar and mix until well blended.
- Spread cream cheese frosting on top of cooled pumpkin bars.
- Refrigerate to keep moist and fresh.

294. Pumpkin Bars Recipe

Serving: 1 | Prep: | Cook: 25mins | Ready in:

Ingredients

- 2 C. flour
- 2 C. sugar
- 2 t. baking powder
- 1 t. baking soda
- 1/2 t. salt
- 2 t. cinnamon
- 1/2 t. cloves
- 4 eggs
- 2 C. pumpkin
- 1 C. vegetable oil
- cream cheese frosting
- 8 oz cream cheese softened
- 1 stick and 2 t butter
- 2 t. vanilla
- 3 1/2 C. powdered sugar
- Mix all ingredients until smooth and creamy.

Direction

- Mix all dry ingredients and set aside.
- Mix wet ingredients.
- Make a well in the dry ingredients and add liquid mixture. Beat well.
- Pour into a greased and floured jelly roll pan. Bake at 350 for 25-30 minutes.
- Spread with cream cheese frosting when cool.

295. Pumpkin Bars With Cream Cheese Frosting Recipe

Serving: 24 | Prep: | Cook: 45mins | Ready in:

Ingredients

- BARS:
- 2 Cups sugar
- 2 Cups flour

- 4 eggs
- 2 Tbsp. baking powder
- 1 tsp. baking soda
- 1/2 tsp. salt
- 1-1/2 tsp. cinnamon
- 1 Cup mazola oil
- 1 can (15oz) pumpkin
- FROSTING:
- 1-1/2 sticks butter, softened
- 1 pkg. (8oz) cream cheese, softened
- 2 tsp. vanilla
- 3-1/2 Cups powdered sugar
- (The frosting ingredients were doubled by my Mother years ago, I'm assuming the original amount didn't cover it to her liking, thought I'd throw this in, I've had a few people ask me.)

Direction

- BARS:
- Preheat oven to 350 degrees.
- Combine all the BAR ingredients in a large bowl & mix until combined.
- Bake in a greased 11x15 pan for 45 minutes or until a toothpick inserted near the center comes out clean.
- Cool completely.
- FROSTING:
- Cream butter & cream cheese together in a large bowl.
- Add vanilla & powdered sugar, mix till smooth.
- If it seems stiff or not spreadable add a little bit of milk.
- Spread over cooled pumpkin bars.

296. Pumpkin Cheese Praline Bars Recipe

Serving: 1 | Prep: | Cook: 30mins | Ready in:

Ingredients

- For pumpkin batter:
- 1 cup Packed brown sugar
- 2 teaspoons ground cinnamon
- 1 teaspoon ground ginger
- 1/2 teaspoon ground cloves
- 1/2 teaspoon baking powder
- 1/2 teaspoon baking soda
- 1/2 cup unsalted butter -- (1 stick)
- 2 eggs
- 1 cup pumpkin puree
- 1 cup all-purpose flour
- For cream cheese batter:
- 8 ounces cream cheese -- room temperature
- 1 egg
- 1 teaspoon vanilla
- 1/3 cup Granulated sugar
- For topping:
- 1/4 cup unsalted butter -- (1/2 stick)
- 1/2 cup Packed brown sugar
- 3/4 cup all-purpose flour
- 3/4 cup Chopped pecans

Direction

- Preheat oven to 350 degrees. Line a 9-by-13-inch baking pan with foil; brush pan with softened butter.
- Prepare pumpkin batter; using an electric mixer on medium speed, mix together brown sugar, cinnamon, ginger, cloves, baking powder and baking soda for about 30 seconds, until evenly combined. Add butter, eggs and pumpkin; beat on medium speed for 2 minutes, until smooth. Scrape bowl with rubber spatula. Add flour all at once; beat on low speed for 30 seconds, until flour is evenly blended in.
- Pour half the pumpkin batter into prepared pan. Reserve other half in a small bowl, scraping mixing bowl well.
- Using the same mixing bowl, prepare cream cheese batter: Beat cream cheese, egg and vanilla on medium speed for about 2 minutes, until fluffy and smooth. Add sugar; beat on medium speed for about 1 minute.
- Spread cream cheese batter over pumpkin batter in pan. Pour reserved pumpkin batter

over cream cheese layer. Using a rubber spatula, cut through the batter several times through the length of the pan, then through the width of the pan, to create a marbled effect.
- Prepare topping: Using an electric mixer on medium speed, beat butter and brown sugar for 2 minutes, until fluffy and light in color. Add flour and pecans; beat on low speed for about 1 minute. The mixture will be crumbly. Sprinkle crumbs evenly over marbled batter.
- Bake for 30 to 35 minutes, reversing the baking pan halfway through baking time. When done, the topping will have begun to brown and the top will feel slightly firm when touched gently with your fingertip.
- Remove from oven; let cool completely on wire rack; cut into bars.
- Store cooled bars in an airtight container for up to 1 week in the refrigerator, or wrap tightly and freeze for up to 2 months.

- Crust
- Combine flour, brown sugar, and butter in a bowl.
- Mix together until crumbly
- Mix in nuts
- Take out 1 C and set aside
- Press remaining mixture in the bottom of a 9x13 baking dish.
- Bake at 350 degrees for 8 minutes
- Filling
- In a mixing bowl cream together cream cheese, sugar and vanilla.
- Mix until very smooth
- Add eggs, pumpkin, allspice and cinnamon.
- Mix well
- Pour over baked crust.
- Sprinkle topping that was set aside over the top
- Bake at 350 for 30 min
- It will be jiggly when done but it will set up as it cools.
- Do not overcook.

297. Pumpkin Cheesecake Bars Recipe

Serving: 24 | Prep: | Cook: 38mins | Ready in:

Ingredients

- CRUST
- 2 C all purpose flour
- 1 1/2 cubes butter
- 1/2 C brown sugar
- 1 C chopped walnuts or pecans
- FILLING
- 2 - 8oz cream cheese (softened)
- 1 1/2 C sugar
- 2 tsp allspice
- 1 tsp vanilla
- 4 eggs
- 3 tsp cinnamon
- 1 C pumpkin

Direction

298. Pumpkin Marshmallow Squares Recipe

Serving: 15 | Prep: | Cook: 5mins | Ready in:

Ingredients

- 50 LARGE MARSHMELLOWS OR 6 CUPS MINIATURE MARSHMELLOWS.
- 1 - 16 OUNCE can pumpkin
- 1 TEASPOON cinnamon
- 2/3 TEASPOON nutmeg
- 1/4 TEASPOON allspice
- 1/4 TEASPOON ginger (OR USE pumpkin pie spice FOR ALL ABOVE spices 2- 2 1/2 TEASPOONS)
- DASH OF cloves
- 1/4 TEASPOON salt
- 3 CUPS WHIPPED DESSERT TOPPING (Dream Whip) 2 ENVELOPES
- 2 CUPS CRUSED graham crackers

- 1/2 CUP butter OR margarine

Direction

- IN A LARGE HEAVY SAUCEPAN, AT LOW HEAT, COMBINE FIRST 8 INGREDIENTS AND STIR UNTIL SMOOTH.
- TAKE OFF HEAT AND COOL AT LEAST 15 MINUTES, BUT WHILE STILL WARM, ADD 3 CUPS OF WHIPPED TOPPING.
- WHILE MIXTURE IS COOLING, MIX GRAHAM CRACKER CRUMBS AND BUTTER TOGETHER AND RESERVE 1/2 CUP FOR TOPPING.
- PAT REMAINING CRUMBS WITH THE BUTTER MIX INTO A 9X13 INCH PAN.
- POUR PUMPKIN MIXTURE OVER CRUMBS.
- TOP WITH ONE CUP MORE OF WHIPPED CREAM AND TOP WITH RESERVED GRAHAM CRACKER CRUMBS.
- REFRIGERATE SEVERAL HOURS OR OVERNIGHT, CUT INTO SQUARES.
- YIELDS 15 - 18 SERVINGS

299. Pumpkin Pie Squares Recipe

Serving: 12 | Prep: | Cook: 45mins | Ready in:

Ingredients

- 18 ounce package yellow cake mix
- 1/2 cup melted butter
- 1 egg
- 16 ounce can pumpkin
- 2 eggs
- 1/2 cup packed light brown sugar
- 2-1/2 teaspoons pumpkin pie spice
- 2/3 cup milk
- 1 teaspoon ground cinnamon
- 1/2 cup chopped pecans
- 1/4 cup butter

Direction

- Reserve 1 cup cake mix.
- Combine remaining mix, melted butter and 1 egg in bowl.
- Mix well and press over bottom of rectangular cake pan.
- Combine pumpkin, eggs, brown sugar, pie spice and milk and pour into pan.
- Mix reserved cake mix, cinnamon, nuts and butter in small bowl.
- Sprinkle over pumpkin layer.
- Bake at 350 for 45 minutes.
- Cool and serve with whipped cream.

300. Pumpkin Squares Recipe

Serving: 15 | Prep: | Cook: 30mins | Ready in:

Ingredients

- FOR cake
- 1 cup flour
- ½ teaspoon baking soda
- ¾ teaspoon ground cinnamon
- ¾ teaspoon ground ginger
- ¼ teaspoon ground nutmeg
- ¼ teaspoon ground allspice
- pinch of cloves
- ½ teaspoon salt
- ½ cup softened butter
- 1 1/3 cups brown sugar
- 1 large egg
- 1 teaspoon vanilla
- 1 cup solid-pack pumpkin
- ½ cup chopped nuts
- ½ cup raisins
- FOR frosting
- 6 ounces white chocolate
- 6 ounces cream cheese
- ¼ teaspoon vanilla
- 3 tablespoons softened butter

Direction

- Make the Pumpkin Squares

- Preheat oven to 350°F. Spray a 13 x 9 pan with vegetable spray or lightly butter.
- Stir together flour and spices. Beat butter in a bowl until creamy. Add brown sugar and beat until light and fluffy. Add egg and vanilla beating until blended. Add flour mixture alternately with pumpkin, beginning and ending with flour. Add the nuts and raisins in with the last bit of flour.
- Spread into prepared pan and bake for 25 to 30 minutes. Cool completely in pan
- Make the frosting
- Melt white chocolate. Let stand until cool, but still liquid.
- Beat cream cheese in a bowl until light and fluffy. Beat in vanilla and butter. Gradually beat in cooled white chocolate and beat until smooth and shiny. If mixture looks curdled, simply continue beating until smooth.
- Spread frosting on pumpkin squares. Refrigerate for 30 minutes or until frosting is set.
- TO SERVE
- Cut into 15 3 x 3 inch squares. We serve these as is, but serve with the ice cream of your choice - maybe a good butter pecan or something spicy like cinnamon.

301. Pumpkin Carrot Snack Bars Recipe

Serving: 16 | Prep: | Cook: 22mins | Ready in:

Ingredients

- 1 cup canned solid-pack pumpkin
- 1 cup shredded carrot
- 1/2 cup sugar
- 1/3 cup dried cranberries or raisins, chopped
- 1/4 cup canola oil
- 2 large eggs add to
- 1 cup whole grain pastry flour
- 1 teaspoon baking powder
- 1 teaspoon ground cinnamon
- 1/2 teaspoon baking soda
- 1/4 teaspoon salt
- 1/4 cup shelled pumpkin seeds or chopped walnuts

Direction

- Preheat the oven to 350°F. Coat a 13" x 9" x 2" baking pan with cooking spray.
- In a large bowl, combine the pumpkin, carrot, sugar, cranberries or raisins, oil, and eggs. Stir until well blended. Add the flour, baking powder, cinnamon, baking soda, and salt. Mix until blended.
- Pour the batter into prepared pan and spread evenly. Sprinkle with pumpkin seeds or walnuts.
- Bake and then cool completely.

302. Pumpkin Spice Bars Recipe

Serving: 9 | Prep: | Cook: 30mins | Ready in:

Ingredients

- 4 eggs
- 2 Cups sugar
- 1 Cup vegetable oil
- 1 Can (16 ounces) pumpkin
- 2 Cups all-purpose flour
- 2 tsp. baking powder
- 2 tsp. ground cinnamon
- 1 tsp. baking soda
- 3/4 tsp. salt
- 1/2 tsp. ground ginger
- 1/4 tsp. ground cloves
- 1/2 Cup raisins
- Cream Cheese Frosting:
- 1 package (3 ounces) cream cheese, softened
- 1/4 Cup plus 2 Tbs. margarine or butter, softened (I reduced this by 2 Tbs. and it was perfect.)
- 1 tsp. vanilla

- 2 Cups powdered sugar
- 1/2 Cup chopped nuts for topping

Direction

- Heat oven to 350 degrees.
- Grease jelly roll pan, 15 1/2 X 10 1/2 X 1-inch.
- Beat eggs, sugar, oil and pumpkin.
- Stir in flour, baking powder, cinnamon, baking soda, salt, ginger and cloves. (I like to have the dry ingredients already mixed in a separate bowl and ready to stir into the rest of the ingredients.)
- Mix in raisins.
- Pour batter into pan.
- Bake until light brown, 25 to 30 minutes.
- Cool on wire rack.
- Frost with Cream Cheese Frosting and sprinkle with nuts.
- Refrigerate any remaining bars.
- Cream Cheese Frosting:
- Mix cream cheese, margarine or butter, and vanilla.
- Gradually beat in powdered sugar until smooth and of spreading consistency. This takes patience, but worth it.

303. Quick Chocolate Cherry Bars Recipe

Serving: 36 | Prep: | Cook: 25mins | Ready in:

Ingredients

- 1 Devils Food cake mix
- 1-21 oz. cherry pie filling
- 1 t. almond extract
- 2 eggs, beaten
- 1/4 c. water
- 1 container chocolate fudge frosting

Direction

- Combine almond extract, eggs and water. Stir into cake mix. Gently stir in pie filling. Pour mixture into a greased and floured, 9×13 inch pan.
- Bake at 350° for 25-30 minutes.
- Cool completely before frosting.

304. Raspberry Linzer Bars Recipe

Serving: 24 | Prep: | Cook: 25mins | Ready in:

Ingredients

- 1 1/2c flour
- 3/4c sugar
- 1/2c plus 2Tbs chopped walnuts, divided
- 1Tbs unsweetened cocoa powder
- 2tsp fresh grated orange zest
- 1/4tsp baking powder
- 1/4tsp baking soda
- 1/4tsp salt
- 1tsp gr. cinnamon
- 1/4tsp gr. nutmeg
- 1/4tsp ground cloves
- 1 lg. egg
- 2Tbs canola oil
- 2Tbs water
- 3/4c seedless raspberry jam
- 1Tbs. orange juice

Direction

- Preheat oven to 350. Coat a 9x9" or 7x11 1/2" pan with cooking spray.
- Combine flour, sugar, 1/2c walnuts, cocoa, orange zest, baking powder, baking soda, salt, cinnamon, nutmeg and cloves in food processor. Pulse until walnuts are finely chopped. Add egg, oil and water; process till moistened. Transfer to prepared pan. Press into even layer. Bake crust until dry to the touch and barely golden, 20-25 mins.
- Whisk jam and orange juice in a bowl. Spread evenly over the crust. Sprinkle with remaining 2Tbs walnuts. Bake the bars until jam bubbles,

10-15 mins longer. Transfer pan to wire rack and cool completely before cutting into bars.

305. Red Velvet Cheesecake Bars From Henrys Deli Recipe

Serving: 15 | Prep: | Cook: 30mins | Ready in:

Ingredients

- CRUST:
- 10-12 chocolate graham crackers squares (about 2.5 oz) crushed
- ¼ cup melted butter
- ¼ cup sugar
- FILING:
- ¾ cup sour cream
- 12 oz cream cheese (softened)
- ¾ cup sugar
- 1 egg & 2 egg yolks (beaten)
- ¼ cup buttermilk
- 1 tsp vanilla
- 1 tsp white vinegar
- 5 tsp unsweetened cocoa powder
- 1 (1 oz) bottle red food coloring
- ICING:
- 4 oz cream cheese (softened)
- 4 tbsp butter (softened)
- 2 cups powdered sugar
- 2 tsp vanilla extract

Direction

- CRUST
- Preheat oven to 350.
- Combine crust ingredients in a bowl and stir thoroughly.
- Place in a well-buttered or greased 9x12 baking dish.
- Flatten out and press with palm of hand or flat bottomed object like a measuring cup or glass.
- Bake for 10 min then remove to cool completely.
- FILLING
- To make the filling, lower oven temp to 300.
- Put sour cream in mixing bowl and mix by itself to coat beater and bowl (makes for easier removal later).
- Add cream cheese and sugar. Mix on medium to high speed until smooth with no lumps.
- Scrape bottom of bowl with spatula to make sure everything is combined.
- Turn mixer to slow or medium speed add eggs, buttermilk, vanilla, and vinegar.
- Mix until combined and scrape bowl again.
- Add cocoa and food coloring.
- Mix on slow; scrape bottom of bowl and mix again until everything is combined and uniform.
- Pour into crust and bake for about 35 minutes.
- When the outside edges are set, but the middle is still a little loose, turn off oven and let it sit in the oven for another 15-20 min. then remove to cool.
- After it has cooled enough that you can handle the pan, place in refrigerator for at least six hours.
- ICING
- Combine together Icing ingredients and spread over cooled cheese cake.
- Makes 12-18 servings

306. Redhead Bars Recipe

Serving: 12 | Prep: | Cook: 30mins | Ready in:

Ingredients

- 1/4 cup light margarine
- 2/3 cup light brown sugar
- 1 tsp vanilla
- 1 medium, over-ripe banana, mashed
- 1 cup flour
- 1 tsp baking powder
- 1/2 tsp salt
- 1 cup grated carrots
- 1/3 cup chopped chocolate (or chocolate chips)

Direction

- Preheat oven to 350, grease an 8" square pan.
- Beat margarine, sugar, vanilla and banana.
- Stir in remaining ingredients except chocolate.
- Sprinkle chopped chocolate over mixture.
- Bake for 30 minutes.

307. Rocky Road Bars Recipe

Serving: 24 | Prep: | Cook: 30mins | Ready in:

Ingredients

- Base
- 1 pouch (1 lb 1.5 oz) Betty Crocker double chocolate chunk cookie mix
- 1/4 cup vegetable oil
- 2 tablespoons water
- 1 egg
- Filling
- 1 package (8 oz) cream cheese, softened
- 1/2 cup granulated sugar
- 1/4 cup butter or margarine, softened
- 2 tablespoons all-purpose flour
- 1 teaspoon vanilla
- 1 egg
- 1/4 cup chopped pecans
- 1 cup semisweet chocolate chips (6 oz)
- 1 1/2 cups miniature marshmallows
- frosting
- 1/2 cup butter or margarine
- 1/4 cup unsweetened baking cocoa
- 1/3 cup milk
- 3 cups powdered sugar
- 1 teaspoon vanilla
- 1 cup chopped pecans

Direction

- Heat oven to 350°F.
- Spray bottom and sides of 13x9-inch pan with cooking spray.
- In large bowl, stir cookie base ingredients until soft dough forms. Press dough in bottom of pan.
- Set aside.
- In large bowl, beat cream cheese, granulated sugar, 1/4 cup butter, the flour, 1 teaspoon vanilla and the egg with electric mixer on medium speed until smooth.
- Stir in 1/4 cup pecans.
- Spread over cookie dough base.
- Sprinkle with chocolate chips.
- Bake 26 to 28 minutes or until filling is set.
- Sprinkle evenly with marshmallows.
- Bake 2 minutes longer.
- In 2-quart saucepan, melt 1/2 cup butter over medium heat.
- Stir in cocoa and milk.
- Heat to boiling, stirring constantly.
- Remove from heat.
- With wire whisk, gradually stir in powdered sugar until well blended. Stir in 1 teaspoon vanilla and 1 cup pecans.
- Immediately pour over marshmallows, spreading gently to cover. Cool 30 minutes.
- Refrigerate about 2 hours or until chilled.
- For bars, cut into 6 rows by 4 rows. Store covered in refrigerator.

308. Rocky Road OREO Bars Recipe

Serving: 20 | Prep: | Cook: 120mins | Ready in:

Ingredients

- 20 OREO chocolate Sandwich cookies 1/4 cup
- (1/2 stick) butter
- 1 pkg. (4-serving size) JELL-O OREO Flavor Instant Pudding & pie filling
- 1-1/2 cups powdered sugar
- 1/3 cup boiling water
- 1/3 cup PLANTERS COCKTAIL peanuts, chopped

- 1/3 cup JET-PUFFED miniature marshmallows
- 2 squares BAKER'S Semi-Sweet baking chocolate

Direction

- FINELY crush cookies; set aside. Microwave butter in large microwavable bowl on HIGH 30 seconds or until butter is melted. Add crushed cookies; mix well. Press crumb mixture firmly onto bottom of 9-inch square pan.
- MIX dry pudding mix, sugar and boiling water until well blended. Pour over crust; spread to completely cover crust. Sprinkle with peanuts and marshmallows.
- PLACE chocolate squares in microwavable bowl. Microwave on HIGH 45 seconds; stir until chocolate is completely melted. Drizzle over pudding mixture. Refrigerate 1 hour or until set. Cut into 20 bars to serve. Store leftover bars in refrigerator.

309. Rustic Nut Bars Recipe

Serving: 12 | Prep: | Cook: 45mins | Ready in:

Ingredients

- 1 tbls. plus 1 1/2 sticks cold butter, divided
- 2 1/3 cups flour
- 1/2 cup sugar
- 1/2 tsp. baking powder
- 1/2 tsp. salt
- 1 egg, lightly beaten
- 2/3 cup honey
- 1/2 cup brown sugar, packed
- 1/4 tsp. salt
- 6 tbls. butter
- 2 tbls. whipping cream
- 1 cup chopped hazelnuts, chopped and toasted
- 1 cup roasted almonds, chopped
- 1 cup cashews, toasted and chopped
- 1 cup pistachios, toasted and chopped

Direction

- Preheat oven to 375.
- Line 13z9 pan with foil and grease with 1 tbsp. butter.
- In mixing bowl, add flour, sugar, baking powder and salt and combine.
- Add remaining butter and mix until resembles coarse crumbs.
- Stir in egg until blended.
- Press firmly into pan.
- Bake 18-20 minutes or until edges are golden brown.
- Cool completely.
- In saucepan over medium heat, bring the honey, brown sugar and salt to boil, stirring until sugar is dissolved.
- Boil without stirring for 2 minutes.
- Add butter and cream.
- Bring to boil, cook and stir constantly for another minute.
- Remove from heat and stir in all the nut ingredients.
- Spread over crust.
- Bake 15-20 minutes or until topping is bubbly.
- Cool completely.

310. Salted Cashew Caramel Bars Recipe

Serving: 24 | Prep: | Cook: 24mins | Ready in:

Ingredients

- Crust
- 1½ cups brown sugar, packed
- 1 cup butter, softened
- 1 teaspoon salt
- 3 cups flour
- 2 cups salted cashews, mixed nuts, peanuts, whatever nut you prefer
- caramel topping

- ½ cup corn syrup
- 2 tablespoons butter
- 1 tablespoon water
- 6 ounces butterscotch chips
- (I would try pnut btter chips!)

Direction

- For the crust, cream together the butter, brown sugar and salt; then blend in the flour. Press mixture into the bottom and up the sides of a 10x15 baking sheet. Bake at 350 degrees for 10 minutes. Prepare topping while crust is baking.
- For the topping, combine all ingredients in a medium saucepan; bring to a boil and then boil gently for 2 minutes, stirring constantly.
- To assemble, remove crust from oven, sprinkle nuts over hot crust, and then pour hot topping over the nuts. Return pan to oven and bake an additional 10 to 14 minutes, until golden brown. Cool completely before cutting into bars.

311. Salted Peanut Marshmallow Bars Recipe

Serving: 15 | Prep: | Cook: 15mins | Ready in:

Ingredients

- Base:
- 1 pound peanut butter sandwich cookies (Nutter-Butter, I assume)
- 1 stick butter, melted
- Topping:
- 2 cups peanut butter chips
- 2/3 cup light corn syrup
- 4 tablespoons butter
- 1 teaspoon vanilla extract
- 2 cups miniature marshmallows
- 2 cups dry roasted peanuts
- 2 cups Rice Krispies cereal

Direction

- Pulverize cookies in food processor until fine crumbs.
- Drizzle in melted butter and process until crumbs clump together.
- Press crumbs into bottom of lightly greased 13x9 pan.
- Bake at 350 degrees for 15 minutes.
- Melt peanut butter chips, corn syrup, 4 tablespoons butter and extract in the microwave, just until chips are melted and mixture can be mixed smooth.
- Spread about ½ of the melted mixture over the hot baked base, being very careful, as the melted mixture will tend to pull away the crust. Work with covering the crust just as soon as the pan is removed from the oven, and it will work best. Use a gentle hand to spread the melted mixture over the crust!
- Top melted peanut butter mixture with marshmallows and return pan to oven.
- Bake until marshmallows puff, about 2 to 4 minutes, then remove pan from oven. Don't let marshmallows brown or they will become crunchy when cooled.
- Toss remaining melted peanut butter chip mixture with the dry roasted peanuts and cereal.
- Drop heaping spoonfuls of peanut/cereal topping over the hot marshmallow layer, then spread it out with a spatula (spray spatula with some non-stick spray to prevent marshmallows from sticking to it). This gets rather tricky, as the mixture will want to pull away the marshmallow layer. My advice is to work quickly on a HOT crust, to keep it all as soft as possible. Have the peanut/cereal topping ready as soon as your remove the crust/marshmallow layer from the oven, plop the topping on the puffed marshmallows and use your buttered fingers or spatula to spread it over the marshmallows gently. If you have some "holes" on the coverage, it's really quite all right - it will still taste fine!
- Cool bars completely before cutting with a knife that has been coated with non-stick spray.

312. Sara Lees Carrot Square Cake Recipe

Serving: 6 | Prep: | Cook: 50mins | Ready in:

Ingredients

- 2 eggs
- 1 teaspoon vanilla
- 6 oz oil
- 1 teaspoon salt
- 1 1/2 teaspoons baking powder
- 2 teaspoons cinnamon
- 1 cup sugar
- 1 1/4 cups all purpose flour
- 1 cup carrots; grate fine
- 1 cup walnuts; well-chopped
- 1/2 cup light raisins; optional

Direction

- Combine first 8 ingredients with electric mixer on medium-high.
- Beat 3 minutes scraping down sides of bowl often.
- Remove beaters. Stir in last 3 ingredients.
- Grease and flour 9" square pan.
- Spread batter evenly in pan.
- Bake at 325~ about 50 minutes.
- Cool in pan about 30 minutes.
- Frost with Cream Cheese Frosting and sprinkle with additional walnuts.
- Contributor: Gloria Pitzer

313. Scarlett OHara Pecan Bars Recipe

Serving: 25 | Prep: | Cook: 40mins | Ready in:

Ingredients

- 1 1/4 cups all-purpose flour
- CRUST INGREDIENTS:
- 1/2 cup butter, softened
- 1/4 cup sugar
- 1/4 cup coarsely chopped pecans
- FILLING INGREDIENTS:
- 3/4 cup dark corn syrup
- 1/3 cup firmly packed brown sugar
- 2 eggs
- 3 tablespoons all-purpose flour
- 1 teaspoon vanilla
- 1/2 teaspoon salt
- 3/4 cup coarsely chopped pecans

Direction

- Heat oven to 350°F. Combine 1 1/4 cups flour, butter and sugar in large bowl. Beat at medium speed, scraping bowl often, until mixture resembles coarse crumbs. Stir in 1/4 cup pecans.
- Press crust mixture evenly onto bottom of ungreased 8 or 9-inch square baking pan. Bake for 18 to 22 minutes or until very light golden brown on edges.
- Meanwhile, combine all filling ingredients except pecans in small bowl; mix well. Stir in pecans. Spread evenly over hot, partially baked crust. Bake for 20 to 30 minutes or until filling appears set and knife inserted 1-inch from edge comes out clean. Cool completely; cut into bars.

314. Scotcholate Bars Recipe

Serving: 24 | Prep: | Cook: 20mins | Ready in:

Ingredients

- 1 stick butter, softened
- 1 cup sugar
- 2 eggs
- 1t vanilla
- 2oz unsweetened chocolate squares, melted
- 2/3 cup cold water
- 1 1/2 cups flour
- 1/2t salt

- 1/2t baking soda
- 12oz butterscotch chips

Direction

- Beat butter and sugar at medium speed until creamy.
- Add eggs and vanilla and mix until combined
- Add chocolate till combined
- Combine dry ingredients and add them alternately with water.
- Beat well for 3-5 minutes until fluffy and colour lightens.
- Pour into greased jelly roll pan then top with butterscotch chips.
- Bake at 350 for about 20 minutes until bars are springy in the centre (more like a cake doneness as compared to under baking brownies)
- Cool completely then cut into bars.

315. Scrumptious Chocolate Layer Bars Recipe

Serving: 36 | Prep: | Cook: 35mins | Ready in:

Ingredients

- Filling:
- 12 oz chocolate chips
- 5 oz Can evaporated milk
- 8 oz cream cheese
- 1/2 ts almond extract
- Crust:
- 3 c flour
- 1 c butter, softened
- 2 eggs
- 1 ts baking powder
- 1/2 ts almond extract

Direction

- Mix chocolate chips, cream cheese and evaporated milk in a saucepan. Cook over low heat, stirring constantly, until mixture is smooth. Remove from heat and stir in 1/2 tsp. almond extract. Mix well; set aside.
- Combine remaining ingredients. Blend well until mixture resembles coarse crumbs.
- Press 1/2 crumbs (not too hard) in greased 9 x 13 pan. Spread with chocolate mixture. Sprinkle remaining 1/2 of crumbs over filling.
- Bake at 375 degrees F for 35-40 minutes or until golden brown. Cool and cut into bars. Makes approx. 36 bars.

316. Simple Apple Squares Recipe

Serving: 12 | Prep: | Cook: 40mins | Ready in:

Ingredients

- 3 large apples, peeled & diced (I had an assortment of red apples on hand.)
- 1 cup pecans, roughly chopped
- 2 cups flour (I used 1/2 whole wheat, 1/2 all purpose flour)
- 1 3/4 cup sugar
- 1 teaspoon baking soda
- 1 teaspoon cinnamon
- 1/2 teaspoon salt
- 2 eggs OR 1/2 cup healthy egg substitute
- 3/4 cup canola oil OR natural applesauce
- 1 teaspoon vanilla

Direction

- Preheat oven to 350F degrees.
- Prep the apples and pecans, set aside. In a large bowl, mix the flour, sugar, soda, cinnamon and salt together. Make a well, pour in eggs, oil, and vanilla. STIR BY HAND. The batter becomes very thick. Fold in the apples and pecans until well mixed. Pour into a well-greased pan. There's enough batter to fill one 9 x 13 inch pan.

317. Sinfully Delicious Caramel Bars Recipe

Serving: 24 | Prep: | Cook: 5mins | Ready in:

Ingredients

- 49 caramels OR 14 OUNCE BAG
- 3 TABLESPOON water
- 5 CUPS crisp rice cereal
- 1 CUP salted peanuts
- 1 (6 OUNCE0 PKG OF chocolate chips
- 1 (6 OUNCE) PKG butterscotch chips

Direction

- PREHAT OVEN TO 200 DEGREES F.
- MELT CARAMELS AND WATER IN A SAUCEPAN OVER LOW HEAT, STIRRING UNTIL SAUCE IS SMOOTH.
- POUR MIXTURE OVER CEREAL AND NUTS.
- TOSS UNTIL WELL COATED
- WITH GREASED FINGERS, PRESS MIXTURE IN GREASED 9 X 13 PAN.
- SPRINKLE WITH BOTH- MORSELS ON TOP.
- PLACE IN OVEN FOR 5 MINUTES OR UNTIL MORSELS ARE SOFTENED,
- SPREAD TO FORM A FROSTING, COOL CUT INTO BARS
- MAKES 24 TO 30 BARS

318. Smore Bars Recipe

Serving: 8 | Prep: | Cook: 30mins | Ready in:

Ingredients

- ½ cup room temperature butter
- ¼ cup brown sugar
- ½ cup sugar
- 1 large egg
- 1 tsp vanilla
- 1 ⅓ cup all-purpose flour
- ¾ cup graham cracker crumbs (whizzed in food processor until fine)
- 1 tsp baking powder
- ¼ tsp salt
- 6 milk chocolate bars
- 1 ½ cup marshmallow crème (not melted marshmallow or fluff)

Direction

- Preheat oven to 350°. Grease an 8-inch square pan.
- Combine and cream together butter, brown sugar, and sugar.
- Beat in the egg and vanilla.
- Whisk together in small bowl flour, graham cracker crumbs, baking powder, and salt.
- Add dry mixture to butter mixture and mix at low speed until combined.
- Divide dough in half. Press half of dough into an even layer on the bottom of the pan.
- Place milk chocolate bars over dough in single layer.
- Spread marshmallow crème over chocolate
- Place remaining half of dough in a single layer on top of marshmallow. Tip: Flatten small pieces of dough into small shingles and layer them together.
- Bake for 30 to 35 minutes, until lightly browned.
- Cool completely before cutting into bars.

319. Smores Bars Recipe

Serving: 24 | Prep: | Cook: 25mins | Ready in:

Ingredients

- 3/4 cup butter
- 2/3 cup sugar
- 1 egg
- 1 teaspoon vanilla
- 18 whole graham crackers, crushed (approx 3 cups)
- 1/2 cup all-purpose flour

- 1/2 teaspoon salt
- 8 milk chocolate bars - 1 1/2 oz each
- 3 1/2 cups miniature marshmallows

Direction

- Heat oven to 350°.
- Beat butter and sugar with electric mixer on medium speed until light and fluffy.
- Beat in egg and vanilla.
- Stir in crushed graham crackers, flour, and salt. Reserve 1 cup of the graham cracker mixture and press remaining mixture over the bottom of a greased 13x9x2-inch baking pan.
- Arrange chocolate bars, in a single layer, over graham cracker crust mixture in the pan.
- Sprinkle with marshmallows.
- Crumbled reserved graham cracker mixture over the marshmallows.
- Bake for 20 to 25 minutes or until golden brown.
- Cool in pan on wire rack for 10 minutes.
- Cut into bars and cool completely.
- Makes about 2 dozen bars.

320. Snicker Bar Cheesecake Recipe

Serving: 8 | Prep: | Cook: 75mins | Ready in:

Ingredients

- 9 ounce package chocolate wafer cookies
- 4 tablespoons butter melted
- 24 ounces cream cheese softened
- 1 cup granulated sugar
- 1 tablespoon vanilla extract
- 4 eggs
- 2 cups heavy cream divided
- 1-1/2 cups snack size Snickers bars

Direction

- Preheat oven to 325.
- In a food processor grind cookies into fine crumbs.
- Add butter and process until well blended.
- Press into bottom and about 1 inch up sides of a 10 inch spring form pan.
- In large bowl beat cream cheese and sugar with electric mixer on medium speed until smooth.
- Beat in eggs one at a time then beat in vanilla extract and 1 cup cream and beat 4 minutes.
- Fold in 1 cup cut up Snickers pieces and pour into pan then bake 1 hour 15 minutes.
- Let cool to room temperature then sprinkle remaining candy pieces over top.
- Refrigerate 5 hours before serving.
- Run knife around edge of pan to loosen cake and remove side of pan.
- Just before serving drizzle fudge topping over cake.
- Whip remaining cream until stiff and spoon a dollop over each slice.

321. Snicker Bars Recipe

Serving: 1 | Prep: | Cook: 16mins | Ready in:

Ingredients

- 1 German chocolate cake mix
- 1 (14 oz) pkg. caramels
- 2/3 C. evaporated milk
- 3/4 C. butter melted
- 1 C. chocolate chips
- 1 C. nuts chopped (optional)

Direction

- Melt caramels with 1/3 C. milk.
- Combine half the cake mix with butter, 1/2 C. milk, and mix with spoon.
- Grease and flour 9x13 baking dish. Spread mixture. Bake at 350 for 6-8 minutes.
- Cover with caramels, chips and nuts. Put remaining cake mix on top. Bake another 10 minutes.

322. Snickers Bar Cheesecake Recipe

Serving: 12 | Prep: | Cook: 80mins | Ready in:

Ingredients

- 1 (9 ounce package) chocolate wafer cookies
- 4 tablespoons butter, melted
- 3 (8 ounce package) cream cheese, softened
- 1 cup sugar
- 4 eggs
- 1 tablespoon vanilla extract
- 2 cup heavy cream
- 1 1/2 pound snack size Snickers bars, each cut into sixths
- Fudge Topping

Direction

- Preheat oven to 325 degrees.
- In a food processor, grind cookies into fine crumbs.
- Add butter and process until well blended.
- Press into bottom and about 1 inch up sides of a 9-1/2-or 10 inch springform pan.
- In a large bowl, beat together cream cheese and sugar with an electric mixer on medium speed until smooth, 1 to 2 minutes.
- Beat in eggs, one at a time.
- Beat in vanilla and 1 cup cream, beat 3 to 4 minutes.
- Fold in 1-1/2 cups cut-up Snickers pieces.
- Turn into a crumb lined pan.
- Bake 1 hour and 15 to 25 minutes, or until cheesecake is almost set but center still jiggles slightly.
- Let cool to room temperature.
- Sprinkle remaining candy pieces over top of cheesecake.
- Refrigerate at least 4 to 5 hours before serving.
- Run a knife around edge of pan to loosen cake and remove springform side of pan.
- Just before serving, drizzle Fudge Topping over cake.
- Whip remaining 1 cup of cream until stiff and spoon a dollop over each slice.

323. Snickers Cheesecake Squares Recipe

Serving: 20 | Prep: | Cook: 40mins | Ready in:

Ingredients

- Crust
- 2 c. crumbs from Oreo Sandwich cookies; (or prepackaged crumbs) or from other chocolate cookies
- 1/4 c. butter or margarine; melted
- Filling
- 2 lb cream cheese; softened
- 1 c. sugar
- 1 tsp vanilla
- 4 eggs
- 4 or 8 to 9 Fun-Size Snickers candy bars-- (2.07 oz.)

Direction

- Preheat oven to 350 degrees.
- For crust:
- Mix crumbs and butter.
- Press into bottom of 9-by 13-inch baking pan.
- For filling:
- Mix cream cheese, sugar and vanilla with an electric mixer on medium speed until well blended.
- Add eggs; mix until blended.
- Gently stir in 1 cup of the chopped candy.
- Pour into crust.
- Sprinkle with remaining chopped candy.
- Bake for 40 minutes or until center is almost set.
- Cool.
- Refrigerate at least three hours.
- Cut into squares.

324. Snickery Squares Recipe

Serving: 16 | Prep: | Cook: 20mins | Ready in:

Ingredients

- For the Crust:
- 1 cup all-purpose flour
- ¼ cup sugar
- 2 TBSP powdered sugar
- ¼ tsp salt
- 1 stick unsalted butter, cut into small pieces and chilled
- 1 large egg yolk, lightly beaten
- For the Filling:
- ½ cup sugar
- 3 TBSP water
- 1 ½ cups salted peanuts
- About 1 ½ cups store-bought dulce de leche
- For the Topping:
- 7 ounces bittersweet chocolate (I use semi), coarsely chopped
- ½ stick unsalted butter, cut into 8 pieces, at room temperature

Direction

- Preheat oven to 350F. Butter an 8 inch square pan and put it on a baking sheet.
- To Make the Crust: Toss the flour, sugar, powdered sugar and salt into a food processor and pulse a few times to combine. Toss in the pieces of cold butter and pulse about 12 times, until the mixture looks like coarse meal.
- Pour the yolk over the ingredients and pulse until the dough forms clumps and curds-stop before the dough comes together in a ball.
- Turn the dough into the buttered pan and gently press it evenly across the bottom of the pan. Prick the dough with a fork and slide the sheet into the oven.
- Bake the crust for 15-20 minutes, or until it takes on just a little color around the edges. Transfer the pan to a rack and cool to room temperature before filling.
- To Make the Filling: Have a parchment or silicone mat-lined baking sheet at the ready, as well as a long-handled wooden spoon and a medium heavy bottomed saucepan.
- Put the sugar and water in the saucepan and cook over medium-high heat, stirring, until the sugar dissolves. Keeping the heat fairly high, continue to cook the sugar, without stirring, until it just starts to color. Toss the peanuts and immediately start stirring.
- Keep stirring, to coat the peanuts with sugar. Within a few minutes, they will be covered with sugar and turn white—keep stirring until the sugar turns back into caramel. When the peanuts are coated with a nice deep amber caramel, remove the pan from the heat and turn the nuts out onto the baking sheet, using the wooden spoon to spread them out as best you can. Cool the nuts to room temperature.
- When they are cool enough to handle, separate the nuts or break them into small pieces. Divide the nuts in half. Keep half of the nuts whole or in biggish pieces for the filling, and finely chop the other half for the topping (I kept mine whole).
- Spread the Dulce de Leche over the shortbread base and sprinkle over the whole candied nuts.
- To Make the Topping: Melt the chocolate in a heatproof bowl set over a saucepan of barely simmering water. Remove chocolate from the heat and gently stir in the butter, stirring until it is fully blended into the chocolate.
- Pour the chocolate over the Dulce de Leche, smoothing it with a long metal icing spatula, then sprinkle over the rest of the peanuts. Slide the pan into the fridge to set the topping, about 20 minutes; if you'd like to serve the squares cold, keep them refrigerated for at least 3 hours before cutting.
- Cut into 16 bars.
- * I used semi-sweet chocolate.
- * I had a really hard time cutting these after refrigerating for only 20 minutes, so I stuck

them in the freezer for a few which made them much easier to cut.

325. So Easy Lemon Bars Recipe

Serving: 36 | Prep: | Cook: 40mins | Ready in:

Ingredients

- 1 roll (18 oz) refrigerated sugar cookies
- 4 eggs, slightly beaten
- 1 1/2 cups sugar
- 1/4 cup all-purpose flour
- 1 tsp baking powder
- 1/4 cup lemon juice
- 1 to 2 TBSP powdered sugar

Direction

- Heat oven to 350.
- Slice cookie dough as directed on package. Arrange slices in bottom of ungreased 13 x 9-inch pan. With lightly floured fingers, press dough evenly in pan.
- Bake 15 to 20 minutes or until light golden brown. Meanwhile, in large bowl, stir together eggs, sugar, flour and baking powder. Stir in lemon juice. Pour mixture over warm crust.
- Bake an additional 20 to 30 minutes or until top is light golden brown. Cool completely, about 1 1/2 hours. Sprinkle with powdered sugar. For bars, cut into 9 rows by 4 rows.

326. Sour Cream Cranberry Bars Recipe

Serving: 16 | Prep: | Cook: 40mins | Ready in:

Ingredients

- 1 cup packed brown sugar
- 1 cup butter softened
- 2 cups quick cooking oats
- 1-1/2 cups cake flour
- 1 teaspoon baking soda
- 2 cups sweetened dried cranberries
- 1 cup sour cream
- 3/4 cup sugar
- 2 tablespoons cake flour
- 1 tablespoon grated lemon peel
- 1 teaspoon vanilla
- 1 egg

Direction

- Preheat oven to 350 then mix brown sugar and butter in large bowl with spoon.
- Stir in oats, flour and baking soda until crumbly.
- Press half of the mixture in bottom of ungreased rectangular pan and bake 10 minutes.
- Mix remaining ingredients in large bowl and pour over baked crust.
- Crumble remaining oats over filling and bake 30 minutes longer then cool completely.

327. Sour Cream Banana Bars Recipe

Serving: 9 | Prep: | Cook: 25mins | Ready in:

Ingredients

- 1 1/2 Cups sugar (I use a little less)
- 1 Cup sour cream (I use Light)
- 1/2 Cup margarine or butter, softened
- 2 eggs
- 1 1/2 Cups mashed bananas (about 3 Large, ripe)
- 2 tsp. vanilla
- 2 Cups all-purpose flour
- 1 tsp. salt
- 1 tsp. baking soda
- 1/2 Cup chopped nuts

- Browned butter Frosting:
- 1/3 Cup margarine or butter
- 3 Cups powdered sugar
- 1 1/2 tsp. vanilla
- About 2 Tbs. milk

Direction

- Heat oven to 375 degrees.
- Grease and flour jelly roll pan, 15 1/2 X 10 1/2 X 1-inch.
- Mix sugar, sour cream, margarine and eggs in a large mixer bowl on low speed, scraping bowl occasionally, 1 minute.
- Beat bananas and vanilla on low speed 30 seconds.
- Beat in flour, salt, and baking soda (I like to have this already mixed in a separate bowl ready to add to the mix) on medium speed, scraping bowl occasionally, 1 minute. Stir in nuts.
- Spread dough in pan.
- Bake until light brown, 20 to 25 minutes.
- Cool; frost with Browned Butter Frosting.
- Cut into bars, about 2 X 1 1/2 inches.
- Brown Butter Frosting:
- Heat margarine over medium heat until delicate brown.
- Mix in powdered sugar. (For best results, use a whisk.)
- Beat in vanilla and milk until smooth and of spreading consistency.

328. Southern Pecan Bars Recipe

Serving: 12 | Prep: | Cook: 30mins | Ready in:

Ingredients

- Crust
- 1 cup flour
- ⅓ cup brown sugar
- ¼ butter, softened
- ¼ cup finely chopped pecans
- ¼ teaspoon baking powder
- Topping
- ¼ cup brown sugar
- 2 tablespoons flour
- ½ teaspoon salt
- ¾ cup white or dark corn syrup (I use white)
- 1 teaspoon vanilla extract
- 2 eggs
- ¾ cup finely chopped pecans (chopping them finely will allow you to cut them into bars easier)

Direction

- In a large bowl, combine all crust ingredients; mix on low speed until crumbly.
- Press crust into an ungreased 9x13 pan.
- Bake at 350 degrees for 10 minutes; remove pan from oven.
- Combine topping ingredients, except pecans; beat on medium speed until well blended.
- Pour topping over hot crust; sprinkle with pecans.
- Bake an additional 20 to 25 minutes, until golden brown.
- Cool completely before cutting into bars.

329. Special K Peanut Butter And Chocolate Bars Recipe

Serving: 40 | Prep: | Cook: 2mins | Ready in:

Ingredients

- 1 cup light corn syrup
- 1 cup white sugar
- 1 cups creamy peanut butter
- 6 cups Special K breakfast cereal
- 12 ounce bag of milk chocolate chips

Direction

- Stir the corn syrup and sugar together in a small saucepan and heat just to boiling (do not boil, as this will cause the bars to become hard

as they cool). Note: I use the microwave and heat until the sugar is dissolved, about 2 minutes on High.
- Remove pan from stovetop or microwave, and stir in the peanut butter; mix ingredients together well.
- Place the cereal in a large bowl.
- Pour syrup mixture over cereal and stir to blend well, making sure all the cereal is coated with the syrup mixture.
- Lightly butter a 10x15 baking sheet (for thicker bars, use a 9x13 pan).
- Firmly press the cereal mixture into the bottom of the pan, being sure to press together any "holes" in the base.
- Melt a 12 ounce bag of milk chocolate chips (I place them in a 2 cup measuring cup and use the microwave to melt them, but you can do it in a saucepan on the stovetop if you prefer). You can also melt a couple 5 ounce chocolate bars instead of chocolate chips.
- Pour melted chocolate over cereal base, and spread to completely cover it.
- Cool completely before cutting into bars.
- VARIATION: For a more intense peanut butter flavor, you can add ¼ cup creamy peanut butter (or more, to your taste) to the melted chocolate.

330. Speedy Brownies

Serving: 8 | Prep: | Cook: 25mins | Ready in:

Ingredients

- 2 cups sugar
- 1-3/4 cups all-purpose flour
- 1/2 cup baking cocoa
- 1 teaspoon salt
- 5 large eggs, room temperature
- 1 cup canola oil
- 1 teaspoon vanilla extract
- 1 cup semisweet chocolate chips

Direction

- In a large bowl, beat the first 7 ingredients. Pour into a greased 13x9-in. baking pan. Sprinkle with chocolate chips.
- Bake at 350° for 30 minutes or until a toothpick inserted in the center comes out clean. Cool in pan on a wire rack.
- Nutrition Facts
- 1 brownie: 155 calories, 8g fat (2g saturated fat), 30mg cholesterol, 75mg sodium, 19g carbohydrate (14g sugars, 1g fiber), 2g protein.

331. Spicy Applesauce Bars Recipe

Serving: 48 | Prep: | Cook: 25mins | Ready in:

Ingredients

- Bars:
- 1 cup sugar
- 1/3 cup butter, softened
- 1 egg
- 1-1/2 cups all-purpose flour
- 1-1/2 cups applesauce
- 1 teaspoon ground allspice
- 1 teaspoon ground cinnamon
- 3/4 teaspoon baking soda
- 1/4 teaspoon salt
- 1/2 cup raisins, soaked in boiling water and drained
- Icing:
- 3 cups powdered sugar
- 1/3 cup sour cream
- 3 Tbsp. butter, softened
- 2 Tbsp. vanilla
- 1/2 cup chopped pecans

Direction

- Heat oven to 350°F.
- Spray 13 x 9 inch baking pan with no-stick cooking spray.
- Set aside.

- Combine sugar, 1/3 cup butter and egg in large bowl.
- Beat at medium speed, scraping bowl often, until creamy.
- Reduce speed to low; add all remaining ingredients except raisins. Beat, scraping bowl often, until well mixed.
- Stir in raisins.
- Spoon batter into prepared pan.
- Bake for 25 to 35 minutes or until toothpick inserted in center comes out clean.
- Cool completely.
- Combine all frosting ingredients except pecans in small bowl.
- Beat at medium speed, scraping bowl often, until smooth.
- Frost cooled bars; sprinkle with pecans or candied sprinkles.
- Cut into bars.

332. Spicy Chocolate Bars Recipe

Serving: 24 | Prep: | Cook: 20mins | Ready in:

Ingredients

- 1 1/2- cups shortening
- 1 1/2- cups sugar
- 1 1/2- cups brown sugar
- 4- eggs
- 2-teaspoon vanilla
- 4-cups flour.sifted
- 2- teaspoon baking soda
- 4- teaspoon cinnamon
- 1-teaspoon cloves
- 1- teaspoon nutmeg
- 2- cups semi-sweet chocolate chips

Direction

- Cream shortening and sugar until fluffy.
- Beat in eggs one at a time.
- Add vanilla.
- Blend in all the dry ingredients. Mix until blended.
- Spread into-- 2. ---ungreased 15 1/2 inch x 10 1/2 inch x1 inch baking sheets.
- Sprinkle chocolate chips over the dough before baking.
- Bake at 350 degrees f. for 20 minutes. EASY.
- Cut into bars while warm, then cool.
- *******************
- Note: for a softer cookie bar use less sugar.

333. Spicy Gingerbread Squares Recipe

Serving: 9 | Prep: | Cook: 45mins | Ready in:

Ingredients

- 2 cups all-purpose flour
- 1/2 cup sugar
- 1/2 tsp salt
- 1 tsp baking soda
- 2 tsp ground ginger
- 1 1/2 tsp ground cardamom
- 1 tsp ground allspice
- 1 Tbsp grated orange peel
- 3 eggs
- 1/2 cup light molasses
- 1 cup buttermilk
- 1 stick butter, melted

Direction

- Stir together first 8 ingredients in a large mixing bowl.
- Put eggs in your mixer bowl and beat with mixer until they are thick and foamy.
- Keep the mixer running and add the molasses in a stream, then the buttermilk.
- Add half of the wet mixture to the dry ingredients and blend well with a spoon.
- Add the rest of the wet mixture in two more parts, beating well by hand after each addition.

- Gradually add the melted butter and beat with a spoon until your batter is blended and smooth.
- Pour into 8 inch square baking pan and bake in preheated 350 oven
- 45 to 50 minutes.

- Store in refrigerator.
- ***
- Forbidden fruit causes many jams.
- ***

334. Spumoni Bars Recipe

Serving: 24 | Prep: | Cook: 20mins | Ready in:

Ingredients

- 1/2 cup powdered sugar
- 1/2 cup shortening
- 2 eggs, separated
- 1 cup all-purpose flour*
- 1/2 cup ground almonds, if desired
- 1 can (14oz) sweetened condensed milk
- 1/4 cup lemon juice
- 1 teaspoon vanilla
- 1/2 cup chopped maraschino cherries, drained
- 1/2 cup granulated sugar
- 1/2 cup roasted diced almonds

Direction

- Heat oven to 350 degrees F.
- Beat powdered sugar, shortening and egg yolks until blended.
- Stir in flour and ground almonds.
- Press in ungreased baking pan, 13x9x2 inches.
- Bake 15 minutes.
- Beat milk, lemon juice & vanilla.
- Stir in cherries.
- Beat egg whites in small mixer bowl until foamy.
- Beat in granulated sugar, 1 tablespoon at a time; continue beating until stiff & glossy. Do not under beat.
- Spread cherry mixture over baked layer.
- Carefully spread meringue over cherry mixture; sprinkle with diced almonds.
- Bake 20 minutes.
- Cut into bars, 2x1 inch, while warm.

335. St Pattys Mint Cheesecake Bars Recipe

Serving: 24 | Prep: | Cook: 55mins | Ready in:

Ingredients

- 1 box Betty Crocker Triple chocolate flavored cake mix
- 1/2 cup butter or maragine, softened
- 3 pkg (8oz) cream cheese, softened
- 1 container(16oz) Betty Crocker Rich & Creamy cream cheese flavored frosting
- 3 eggs
- 6-8 drops green food coloring
- 3-4 drops Wilton creme de menthe Candy Flavoring
- 1-10oz pkg Toll House dark chocolate & mint Morsels, divided

Direction

- Heat oven to 325 degrees. In a large bowl, beat cake mix and butter with electric mixer on low speed until crumbly; reserve 1 cup. In bottom of ungreased 13x9-inch pan, press remaining crumb mixture. Bake for 10 minutes. Remove from oven, cool slightly.
- In the same bowl, beat cream cheese and frosting with electric mixer on medium speed until smooth. Add in eggs, one at a time, until blended. Add 6-8 drops of green food coloring, or more depending on how dark you want the batter. Mix well. Then add 3-4 drops of candy flavoring, mix well and taste to adjust if more is needed to your preference. Pour over crust; sprinkle with reserved crumb mixture. Top with 1 cup of Toll House Morsels, reserving the rest of the bag for finishing touches.

- Bake about 45 minutes (about 42 minutes for dark or non-stick pan) or until set. Cool completely. Cover and refrigerate at least 2 hours or until chilled. Reserved morsels: In a small microwaveable bowl, add morsels and heat in microwave in 45 second intervals, stirring until completely melted and smooth. Place melted chocolate into a Ziploc bag and clip a small corner, then drizzle over cooled bars.
- For bars, cut into 6 rows by 6 rows. Store in refrigerator. Enjoy.

336. Sticky Carrot Squares Recipe

Serving: 16 | Prep: | Cook: 2hours | Ready in:

Ingredients

- 2 tbsp ground flaxseed
- ⅓ cup hot water
- ½ cup unsweetened apple butter
- ⅓ cup unsweetened almond milk
- ½ cup canola oil
- ¾ cup xylitol
- ¼ tsp liquid stevia
- ½ tsp sea salt
- 2 tsp cinnamon
- ½ tsp ginger
- ½ tsp nutmeg
- ¼ tsp cardamom
- 1 ¼ cups gluten free all purpose flour (I used Artisan Gluten Free Flour Blend)
- ½ tsp guar gum
- 2 tsp baking powder
- 1 tsp baking soda
- 8 medium-large carrots, finely grated
- ¼ cup raisins
- ¼ cup slivered almonds, plus additional almonds for garnish

Direction

- Preheat the oven to 350F and line a 9" square pan with a "sling" of greased foil.
- In a bowl, whisk together flaxseed, water, apple butter, almond milk, oil, xylitol, stevia, salt and spices until thoroughly combined.
- Add the flour, guar gum, baking powder and baking soda. Stir to combine well.
- Fold in carrots, raisins and measured almonds.
- Scrape into the pan and smooth the top. Sprinkle with additional almonds.
- Bake for 30 minutes.
- Cover pan tightly with foil and return to the oven for 15 minutes.
- Remove bars from the pan (use the "sling") and cut into 16 pieces - these will still be gooey.
- Place pieces on a parchment or silicone lined baking sheet and bake 30 minutes.
- Cool on the sheet, then store in an airtight container in the fridge up to 5 days.

337. Strawberry Cheesecake Bars Recipe

Serving: 32 | Prep: | Cook: 18mins | Ready in:

Ingredients

- 1- pouch (pkg)Betty Crocker sugar cookie mix
- 1/3 -cup butter, melted
- 2- tablespoons flour
- 2- packages (8 oz each) cream cheese, softened
- 3/4- teaspoon vanilla
- 2- eggs
- 3/4- cup strawberry spreadable fruit

Direction

- Heat oven to 350°F.
- Mix together cookie mix, butter, flour and 1 egg.
- Press in greased 13x9-inch pan.
- Bake 15 to 18 minutes until light golden brown. Cool 15 minutes.

- Beat cream cheese, sugar, vanilla and 2 eggs until smooth.
- Spread over cookie crust.
- Spoon spreadable fruit in 3 lines the length of the pan.
- Use knife to pull spread from side to side through cream cheese mixture at 1-inch intervals.
- Bake 25 to 30 minutes until filling is set.
- Refrigerate to chilled, about 2 hours. Cut into bars.
- Makes 32 bars.

338. Stuffed Chocolate Chip Cookie Bars Recipe

Serving: 8 | Prep: | Cook: 20mins | Ready in:

Ingredients

- 2 pkgs. of chocolate chip cookie dough
- 1 - 8 oz package of cream cheese
- 2 eggs

Direction

- Pat 1 package of cookie dough into a 13 X 9" pan.
- Then mix the cream cheese and eggs together until smooth. Pour over the cookie dough.
- Take the 2nd package of cookie dough and drop spoonfuls onto of the cream cheese mixture until covered. Bake as instructed on cookie dough package.
- Let cool completely and then cut into bars.

339. Sunshine Lemon Or Lime Bars Recipe

Serving: 24 | Prep: | Cook: 30mins | Ready in:

Ingredients

- 1 pkg lemon cake mix
- 1/2 cup (1 stick) butter, softened
- 1 large egg
- 1 (14 oz) can sweetened condensed milk (like Eagle Brand)
- 1/2 cup lemon juice (juice from about two large limes/lemons)
- Zest from two limes/lemons

Direction

- Preheat oven to 350 °F.
- Stir together cake mix, butter, egg and half the lime/lemon zest. Spread mixture evenly into bottom of a 13x9-inch baking pan.
- Blend together sweetened condensed milk, lemon juice and remaining zest.
- Pour mixture over top of cake mix mixture.
- Bake for 23 to 27 minutes. Cool completely.
- Cut into 1 1/2x3 1/4-inch bars.

340. Super Lemony Lemon Bars Recipe

Serving: 24 | Prep: | Cook: 40mins | Ready in:

Ingredients

- 12 tablespoons (1 1/2 sticks), plus 1 tablespoon cold unsalted butter
- 1 3/4 cups plus 3 tablespoons all-purpose flour
- 2/3 cup confectioners' sugar, plus more for garnish
- 1/4 cup cornstarch
- 3/4 teaspoon salt plus a pinch
- 4 eggs, lightly beaten
- 1 1/3 cups granulated sugar
- 1 1/2 teaspoons lemon zest
- 2/3 cup fresh lemon juice, strained
- 1/4 cup whole milk
- 2 tablespoons limoncello, or other lemon-flavored liqueur, optional

Direction

- Lightly butter a 9 by 13-inch baking dish with 2 teaspoons of the butter and line with 1 sheet of parchment paper. Butter the top of this sheet of paper with 1 teaspoon of the remaining butter and then lay a second sheet of parchment or waxed paper crosswise over the first sheet. The parchment should be cut large enough so that the sides are even with the top of the baking dish; this extra paper will function as handles to help you remove the lemon squares from the pan later. Set pan aside.
- In a large bowl combine 1 3/4 cups of the flour, 2/3 cup of the confectioners' sugar, the cornstarch, and 3/4 teaspoon of the salt and mix thoroughly.
- Cut the remaining 12 tablespoons of butter into small pieces and add to the flour mixture. Using your hands, 2 forks, or a pastry blender, work the butter into the flour mixture until the mixture resembles coarse meal.
- Transfer the butter-flour mixture to the prepared baking dish and press into an even 1/4-inch layer along the bottom and partly up the sides of the pan. Refrigerate for 30 minutes.
- While the crust is chilling, preheat the oven to 350 degrees F.
- Bake the crust until golden brown, about 20 to 25 minutes.
- While the crust is baking, assemble the filling by combining the eggs, granulated sugar, flour, and lemon zest in a medium bowl and whisking until smooth. Stir in lemon juice, milk, optional Limoncello, and remaining pinch of salt and mix well.
- When the crust is golden brown, remove it from the oven and reduce the oven temperature to 325 degrees F. Stir the lemon mixture again, then pour onto the warm crust. Bake until the filling is set, about 20 minutes.
- Transfer to a wire rack to cool completely. Grasp the waxed paper that lines the 2 longest sides of the baking dish and remove the bars from the pan by pulling up gently. The entire dessert should easily dislodge and come away from the pan. Transfer to a cutting board and, using a clean knife, cut into squares, wiping knife after each cut. Place a small amount of confectioners' sugar into a small sieve, and sprinkle the bars with the sugar. Serve immediately, or refrigerate, wrapped with plastic wrap, up to 2 days, until ready to serve.

341. Sweet And Salty Chewy Pecan Bars Recipe

Serving: 16 | Prep: | Cook: 32mins | Ready in:

Ingredients

- 1 pkg. (16.5 oz.) NESTLÉ® TOLL HOUSE® Refrigerated chocolate chip Cookie Bar Dough, divided
- 1 tablespoon butter, melted
- 3/4 cup chopped pecans
- 1 tablespoon granulated sugar
- 1/4 teaspoon salt
- 1/3 cup NESTLÉ® TOLL HOUSE® Semi-sweet chocolate Morsels
- 2 tablespoons caramel sauce

Direction

- PREHEAT oven to 350° F. Grease 8-inch-square baking pan.
- PRESS 3/4 package (18 squares) cookie dough into prepared baking pan and refrigerate remaining 1/4 package (6 squares) cookie dough.
- BAKE for 10 minutes; remove from oven.
- COMBINE butter, nuts, sugar and salt in small bowl until coated. Sprinkle over dough. Top with teaspoonfuls of remaining cookie dough; pressing down gently. Sprinkle with morsels.
- BAKE for an additional 22 to 24 minutes or until edges are browned and set. Cool 30 minutes in pan on wire rack.
- DRIZZLE caramel sauce over bar. Cool completely in pan on wire rack. Cut into bars.
- TIPS

- For chewier caramel top, microwave 6 unwrapped caramel candies with 1 teaspoon milk for 20 to 30 seconds or until melted; stir until smooth. Drizzle sauce over bar.
- Toasted pecans may also be used, if desired.

342. THEYLL NEVER BELIEVE IT CAKE SQUARES Recipe

Serving: 16 | Prep: | Cook: 35mins | Ready in:

Ingredients

- 2 tablespoons chocolate chips
- 1/4 cup walnuts
- 1 15 oz can black beans, drained and rinsed
- 4 eggs (or egg beaters)
- 1/4 cup baking cocoa
- 1 tsp. baking powder
- 2 tsp. vanilla
- 1/2 teaspoon almond extract
- 1 medium/large red apple, cored, but skin left on, cut in chunks
- 1/4 cup granular Splenda - optional if you like a sweeter taste

Direction

- Preheat oven to 350 degrees.
- Put the chocolate chips and walnuts in the blender and blend until ground. Set aside.
- Mix the rest of the ingredients in the blender until smooth.
- Pour into a sprayed 8x8 pan (non-stick spray is essential.)
- Top with walnut - chocolate chip mixture.
- Bake about 35 minutes, until top springs back when lightly touched.
- Chill for a couple of hours before cutting into bars.

343. Tarzan Ape Man Bars Recipe

Serving: 24 | Prep: | Cook: 25mins | Ready in:

Ingredients

- 1 cup flour
- 1/2 cup whole wheat flour
- 1/2 cup rolled oats (old-fashioned or "quick", not instant)
- 1/2 tbsp baking powder
- 1/2 tsp baking soda
- 1 tsp pumpkin pie spice (a blend of cinnamon, nutmeg, ginger and cloves)
- 2 tbsp canola oil
- 2/3 cup brown sugar
- 2 tbsp honey
- 2 tbsp unsweetened applesauce
- 1 cup sour cream (light's fine, NI is for 14% M.F.)
- 1 tbsp vanilla
- 6 oz silken tofu (I use Mori-Nu lite), pureed
- 3 medium-large bananas, mashed
- walnuts or chocolate chips for topping (optional, not included in NI)

Direction

- Preheat oven to 350F, grease and line a 9x13" pan or two 8" pans.
- Whisk together flours, oats, baking powder, baking soda and pie spice in a medium bowl. Set aside.
- In a large bowl beat together oil, brown sugar, honey and applesauce until smooth.
- Add sour cream, vanilla and tofu puree and again beat smooth.
- Add flour and bananas in alternate batches, starting and ending with dry.
- Pour batter into prepared pan(s), top if desired.
- Bake 25 minutes, rotating pans after 15 minutes.
- Cool completely in pans (or chill if possible) before cutting.

344. Thick And Custardy Lemon Bars Recipe

Serving: 12 | Prep: | Cook: 20mins | Ready in:

Ingredients

- Crust, mix and press into 9x13 pan bake for 20-25 minutes @ 350
- (when I make any of my cookie bars I usually do not bake the full amount of time given. They will bake with the topping yet. I bake this only 15 or 20 minutes. It makes them more delicate and crumbly as well)
- 2 ¼ cups flour
- 1 cup butter, soften and remember use sweet!
- ½ cup 10X sugar
- Beat:
- 2 cups sugar
- ½ cup lemon juice
- 4 large eggs
- Peel of one lemon
- ¼ cup flour
- Pour onto crust

Direction

- Bake 20 minutes
- Cool and sift 10X
- For a variation. You can also top the bars with 10X sugar mixed with lemon juice and coat the top of the bars with this instead of just 10x sugar.

345. Three Layer Lemon Bars Recipe

Serving: 16 | Prep: | Cook: 40mins | Ready in:

Ingredients

- 1 stick salted butter softened
- 1/4 cup confectioners' sugar
- 1 teaspoon vanilla extract
- 1 cup all-purpose flour
- 8 ounces cream cheese softened
- 1-1/2 cups confectioners' sugar
- 1 large egg
- 1 teaspoon lemon extract
- 4 large egg yolks
- 1 tablespoon cornstarch
- 3/4 cup granulated sugar
- 3/4 cup water
- 2 tablespoons salted butter softened
- 2 teaspoons grated lemon peel
- 1/4 cup fresh lemon juice
- 2 tablespoons confectioners' sugar

Direction

- Preheat oven to 325.
- Cream butter and sugar in medium bowl with electric mixer set on high speed.
- Add vanilla and mix until combined.
- Add flour and mix at low speed until fully incorporated then press dough evenly into bottom of square baking pan.
- Refrigerate until firm.
- Prick shortbread crust with fork and bake for 30 minutes.
- Cool on rack to room temperature.
- Prepare cream cheese filling while crust is baking.
- Beat cream cheese and sugar until smooth in medium bowl with electric mixer set on high speed.
- Add egg and lemon extract and beat on medium speed until light and smooth.
- Cover bowl tightly and refrigerate.
- Blend egg yolks with the cornstarch and sugar in medium non-aluminum saucepan.
- Place over low heat and slowly whisk in water and lemon juice.
- Increase heat to medium low and cook stirring constantly until mixture thickens enough to coat the back of a spoon.
- Remove from heat.
- Add lemon peel and butter and cool for 10 minutes.

- Spread chilled cream cheese filling evenly over cooled shortbread crust with spatula.
- Spread lemon curd evenly over cream cheese filling.
- Place pan in center of oven and bake 40 minutes.
- Cool to room temperature on rack.
- Chill in refrigerator 1 hour before cutting into bars.
- Dust top with confectioners' sugar.

346. Tiramisu Cookie Bars Recipe

Serving: 24 | Prep: | Cook: 60mins | Ready in:

Ingredients

- Bars
- 3/4 cup Gold Medal® all-purpose flour
- 1/2 cup butter or margarine, softened
- 1/4 cup powdered sugar
- 1 cup granulated sugar
- 3/4 cup whipping cream
- 1/4 cup butter or margarine, melted
- 3 tablespoons Gold Medal® all-purpose flour
- 1 tablespoon instant coffee granules or crystals
- 1/2 teaspoon vanilla
- 2 eggs
- 3 oz semisweet baking chocolate, grated (about 1 1/4 cups)
- frosting
- 1 package (3 oz) cream cheese, softened
- 1/4 cup whipping cream
- chocolate curls, if desired

Direction

- 1. Heat oven to 350°F. In medium bowl, beat 3/4 cup flour, 1/2 cup softened butter and the powdered sugar with electric mixer on medium speed until soft dough forms. Spread evenly in bottom of ungreased 8-inch square pan. Bake 10 minutes.
- 2. Meanwhile, in medium bowl, beat remaining bar ingredients except grated chocolate with wire whisk until smooth.
- 3. Sprinkle 1 cup of the grated chocolate over hot baked crust. Pour egg mixture over chocolate.
- 4. Bake 40 to 45 minutes or until golden brown and set. Cool completely in pan on cooling rack, about 1 hour 15 minutes.
- 5. In medium bowl, beat cream cheese and 1/4 cup whipping cream on medium speed about 2 minutes or until fluffy. Spread over cooled bars. Sprinkle with remaining grated chocolate. For bars, cut into 6 rows by 4 rows. Garnish each with chocolate curl. Store covered in refrigerator.

347. Tiramisu Squares Recipe

Serving: 15 | Prep: | Cook: 3mins | Ready in:

Ingredients

- 1 envelope unflavored gelatin
- 1/4 cup cold water
- 1 prepared marble or chocolate pound cake (14 oz)
- 3 tablespoons coffee liqueur
- 16 ounces cream cheese
- 1 container ricotta cheese (15 oz)
- 1 1/2 cups confectioners sugar
- 3 tablespoons unsweetened cocoa powder
- 1 cup mini chocolate pieces
- unsweetened cocoa powder for dusting

Direction

- Soften gelatine in water in heat proof dish, 3 minutes; place dish in skillet of simmering water; stir gelatine to dissolve.
- Slice cake into scant 1/2 inch thick slices.
- Fit slices in bottom of a 13 x 9 x 2 inch baking pan in single layer, cutting and adding scraps to fit snugly.
- Drizzle liqueur over cake.

- Process cream cheese, ricotta, sugar and cocoa in food processor until smooth.
- Add gelatine mixture, processing to blend.
- Add chocolate pieces, process just to combine.
- Scrape into prepared pan, spreading over cake.
- Cover with plastic wrap and chill for 3 hours or until set.
- Dust with cocoa; cut into squares.
- 15 squares

348. Toffee Almond Turtle Bars Recipe

Serving: 24 | Prep: | Cook: 37mins | Ready in:

Ingredients

- 1- cup bleached all-purpose flour
- 2- tablespoons unsweetened cocoa powder
- 1/4-- teaspoon baking powder
- 1/8 - teaspoon salt
- 5- packages (1.4 ounces each) milk chocolate candy bars with toffee (like heath bars) chopped
- 1/2 - pound (2 sticks) unsalted butter, melted and cooled to tepid.
- 4- ounces unsweetened chocolate, melted and cooled to tepid.
- 4- large eggs
- 1 3/4- cups plus 2 - tablespoons superfine sugar
- 2- teaspoons vanilla extract-
- 1/2-cup chopped or slivered almonds
- Topping ………
- Please use my turtle topping in my recipes…………adding nuts if you want them on top
- Plus 2 pkgs of the Heath candy bars cut into chunks…..

Direction

- Preheat oven to 325 degrees F. spray lightly the inside of a 9x9x2inch baking pan with a non-stick cooking spray.
- Sift the flour, cocoa powder, baking powder, and salt onto a sheet of waxed paper.
- Ina small bowl, toss the chopped toffee with 1/2 teaspoon of the sifted mixture.
- In a medium size mixing bowl, whisk the melted butter and melted chocolate until smooth.
- In a large mixing bowl, whisk the eggs until blended, about 15 seconds.
- Add the sugar and whisk until combined, about 45 seconds to 1 minute.
- Blend in vanilla and melted butter- chocolate mixture.
- Sift the flour mixture over and stir to form a batter, mixing thoroughly until all is blended well
- Stir in the chopped toffee and almonds.
- Pour into the prepared pan and smooth top.
- Bake at 325 f. for 33- 37 minutes or until set.
- Let stand on a cooling rack in pan .until completely cooled.
- Spoon and spread the topping randomly over the chocolate bar base.
- After 1 minute sprinkle the almonds and toffee on top. Let it stand for 1 hour before cutting
- Makes 2 dozen bars.

349. Toffee Pumpkin Squares Recipe

Serving: 1 | Prep: | Cook: 40mins | Ready in:

Ingredients

- 1 cup sifted flour
- 1/2 cup quick oats
- 1/2 cup light brown sugar
- 1/2 cup butter
- 1 (1 pound) can pumpkin
- 1 (13 ounce) can evaporated milk
- 1/2 teaspoon salt

- 2 eggs
- 3/4 cup granulated sugar
- 1/4 teaspoon ground cloves
- 1/2 teaspoon ground ginger
- 1 teaspoon cinnamon
- 1/2 cup chopped pecans
- 1/2 cup light brown sugar
- 2 tablespoons melted butter

Direction

- Combine flour, oats, brown sugar and butter in mixing bowl until crumbly. Press into ungreased 13 x 9 x 2-inch pan. Bake at 350 degrees for 15 minutes.
- Combine pumpkin, milk, eggs, sugar, salt and spices.
- Beat well. Pour into crust. Bake for 20 minutes at 350 degrees F.
- Combine pecans, brown sugar and butter. Sprinkle over pumpkin filling.
- Return to oven and bake 15 to 20 minutes. Cool before cutting.

350. Triple Chocolate Cherry Bars Recipe

Serving: 48 | Prep: | Cook: 40mins | Ready in:

Ingredients

- 1 box Betty Crocker® SuperMoist® chocolate fudge cake mix
- 1 can (21 oz) cherry pie filling
- 2 eggs, beaten
- 1/2 bag (12-oz size) miniature semisweet chocolate chips (1 cup)
- 1 container Betty Crocker® Whipped chocolate frosting

Direction

- 1. Heat oven to 350°F (325°F for dark or non-stick pan). Grease and flour 15x10x1-inch or 13x9-inch pan, or spray with baking spray with flour.
- 2. In large bowl, gently mix dry cake mix, pie filling, eggs and chocolate chips with rubber scraper; break up any undissolved cake mix by pressing with scraper. Carefully spread in pan.
- 3. Bake 15x10x1-inch pan 25 to 30 minutes, 13x9-inch pan 35 to 40 minutes, or until toothpick inserted in center comes out clean. Cool completely, about 1 hour. Frost with frosting. For bars, cut into 8 rows by 6 rows.

351. Turtle Bars Recipe

Serving: 8 | Prep: | Cook: 30mins | Ready in:

Ingredients

- Crust
- 4 cups flour
- 2 cups light brown sugar, packed
- 1 cup butter, room temp.
- 2 cups pecans
- caramel layer:
- 1 1/2 cups butter
- 1 cup light brown sugar, packed
- 2 cups semisweet chocolate chips

Direction

- Preheat oven to 350.
- Crust
- Add flour, sugar and butter to mixing bowl.
- Mix well.
- Pat firmly into 9 x 13-inch pan.
- Sprinkle pecans on top.
- Caramel layer:
- In heavy pan over medium heat, cook butter and sugar, stirring constantly until it comes to boil.
- Boil 1 minute.
- Pour over crust.
- Bake 23 to 25 minutes.
- Sprinkle chocolate chips over top.
- Let melt a little.

- Take knife and swirl chocolate to marbleize.
- Cool completely before cutting.

352. Turtle Fudge Bars Recipe

Serving: 30 | Prep: | Cook: 37mins | Ready in:

Ingredients

- Crust:
- 1 pkg. graham crackers (approximately 10 crackers)
- 1 C. walnuts or pecans
- 1/2 C. butter or margarine, melted
- Fudge:
- 2 1/2 C. sugar
- 1/4 C. butter or margarine
- 1 small can sweetened condensed milk
- 1 jar marshmallow fluff
- 3/4 tsp. salt
- 3/4 tsp vanilla
- 1 12 oz. pkg. chocolate chips
- Topping:
- caramel flavored icecream topping
- handful of walnuts or pecans

Direction

- Crust:
- Using a food processor, chop walnuts and graham crackers until they are finely chopped. Pour into a medium sized cake pan. Add butter, and mix thoroughly. Press into bottom of pan. Cool completely. (For faster cooling, refrigerate)
- Fudge:
- Combine sugar, butter, condensed milk, marshmallow fluff and salt in medium sized pan. Stir over low heat until blended.
- Bring to a boil over moderate heat, being careful not to mistake air bubbles for boiling. Then boil slowly, stirring constantly, for 5 minutes. (To softball stage)
- Remove from heat. Stir in chocolate chips and vanilla, until chocolate is melted.
- Remove cake pan from refrigerator, and pour fudge into cake pan, spreading over crust.
- Cool completely, until fudge is set.
- Topping:
- When fudge layer is set and cooled, spread caramel topping over top of fudge.
- Sprinkle desired amount of walnut pieces over caramel topping and serve.

353. ULTIMATE RICE KRISPY SQUARES Recipe

Serving: 1 | Prep: | Cook: | Ready in:

Ingredients

- 1 C. corn syrup
- 1 C. granulated sugar
- 6 to 7 C. rice Krispy cereal
- 1 C. peanut butter
- 1 C. butterscotch chips
- 1 C. semisweet chocolate chips

Direction

- Cook corn syrup and sugar together in a saucepan over medium heat until the sugar crystals are dissolved.
- In a large mixing bowl, combine Rice Krispy cereal and peanut butter. Pour corn syrup mixture over the top and mix well. Pour into a 13 x 9-inch pan.
- Melt butterscotch chips and chocolate chips together and spread over the warm mixture in the pan. Put in the refrigerator until set and cut into squares.

354. Walnut Easy Bars Recipe

Serving: 24 | Prep: | Cook: 19mins | Ready in:

Ingredients

- 1 egg
- 1 cup brown sugar
- 1 tsp. vanilla extract
- 1/2 cup all-purpose flour
- 1/4 tsp. baking soda
- 1 cup chopped walnuts

Direction

- Preheat oven to 350 degrees.
- Mix together the egg, sugar and vanilla. Quickly mix in the flour and baking soda. Stir in walnuts. Spread in a greased 8-inch pan. Bake for 18 to 20 minutes.
- Cookies should be soft in the center when removed from the oven. Cool. Cut into bars.
- Makes about 2 dozen or more, depending on size cut.

355. White Christmas Fudge Bars Recipe

Serving: 35 | Prep: | Cook: 5mins | Ready in:

Ingredients

- 2 1/2 cups confectioners sugar
- 2/3 cup milk
- 1/4 cup butter or margarine
- 12 ounces white chocolate, coarsely chopped
- 1/2 teaspoon almond extract (optional)
- 3/4 cup dried cherries, cranberries, or apricots, coarsely chopped
- 3/4 cup toasted almond slices

Direction

- Line an 8-inch square pan with foil; grease foil.
- Mix confectioners' sugar and milk in a heavy 3-quart saucepan. Over medium heat, add butter and stirring constantly, bring to boil. Without stirring, boil constantly for 5 minutes.
- Over low heat, add chocolate and almond extract.
- Stir then whisk until chocolate melts and mixture is smooth.
- Stir in dried cherries and toasted almonds.
- Pour mixture into prepared pan.
- Refrigerate 2 hours until firm. Invert pan, peel off foil and cut into 1-inch squares. Garnish as desired.
- To toast almonds, spread in a single layer on cookie sheet with a rim.
- Bake in 350 F oven for 5-10 minutes, shaking pan occasionally, until they begin to brown.

356. Whole Wheat Banana Bars Recipe

Serving: 20 | Prep: | Cook: 22mins | Ready in:

Ingredients

- 1/2 cup all purpose flour
- 1/2 cup whole wheat flour
- 1 tbsp toasted wheat germ
- 1/2 tsp cinnamon
- 1 tsp. baking powder
- 1/8 tsp. salt
- 1 beaten egg
- 1/2 cup brown sugar
- 1/3 cup milk
- 1/4 cup cooking oil
- 1/2 tsp. vanilla
- 1 ripe medium mashed banana
- 1/3 cup dried fruit bits

Direction

- Grease an 11x7x1-1/2 inch baking pan; set aside.
- In a bowl combine all-purpose flour, whole wheat flour, wheat germ, baking powder, cinnamon, and salt; set aside.
- In another bowl stir together egg, sugar, milk, oil, and vanilla. Stir in banana and fruit bits. Add banana mixture to flour mixture, stirring to combine. Spread batter evenly pan.

- Bake in a 350* oven for 20 to 25 min. or until wooden toothpick comes out clean.
- Cool in pan cut into bars.

357. Whole Wheat Blueberry Bars Recipe

Serving: 1215 | Prep: | Cook: 35mins | Ready in:

Ingredients

- 1 1/3 cups whole-wheat flour
- 1/2 teaspoon baking powder
- 1/2 teaspoon baking soda
- 1/2 teaspoon salt
- 1 cup brown sugar
- 2 tablespoons butter -- softened
- 2 tablespoons vegetable oil
- 1 large egg
- 1 teaspoon vanilla
- 3 tablespoons whole-wheat flour
- 1/2 cup granulated sugar
- 2 tablespoons all-purpose flour
- 1 teaspoon grated lemon rind
- 2 cups blueberries -- picked clean
- 1 tablespoon lemon juice

Direction

- 1. Preheat oven to 350 degrees. Spray 9 x 13 pan with pan spray.
- 2. Stir together 1 1/3 cup whole wheat flour, baking powder, soda & salt; set aside. In mixer beat together brown sugar, butter, oil, egg & vanilla until smooth, making sure no lumps of brown sugar remain. Add the dry ingredients & stir until well- blended; the mixture will be firm. Reserve 1/2 cup (packed) for topping.
- 3. Place remaining dough in pan & cover with a piece of plastic wrap & use it to press dough into the bottom of prepared pan. Remove plastic wrap; bake at 350 degrees for 15 minutes or until puffed & golden.
- 4. Using fingertips, gradually mix remaining 3 tablespoons flour into reserved 1/2 cup of topping until it gets crumbly. Set aside.
- 5. Combine sugar, all-purpose flour & zest; set aside. Combine blueberries & lemon juice in saucepan; cook stirring over medium heat until berries begin to exude juice. Add sugar mixture & stir until the filling reaches a simmer & thickens.
- 6. With a wooden spoon, push down the higher outside edges of the baked crust; pour hot filling over it & spread all the way to the sides of the dish. Sprinkle with topping. Bake 15 to 20 minutes or until topping is golden.
- 7. Transfer to a rack & let cool, covered with a kitchen towel to soften crumbs slightly. Cut into 24 bars. Dust with confectioners' sugar & serve.

358. Yummie No Bake Cereal Bars Recipe

Serving: 1 | Prep: | Cook: | Ready in:

Ingredients

- 1 cup white corn syrup
- 1 cup sugar
- 1 1/4 cup peanut butter
- 6 cups Rice Krispies cereal
- 1 bag semi sweet choc chips (2 cups)
- Immediately press into pan (at desired thickness)

Direction

- 1. Lightly butter 13x9 inch pan, in sauce pan heat corn syrup and sugar to boiling over medium high heat, stirring constantly.
- Cook until sugar is dissolved, remove from heat. Add 1 cup of Peanut Butter, stir until smooth. Add Cereal mix well.
- 2. Melt choc chips and 1/4 PB in bowl in Microwave for 30-40 seconds stirring every 10

- seconds. Pour over cereal bars and cover to the edges.
- Cool in fridge for 30 minutes or on the counter until firm. Cut to size serve and Enjoy....
- Pour into a greased and floured 9 x 13 pan. Bake at 350° for 30-35 minutes.
- Blend frosting ingredients and beat till smooth. Frost bars when cool, and cut into desired sizes. Makes approx. 20 servings.

359. Zucchini Bars With Almond Cream Cheese Frosting Recipe

Serving: 20 | Prep: | Cook: 30mins | Ready in:

Ingredients

- BARS:
- 2 cups sugar
- 1 cup oil
- 3 eggs
- 2 cups flour
- 1 teaspoon cinnamon
- 1 teaspoon salt
- 1 teaspoon baking soda
- 2 teaspoons baking powder
- 1 teaspoon vanilla
- 2 cups shredded zucchini
- 1 small carrot, shredded
- 3/4 cup rolled oats (or nuts)
- FROSTING:
- 1/2 cup softened butter or butter flavored shortening (to help hold up to the heat)
- 1/4 teaspoon almond extract (a little goes a long way!)
- 2 teaspoons vanilla
- 2 1/2 cups powdered sugar
- 1 package (3 oz.) softened cream cheese
- (you can thin the frosting down with some cream or milk)

Direction

- Mix together oil and sugar, eggs and vanilla, mixing well.
- Add dry ingredients and fold in zucchini, carrot and nuts. (Note, if you sift the flour, you will get a much lighter, higher cakelike bar)

360. Zucchini Bars With Spice Frosting Recipe

Serving: 24 | Prep: | Cook: 30mins | Ready in:

Ingredients

- zucchini Bars:
- 2/3 C packed brown sugar
- 1/4 C margarine or butter, softened
- 1 egg
- 1/2 tsp. vanilla
- 1 C all-purpose flour
- 1 tsp. baking soda
- 1/2 tsp. ground cinnamon
- 1/2 ground cloves
- 1 C shredded zucchini, drained
- 1/2 C chopped nuts
- spice Frosting:
- 3/4 C powdered sugar
- 1 tbl. margarine or butter, softened
- 3 to 4 Tbl. milk
- 1/8 tsp. ground cloves

Direction

- Heat oven to 350 degrees.
- Grease square pan, 8X8X2-inches or 9X9X2-inches.
- Mix brown sugar, margarine, egg and vanilla in large bowl.
- Stir in flour, baking soda, cinnamon and cloves.
- Stir in zucchini and nuts.
- Spread batter in pan.
- Bake 25 to 30 minutes or until toothpick inserted in center comes out clean.
- Cool completely.

- Prepare Spice Frosting and spread on bars.
- Spice Frosting:
- Mix all ingredients until smooth and of spreading consistency.

- Halve the cake lengthways and cut each half into 3 layers. Sandwich the layers with the three-quarters of the chocolate filling. Spread the remainder over the cake and mark a wavy pattern on the top. Press the almonds on the sides.

361. Chocolate Bar Cake Recipe

Serving: 8 | Prep: | Cook: 35mins | Ready in:

Ingredients

- 7 eggs
- 200g/ 1 ¾ cups caster sugar
- 150g/ 1 ¼ cups flour
- 50g/ ½ cup cocoa powder
- 50g/ 4 tbsp butter, melted
- Filling:
- 200g/ 7 oz Plain chocolate
- 125g/ ½ cup butter
- 50g/ 4 tbsp icing sugar
- Decoration:
- 75g/ 10tbsp toasted flaked almonds, crushed lightly

Direction

- Grease a deep 23cm/ 9inch square cake pan and line the base with baking parchment.
- Whisk the eggs and sugar in a mixing bowl for 10 minutes, until very light and foamy and the whisk leaves a trail when lifted.
- Sieve the flour and cocoa powder together and fold half into the mixture. Drizzle over the melted butter and fold in the rest of the flour and cocoa. Pour into the prepared pan and bake in a preheated oven 350F, for 30-35 minutes. Leave to cool in the pan
- Slightly and then remove and cool completely on a wire rack.
- To make the filling, melt the butter and chocolate together, then remove from the heat and stir in the icing sugar, leave to cool, and then beat until thick enough to spread.

362. Chocolate Mint Bars Recipe

Serving: 12 | Prep: | Cook: 40mins | Ready in:

Ingredients

- 3/4 cup margarine
- 1 cup sugar
- 4 eggs
- 1 teaspoon vanilla
- 16 ounces chocolate syrup (1 can)
- 1 1/4 cups flour
- 2 cups powdered sugar
- 2 teaspoons milk
- 1/4 teaspoon peppermint extract
- 1/2 teaspoon vanilla extract
- 5 drops green food coloring
- 3 ounces cream cheese
- 1 cup chocolate chips
- 6 tablespoons margarine

Direction

- Preheat oven to 350 F. Mix together 3/4 cup margarine, 1 cup granulated sugar, all 4 eggs, the vanilla extract, the can of chocolate syrup, and the flour until smooth. Pour into a 13 x 9 greased pan and bake for 20 minutes or until cooked through.
- In a separated bowl mix together the powdered sugar, milk, peppermint extract, food coloring, and cream cheese. Spread over the cooled cake. Refrigerate until hard.
- Combine the chocolate chips and remaining 6 tablespoons of margarine in a microwave safe bowl and microwave at 50% power for 1 minute. Let cool and spread on top of dessert.

- Refrigerate until just before serving. Cut into small squares to serve.

363. Coconut Syrup Squares Recipe

Serving: 28 | Prep: | Cook: 35mins | Ready in:

Ingredients

- 5 eggs
- 3/4 cup sugar
- 1 tsp vanilla
- 1 cup plain yogurt
- 1 cup plain flour
- 1 tsp baking powder
- 1 cup semolina
- ¾ cup unsweetened coconut
- Syrup:
- 1 1/2 cup superfine sugar.
- 1 1/2 cup water.

Direction

- Heat sugar and water over medium heat till sugar is dissolved, then boil for 3 minutes and let it cool.
- Preheat oven to 375f, position rack in center of oven. Grease a 9 inch x 1/2 inch in height pan or heatproof glass dish with ghee or melted butter.
- Beat eggs, vanilla and sugar until thick and pale in color. Add yogurt and beat until just combined. Sift together the plain flour, baking powder and semolina and fold in two batches over the eggs mixture. Add coconut and fold again. Pour in prepared pan and smooth top. Bake for 35 minutes until springy to the touch and a skewer inserted in the center comes out clean. Remove from oven and pour cold syrup over the top. Let cool completely. Cut into squares. Sift icing sugar over the top.

364. Frosted Banana Cake Bars Recipe

Serving: 16 | Prep: | Cook: 27mins | Ready in:

Ingredients

- bars
- 2 ripe bananas
- 1 cup granulated sugar
- 1/3 cup vegtable oil
- 2 eggs or egg beaters
- 1 cup of flour
- 1 teaspoon baking powder
- 1/2 teaspoon baking soda
- 1/2 teaspoon cinnamon
- 1/4 teaspoon salt
- frosting (optional)
- 1 package of creamcheese (regular, fat free)
- 1/3 cup i cant believe its not butter light
- 1 teaspoon vanilla
- 2 cups powdered sugar

Direction

- Heat oven to 350°F. Grease bottom and sides of rectangular pan, 13x9x2 inches, with shortening. In large bowl, mix granulated sugar, bananas, oil and eggs with spoon. Stir in flour, baking powder, baking soda, cinnamon and salt. Spread in pan.
- Bake bars 25 to 30 minutes or until toothpick inserted in center comes out clean. Cool completely, about 1 hour.
- Meanwhile, in medium bowl, mix cream cheese, butter and vanilla with electric mixer on medium speed until blended. Gradually beat in powdered sugar with spoon, scraping bowl occasionally, until smooth and spreadable.
- Spread cooled bars with Cream Cheese Frosting. For bars, cut into 6 row by 4 rows. Store covered in refrigerator.

365. Yummy Healthy Apple Oat Bars Recipe

Serving: 18 | Prep: | Cook: 40mins | Ready in:

Ingredients

- 2 cups wholemeal SR flour
- 1 tsp bi-carb soda
- 2 tsp allspice
- 1 tsp cinnamon
- 1 cup rolled oats
- 1/3 cup sultanas
- 2 apples, grated
- 1 egg
- ½ cup yoghurt
- ¼ cup yoghurt juice*
- 1/3 cup honey

Direction

- - Preheat oven to 150°C (300F)
- - In a large bowl, mix together flour, soda, spices, oats, sultanas and apple.
- - In a separate bowl, whisk together the remaining ingredients.
- - Add wet mixture to dry mixture and, using a metal spoon, fold to gently combine. Don't overmix.
- - Spoon into a lined 16 x 28 cm pan and bake for 40-50 minutes, until a skewer comes out clean.
- - Cool completely before slicing.

Index

A

Almond 3,4,5,7,11,12,13,26,66,91,102,129,171,176

Apple 3,5,6,7,14,15,16,17,40,76,86,96,125,129,155,162,179

Apricot 3,11,17,18,19,20

B

Baking 43

Banana 3,4,6,7,22,23,24,25,33,52,119,142,160,174,178

Blueberry 3,4,5,7,26,27,28,29,70,72,87,112,175

Bran 4,63,84,96,166

Brie 98

Brown sugar 18

Butter 3,4,5,6,7,8,9,10,12,17,18,33,34,40,44,50,51,57,58,60,61,65,67,73,75,82,83,85,86,89,95,101,122,126,127,128,129,130,132,133,135,136,137,138,139,140,153,159,161,167,175

C

Cake 3,4,5,6,7,12,30,37,38,46,53,71,74,89,97,99,104,106,123,140,154,177,178

Caramel 3,4,5,6,7,40,41,42,43,44,45,46,53,54,64,65,84,136,137,152,156,172

Carrot 3,4,6,7,13,45,46,148,154,165

Cashew 3,4,6,7,34,41,42,46,53,126,152

Cheese 3,4,5,6,7,14,22,23,24,25,27,42,45,46,48,50,54,55,56,57,62,70,72,75,76,107,110,111,132,143,144,145,146,148,149,150,154,157,158,164,165,176,178

Cherry 4,5,6,7,49,50,65,66,88,117,149,172

Chips 4,50

Chocolate 3,4,5,6,7,10,11,29,30,37,51,52,53,54,55,56,57,58,59,60,61,62,63,64,65,66,67,73,81,82,83,84,88,89,92,99,107,108,113,115,118,123,127,128,129,135,137,138,149,155,161,163,166,172,177

Cider 14

Coconut 3,4,5,6,7,12,57,69,70,71,72,73,85,94,128,142,178

Coffee 4,5,72,73,97

Cola 6,142

Crackers 106

Cranberry 4,7,74,75,160

Cream 3,4,5,6,7,22,23,26,27,31,32,35,37,38,44,45,46,49,50,57,74,75,76,77,78,79,85,87,92,96,103,106,110,119,121,129,132,144,145,148,149,154,160,163,164,169,176,178

Crumble 41,54,55,56,76,78,86,157,160

Curd 112

Custard 5,7,110,169

D

Date 5,78,80,97

E

Egg 4,25,53

F

Fat 36,82

Flour 165

Fruit 5,85,89

Fudge 4,5,6,7,25,45,62,90,114,158,173,174

G

Gin 5,7,92,93,163

H

Hazelnut 5,105

Honey 3,5,22,102

I

Icing 3,5,12,26,86,106,129,131,150,162

J

Jam 81,95
Jelly 6,139
Jus 84,89,157,158

L

Lemon 4,5,6,7,47,78,87,109,110,111,112,113,121,122,129,160,166,169
Lime 5,7,105,166

M

Macadamia 6,114,115,128
Macaroon 4,58
Marshmallow 3,5,6,7,30,99,103,119,146,153
Marzipan 6,120
Milk 6,79,96,99,123
Mint 4,6,7,58,125,164,177
Muffins 6,118

N

Nougat 4,59
Nut 3,4,5,6,7,20,31,33,52,56,71,78,80,83,84,89,94,95,118,128,129,130,131,152,153,162

O

Oatmeal 3,4,6,19,49,127,143
Orange 3,13,16

P

Pastry 3,15
Peanuts 3,26
Pear 4,74,75
Pecan 4,6,7,62,141,154,161,167

Peel 40,169
Pie 3,4,6,15,39,49,119,125,147
Pineapple 6,142,143
Popcorn 3,28
Praline 3,5,6,10,92,104,143,145
Pulse 11,149
Pumpkin 4,5,6,7,62,81,92,144,145,146,147,148,171

R

Raspberry 4,5,7,62,81,111,149
Rice 3,17,36,65,118,131,140,141,153,173,175
Ricotta 3,28

S

Salt 7,152,153,167
Shortbread 5,6,81,98,112,124
Strawberry 7,165
Syrup 7,178

T

Toffee 4,7,52,64,100,171

V

Vegan 6,122
Vegetable shortening 140

W

Walnut 3,5,7,20,29,52,81,173

Z

Zest 166

L

lasagna 45

Conclusion

Thank you again for downloading this book!

I hope you enjoyed reading about my book!

If you enjoyed this book, please take the time to share your thoughts and post a review on Amazon. It'd be greatly appreciated!

Write me an honest review about the book – I truly value your opinion and thoughts and I will incorporate them into my next book, which is already underway.

Thank you!

If you have any questions, **feel free to contact at:** *author@bisquerecipes.com*

Susan Perrin

bisquerecipes.com

Made in United States
North Haven, CT
08 June 2024